Better Homes and Gardens

Annual Recipes 2013

CHERRY-BERRY
SHORTCAKE STARS,
PAGE 191

From the editor

This cookbook covers the bases from 30-minute meals to special-occasion menus, with a common theme of freshness, familiarity, and fun.

The *Merriam-Webster Online* dictionary defines "fresh" as something "newly produced, made or gathered." That pretty much sums up what we as editors and designers do with every issue of *Better Homes and Gardens* magazine: Share the best new ideas for making your lives better, easier, and more beautiful. The best new food ideas we discovered this year are featured in this collection of recipes from the 2013 issues of the magazine.

One of the year's most exciting events was the publication of *Better Homes and Gardens Fresh*, a big, gorgeous cookbook with more than 300 recipes "for enjoying ingredients at their peak." *Fresh* perfectly expresses the philosophy that informs every recipe we create, test and taste—to get the very best from every ingredient and from every moment while enjoying good food with family and friends. For a sampling of the fabulous seasonal foods featured in *Fresh*, check out pages 152–157. Take a taste of Strawberry and Arugula Salad with Manchego Fricos, Grilled Zucchini Salad with Mozzarella and Dill, Grilled Romaine Salad Tomato and Corn Tumble, or Succotash Salad with Buttermilk Avocado Dressing.

Although the publication of *Fresh* was a one-time special event, every month the magazine pages contain regular features that bring your busy life together with food that is fresh, familiar, and fun—and that help you manage your time and money. In our Home Cooking feature, food professionals share their expertise; Delicious Every Day lends a hand in getting a delicious, nutritious meal on the table on even the busiest weeknights; and Dinner on a Dollar helps you and your family eat well on a budget.

In January, start the year (and your morning) with some very special breakfasts. Wake up to Sweet Potato Biscuit Sandwiches with Ham and Redeye Gravy (page 12) or, on the sweeter side, with citrus-topped Greek Yogurt and Cornflakes Tart. In June, gather friends for a fresh and easy backyard feast featuring Grilled Corn with Smoky Lime Butter (page 143) and Cucumber-Honeydew Salad with Feta (page 148).

In the fall and winter months, get inspired for seasonal celebrations with fabulous desserts such as Maple Pumpkin Pie with Salted Pecan Brittle (page 286), artful Chocolate-Cinnamon Pear Loaf Cake (page 290), or nostalgic fluffy pink frosting-filled Coconut Snowballs (page 303).

Whatever the occasion, we hope you enjoy these fresh new ideas for making the most of family mealtime—and the time spent in the kitchen creating it.

Gayle

Gayle Goodson Butler, Editor in Chief
Better Homes and Gardens magazine

Annual Recipes 2013

Test Kitchen

Our seal assures you that every recipe in *Better Homes and Gardens* Annual Recipes 2013 has been tested in the Better Homes and Gardens Test Kitchen. This means that each recipe is practical and reliable, and meets our high standards of taste appeal. We guarantee your satisfaction with this book for as long as you own it.

All of us at Meredith Consumer Marketing are dedicated to providing you with information and ideas to enhance your home. We welcome your comments and suggestions. Write to us at: Meredith Consumer Marketing, 1716 Locust St., Des Moines, IA 50309-3023.

Pictured on front cover:
Cherry-Blackberry Pie, page 187

MEREDITH CONSUMER MARKETING
Vice President, Consumer Marketing: Janet Donnelly
Consumer Marketing Product Director: Heather Sorensen
Consumer Marketing Product Manager: Wendy Merical
Business Director: Ron Clingman
Senior Production Manager: Al Rodruck

WATERBURY PUBLICATIONS, INC.
Editorial Director: Lisa Kingsley
Associate Editor: Tricia Bergman
Creative Director: Ken Carlson
Associate Design Director: Doug Samuelson
Contributing Copy Editors: Terri Fredrickson, Peg Smith
Contributing Indexer: Elizabeth T. Parson

BETTER HOMES AND GARDENS MAGAZINE
Editor in Chief: Gayle Goodson Butler
Creative Director: Michael D. Belknap
Senior Deputy Editor: Nancy Wall Hopkins
Editorial Assistant: Renee Irey

MEREDITH NATIONAL MEDIA GROUP
President: Tom Harty

MEREDITH CORPORATION
Chairman and Chief Executive Officer: Stephen M. Lacy

In Memoriam: E.T. Meredith III (1933–2003)

LESSONS LEARNED Remember the old adage *If you're going to do something at all, do it right.* What's better than experts to guide you to success? This year's *Better Homes and Gardens® Annual Recipes* features chefs, cookbook authors, and professional foodies who share their best recipes, skillful techniques, and years of experience—because your time in the kitchen should be rewarding and delicious. Try bright summer salads that are more than simply greens, an innovative city brunch with country recipes, unforgettable sauces and rubs for backyard cookouts, plus luscious holiday recipes for memorable celebrations. With this book as your kitchen companion, folks will ask how you became such an amazing cook!

Look for

Monthly Features Each chapter showcases innovative seasonal recipes to add to your cooking repertoire. In February, baker extraordinaire Dorie Greenspan shows how to work with chocolate to create little bites of wonderful that are meant to be shared. For chef and cookbook author Robin Asbell, eating well means using nutrition-packed grains, and in March she shares versatile recipes so you, too, can go with the grain. Award-winning author Grace Young finds culinary magic with stir fries that are easy on the wallet and allow for creativity. These one-dish wonders get dinner on the table pronto. Trisha Yearwood, who leads a double life as a celebrated country singer and best-selling cookbook author, shares her passion for Southern comfort food with doable recipes for family gatherings.

Home Cooking Food professionals share their expertise with new takes on favorite recipes—and plenty of inspiration for you to be your creative best. Spring baking gets a fresh-from-the-jar twist with jams, jellies,

and preserves. New spins on humble pasta salads create anything but ho-hum potluck food. And learn simple techniques for the perfect roasted chicken, with flavorful changes for variety to suit any taste.

Dinner on a Dollar Feeding a hungry family on a budget without sacrificing flavor is the focus of this feature. You'll find savory main dishes that are delicious, packed with nutrition, and save a few cents.

Delicious Every Day Because weeknight cooking can be a challenge, Delicious Every Day answers "What's for dinner?" with recipes that call for fresh ingredients, simple prep, and the reward is knowing that, even on the busiest days, you can make a great-tasting meal that your family will love.

Recipe Icons Helpful recipe icons indicate whether a recipe is Fast (30 minutes or less), Kid Friendly, or Low Fat (see nutrition guidelines on page 335).

SPICE AND HONEY
ROASTED CARROTS,
PAGE 119

contents

2013

74

230

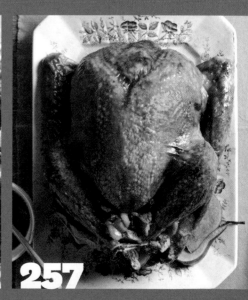

257

**QUINOA-PUMPKIN
SEED GRANOLA**

NEW YEAR'S REINVENTIONS City brunch meets country breakfast in dishes that can be savored any time of day. And take the cold out of winter with hot-out-of-the-oven dinners.

12

23

25

Breakfast Special 24/7

Served at the start of the day, for dinner, or as a midnight snack, these delicious twists on the traditional morning menu will wake up your taste buds.

Pork and Hot Pepper Hash

This meat-and-potatoes pleaser goes just as well with a cold brew as it does with OJ.

PREP 20 min. STAND 15 min.
COOK 20 min.

- 1 cup loosely packed fresh cilantro leaves, finely chopped
- 1 poblano pepper*, seeded and finely chopped
- 1 jalapeño pepper*, seeded and finely chopped
- 1 clove garlic, minced
- 1¼ lbs. ground pork
- 3 Tbsp. lime juice
- 1 lb. baby Yukon gold potatoes, halved or quartered
- ½ tsp. salt
- ¼ tsp. ground black pepper and/or crushed red pepper
- ¼ cup chicken broth (optional)
- 4 eggs, cooked sunny-side up in 1 Tbsp. butter (see Sunny-Side Success, right)
  Sliced red and/or green jalapeño peppers* (optional)
  Fresh cilantro sprigs (optional)
  Bottled green hot pepper sauce
  Lime wedges

1. In a large bowl combine cilantro, poblano pepper, jalapeño pepper, and garlic. Add pork and lime juice. Gently mix to combine. Set aside for 15 minutes to blend flavors.

2. Meanwhile, in a large saucepan cook potatoes in boiling salted water, covered, for about 10 minutes or just until just tender. Drain.

3. In a large skillet cook pork mixture until pork begins to brown. Stir in potatoes; sprinkle with salt and pepper. Cook for 5 to 7 minutes more or until pork is cooked through and potatoes are tender, turning occasionally. For moist hash, stir in chicken broth, if desired.

4. Serve eggs over hash. Top with sliced peppers and additional cilantro, if desired. Pass bottled green hot pepper sauce and lime wedges. Makes 4 servings.

*Because hot peppers contain oils that may burn skin and eyes, wear plastic gloves when working with them. If using bare hands, wash well afterward with soap and water.

EACH SERVING *500 cal, 33 g fat, 110 mg chol, 418 mg sodium, 24 g carb, 4 g fiber, 27 g pro.*

SUNNY-SIDE SUCCESS
Practice a little patience is all you need to whip up picture-perfect sunny-side up eggs.

- In a skillet melt butter over medium heat. Break eggs into the skillet; sprinkle with a bit of salt and pepper.

- Reduce heat to low. If the heat is too high, the eggs will scorch. Cook eggs for 3 to 4 minutes.

- To keep the eggs moist, spoon some of the butter over them as they cook. The hot butter will also firm up the yolks while the undersides cook.

Biscuits loaded with the flavor of sweet potatoes and cheddar cheese are stuffed with ham, fluffy eggs, and bacon. The surprise flavor? Redeye gravy made the old-fashioned way—using coffee and a hint of bacon drippings.

PERFECT SCRAMBLE
The secret to tender, buttery eggs? Don't overcook them.

• For extra moisture and richness, whisk a little milk, buttermilk, or sour cream into the eggs before cooking.

• To cook, in a skillet melt 1 Tbsp. butter; pour eggs into skillet. Let them stand for 20 to 30 seconds, or until the eggs along the bottom begin to set.

• With a spatula, lift and fold the cooked part toward the center, allowing uncooked eggs to flow to edge, repeat until eggs are cooked through but still glossy.

• Serve immediately so they don't continue cooking and dry out.

Sweet Potato Biscuit Sandwiches with Ham and Redeye Gravy

Redeye gravy, that Southern specialty made with coffee, infuses the ham slices with bold, rich flavor—a wonderful complement to light, flaky, slightly sweet biscuits.

PREP 45 min. BAKE 12 min.
COOK 15 min. OVEN 450°F

3	cups all-purpose flour
1	Tbsp. baking powder
1	Tbsp. sugar
1	tsp. salt
¾	tsp. cream of tartar
¼	tsp. cayenne pepper
⅓	cup butter
1	cup shredded cheddar cheese
1	cup milk
½	cup mashed cooked sweet potato
4	slices bacon
1	¼-inch-thick fully cooked ham slice (about 5 oz.), cut into 4 equal pieces
1	cup strong coffee
¼	cup peach preserves
4	eggs, scrambled (see Perfect Scramble, left)
	Fresh flat-leaf Italian parsley

1. Preheat oven to 450°F. For sweet potato biscuits, in a large bowl combine flour, baking powder, sugar, salt, cream of tartar, and cayenne pepper. Using a pastry blender, cut in butter until mixture resembles coarse crumbs. Stir in cheese. Make a well in the center of the flour mixture. In a small bowl combine milk and sweet potato. Add sweet potato mixture to flour mixture. Using a fork, stir just until dough is moistened.
2. Turn out dough onto a well-floured surface. Knead gently 10 to 12 strokes. Pat or lightly roll dough to a ¾-inch-thick rectangle (about 9×5 inches). Cut into 8 pieces. Place biscuits 1 inch apart on a large baking sheet. Bake for 12 to 14 minutes or until lightly browned.*
3. Meanwhile, in a large skillet cook bacon until crisp. Drain on paper towels, reserving 1 Tbsp. bacon fat in skillet. Add ham to skillet; cook 5 minutes or until well-browned on both sides. Add coffee to skillet with ham, stirring to scrape up any browned bits. Simmer, uncovered, just until coffee begins to thicken and glaze the ham. Remove ham from skillet.
4. Split biscuits. Top bottoms with ham, peach preserves, scrambled eggs, bacon, parsley, and biscuit tops. Makes 4 servings.
*This recipe uses 4 of the 8 biscuits. Bake and cool completely, then wrap and freeze any leftover biscuits for another use. To reheat, thaw biscuits and wrap in foil. Bake at 350°F for 10 minutes.
EACH SERVING *595 cal, 28 g fat, 261 mg chol, 1,398 mg sodium, 60 g carb, 3 g fiber, 26 g pro.*

SALSA BLOODY MARY

EGGS AND GREENS
BREAKFAST PIZZA

This is the dish you'll crave after a night of New Year's revelry—or on a frosty Friday night curled up at home. Add spicy sausage for heat, or make it meatless with a soft-set egg and a sprinkle of Parmesan on the greens. Serve it with a Salsa Bloody Mary— there's always something to celebrate!

KID FRIENDLY

Eggs and Greens Breakfast Pizza

PREP 25 min. STAND 30 min.
BAKE 16 min. OVEN 400°F/450°F

- 4 eggs
- 8 oz. hot or sweet Italian sausage (remove casings if present)
- 4 7-inch Greek flatbread or pita bread rounds
- 1 cup pizza sauce or thick marinara sauce
- ½ cup shredded mozzarella cheese (2 oz.)
- ½ cup shredded cheddar cheese (2 oz.)
- ½ cup thinly sliced red onion
- 4 cups torn arugula
- 1 Tbsp. olive oil
- 1 tsp. lemon juice
- 1 to 2 Tbsp. grated Parmesan cheese

1. Let eggs stand at room temperature for 30 minutes. Preheat oven to 400°F. Line a baking sheet with foil; set aside. In a large skillet cook sausage over medium heat until brown, using a wooden spoon to break up meat as it cooks. Drain off fat.

2. Meanwhile, place flatbreads directly on oven rack. Bake for 4 to 6 minutes or until lightly toasted, turning once. Arrange flatbreads on the prepared baking sheet. Increase oven to 450°F.
3. Spread one-fourth of the pizza sauce over each flatbread. Sprinkle with mozzarella and cheddar cheeses, cooked sausage, and onion. Break an egg into a small dish*; make a small indentation in the center of one pizza and pour the egg into the indentation. Repeat with the remaining eggs and pizzas. Bake for 12 to 15 minutes or until egg whites are set and yolks begin to thicken.
4. In a medium bowl toss together arugula, oil, lemon juice, and ⅛ tsp. each salt and pepper. Sprinkle arugula salad with Parmesan cheese; serve with pizzas. Makes 4 servings.
*This is in case the yolk breaks when you crack the egg. If it does, start over with another egg.

EACH SERVING *593 cal, 30 g fat, 250 mg chol, 1,122 mg sodium, 45 g carb, 3 g fiber, 30 g pro.*

Salsa Bloody Mary Blend 2 cups tomato juice, 1 cup purchased salsa, 2 Tbsp. lime juice, 2 tsp. horseradish, and ¼ tsp. celery salt to desired consistency. Add a splash of vodka, if desired. Serve over ice with cucumber spears or celery sticks. Makes 4 drinks.

This refreshing tart is simply stunning—whether for brunch or dessert, where humble cereal gets a star-power makeover. Pat the flakes into a crunchy crust, then top with a honey-sweetened yogurt filling that sets up overnight in the fridge. Top with warm marmalade and orange slices, and breakfast is ready.

KID FRIENDLY

Greek Yogurt and Cornflakes Tart

This tart is a canvas for whatever fruit is in season. In winter, top it with juicy orange slices and orange marmalade. Come spring and summer, swap in a handful of berries and strawberry preserves or apricot slices and peach jam.

PREP **20 min.** BAKE **8 min.**
CHILL **4 to 24 hrs.** OVEN **375°F**

- 1½ cups crushed cornflakes (about 5 cups whole flakes)
- ⅓ cup butter, melted
- 3 Tbsp. packed brown sugar
- 1 envelope unflavored gelatin
- ¼ cup water
- 1¼ cups plain Greek yogurt
- ½ cup milk
- ¼ cup honey
- 1 tsp. vanilla
- 4 small oranges or clementines or 2 medium oranges
- ¼ cup orange marmalade

1. Preheat oven to 375°F. In a medium mixing bowl combine cornflakes, melted butter, and brown sugar. Press into the bottom and up the sides of a 14×5×1-inch or 11×8×1-inch fluted tart pan with a removable bottom. Bake for 8 to 10 minutes or until golden brown. Cool on a wire rack.

2. Meanwhile, in a 1-cup glass measure sprinkle gelatin over the water; let stand several minutes to soften. Microwave on 100 percent power (high) for 20 seconds or until gelatin is dissolved, stirring twice. For filling, in a large bowl whisk together yogurt, milk, honey, and vanilla; whisk in dissolved gelatin. Pour filling into prepared crust. Chill for 4 to 24 hours.

3. Peel oranges and very thinly slice. Remove and discard any seeds.

4. Remove tart from pan; sprinkle any loose crust pieces on edges of tart. Arrange orange slices on tart. In a small saucepan heat marmalade just until melted; brush or drizzle on oranges. Cut crosswise or in wedges to serve. Makes 8 servings.

EACH SERVING *298 cal, 11 g fat, 34 mg chol, 224 mg sodium, 42 g carb, 2 g fiber, 10 g pro.*

ORANGE-RICOTTA
PANCAKES

Orange-Ricotta Pancakes

When you stir the wet ingredients into the flour mixture, the batter should look slightly lumpy. Don't overmix, or the pancakes will be tough.

PREP 25 min. COOK 3 min. per batch

1½ cups all-purpose flour
½ cup cornmeal
2 Tbsp. sugar
1 tsp. baking powder
½ tsp. baking soda
½ tsp. salt
1 cup milk
½ cup ricotta cheese
¼ cup orange juice
2 eggs
2 tsp. finely shredded orange peel
1 recipe Raspberry-Orange Syrup

1. For pancakes, in a large mixing bowl combine flour, cornmeal, sugar, baking powder, baking soda, and salt. In a medium bowl whisk together milk, ricotta, orange juice, eggs, and orange peel. Add milk mixture to flour mixture; stir just until combined.
2. Preheat a griddle over medium heat; brush lightly with butter. Add ¼ to ⅓ cup batter per pancake. Cook about 2 minutes; turn over when surfaces are bubbly and edges are slightly dry. Cook 1 to 2 minutes more or until done.
3. Spoon Raspberry-Orange Syrup over pancakes. Garnish with additional fresh raspberries. Sprinkle with powdered sugar, if desired. Makes 10 to 12 pancakes.
Raspberry-Orange Syrup In a small saucepan combine 1 cup sugar, ½ cup orange juice, and 1 Tbsp. lemon juice. Bring to boiling, stirring to dissolve sugar. Reduce heat; simmer about 10 minutes or until syrupy. Stir in 1 pint fresh raspberries.

EACH SERVING (*2 pancakes and about ¼ cup syrup*) *527 cal, 9 g fat, 97 mg chol, 551 mg sodium, 99 g carb, 5 g fiber, 13 g pro.*

QUINOA-PUMPKIN SEED GRANOLA

Quinoa-Pumpkin Seed Granola

Rinse and drain quinoa (pronounced KEEN-wah) before cooking to remove the grain's natural coating, which has a slightly bitter taste.

PREP 20 min. BAKE 20 min.
COOL 15 min. OVEN 350°F

¾ cup uncooked quinoa, rinsed and well-drained
½ cup raw pumpkin seeds (pepitas)
½ cup whole and/or slivered almonds
¼ cup flaxseed
¼ cup honey
2 Tbsp. canola oil
1 tsp. ground cinnamon
½ tsp. coarse salt
¾ cup dried cherries, cranberries, golden raisins, and/or snipped dried apricots
Baked apples (optional)
Milk (optional)

1. Preheat oven to 350°F. In a large bowl combine quinoa, pumpkin seeds, almonds, and flaxseed. In a small microwave-safe bowl heat honey on 100 percent power (high) for 20 seconds. Stir in oil, cinnamon, and salt. Pour honey mixture over quinoa mixture; toss to coat. Spread in a 15×10×1-inch baking pan.
2. Bake, uncovered, for 20 minutes or until golden brown, stirring twice. Stir in dried fruit. Cool for 15 minutes in the pan. Spread out on foil. Cool completely, breaking up any large pieces. Transfer to an airtight container. Store up to 2 weeks in the refrigerator. If desired, serve over baked apples with milk. Makes 13 (¼-cup) servings.

EACH SERVING *191 cal, 11 g fat, 0 mg chol, 94 mg sodium, 22 g carb, 3 g fiber, 6 g pro.*

These breakfast sandwiches of sweet Hawaiian-style buns, filled with provolone cheese, sliced pear, and smoked chicken sausage are cooked à la french toast and served with maple syrup for a sweet finish.

KID FRIENDLY | **FAST**

French-Toasted Sausage and Pear "Hot Dogs"

To keep french toast warm, place in a rectangular baking dish and set in a 200°F oven.

PREP 25 min. COOK 6 min. per batch

- 12 oz. fully cooked applewood smoked chicken sausage links
- 1 Tbsp. vegetable oil
- 2 eggs
- ½ cup half-and-half or light cream
- 1 Tbsp. sugar
- 1 tsp. vanilla
- ⅛ tsp. ground cinnamon
- ⅛ tsp. ground nutmeg
- 6 Hawaiian sweet hot dog buns or regular hot dog buns, split
- 2 Tbsp. honey (if using regular hot dog buns)
- 6 thin slices provolone cheese
- ½ medium red pear, cored and thinly sliced
- 1 to 2 Tbsp. butter or vegetable oil
  Maple syrup (optional)

1. Slice chicken sausage lengthwise into ¼- to ½-inch-thick pieces. In a large skillet heat 1 Tbsp. oil over medium-high heat. Brown sliced chicken sausage on both sides. Drain on paper towels. Wipe out skillet with paper towels; set aside.
2. Meanwhile, in a shallow dish whisk together eggs, half-and-half, sugar, vanilla, cinnamon, and nutmeg; set aside.
3. If using regular hot dog buns, drizzle cut sides of buns with honey. Add a slice of cheese to each bun. Fill with sliced chicken sausage and pear. Secure buns with wooden toothpicks.

4. In the large skillet heat butter over medium heat. Dip three of the filled buns in egg mixture; add to skillet. Cook until well browned, about 3 to 4 minutes per side. Repeat with remaining filled buns. Remove toothpicks. Serve with maple syrup, if desired. Makes 6 servings.

EACH SERVING *551 cal, 23 g fat, 159 mg chol, 734 mg sodium, 63 g carb, 1 g fiber, 23 g pro.*

Delicious Every Day

Fresh and easy ideas for dinner.

ROASTED PORK TENDERLOIN WITH RED PEPPER PESTO

Roasted Pork Tenderloin with Red Pepper Pesto

PREP 20 min. ROAST 25 min.
STAND 5 min. COOK 8 min.
OVEN 425°F

- 3 cloves garlic, cut into thin slivers
- 2 Tbsp. snipped fresh oregano
- 1 tsp. smoked paprika
- 1 1-lb. pork tenderloin
- 4 Tbsp. olive oil
- 3 large red sweet peppers, cut into wedges
- 2 cloves garlic, minced
  Fresh oregano

1. Preheat oven to 425°F. In a small bowl combine slivered garlic, oregano, smoked paprika, ¼ tsp. salt, and ¼ tsp. ground black pepper. Brush pork with 1 Tbsp. of the olive oil; press garlic mixture evenly onto all sides. Place on a rack in a shallow roasting pan.
2. Roast, uncovered, for 25 to 30 minutes or until an instant-read thermometer registers 145°F. Cover with foil; let stand 5 minutes.
3. Meanwhile, heat a large nonstick skillet over medium-high heat. Add pepper wedges. Cook 8 to 10 minutes, turning occasionally until peppers are well-browned. Remove from heat.
4. For pesto transfer one-third of the peppers to a blender or food processor. Add minced garlic and remaining 3 Tbsp. olive oil. Process until almost smooth. Add additional oil, if necessary, for pesto consistency. Season to taste with salt and ground black pepper. Serve pork with red pepper pesto and roasted pepper wedges. Sprinkle with fresh oregano. Makes 4 servings.
EACH SERVING *293 cal, 18 g fat, 74 mg chol, 354 mg sodium, 7 g carb, 2 g fiber, 25 g pro.*

FLAVOR SECRET

Make sure to reach for smoked paprika—which is different from the spice labeled "paprika". It adds a touch of heat and earthy smokiness. And garlic slices roast up perfectly to lend a subtle bite.

STEAK WITH FENNEL AND BEANS

Steak with Fennel and Beans

START TO FINISH 47 min.

- 1 Tbsp. olive oil
- 2 10- to 12-oz. beef shoulder petite tenders
- 1 small fennel bulb, plus 2 Tbsp. reserved feathery fronds
- ½ cup reduced-sodium beef broth
- 1 medium onion, chopped (½ cup)
- 1 cup grape tomatoes, halved
- 2 cloves garlic, minced
- 1 Tbsp. fennel seeds, coarsely crushed
- 1 15-oz. can cannellini (white kidney) beans, rinsed and drained
- 2 Tbsp. balsamic vinegar

1. In a large skillet heat the oil over medium-high heat. Season steaks with salt and pepper and add to the pan. Cook about 12 minutes* each side or until medium-rare (145°F). Remove steaks; cover with foil. Let stand 10 minutes before slicing.
2. Meanwhile, use a sharp knife to cut off the fennel stalks (about 1 inch above the bulb). Discard stalks, reserving 2 Tbsp. feathery fronds. Cut a thin slice off the root end of the bulb. Cut bulb into thin wedges. Cut away and discard tough core from each wedge.
3. Add broth to the hot skillet. Cook and stir, scraping up browned bits from the bottom of the pan. Add fennel wedges; cook 4 minutes. Add onion, tomatoes, garlic, and fennel seeds; cook about 5 minutes or just until vegetables are tender. Add beans and balsamic vinegar; cook 3 minutes more. Sprinkle with fennel fronds. Serve beans, vegetables, and their pan juices with sliced steak. Makes 4 servings.
*If steak browns too quickly, reduce heat to medium.
EACH SERVING *350 cal, 13 g fat, 79 mg chol, 473 mg sodium, 26 g carb, 8 g fiber, 37 g pro.*

FLAVOR SECRET

That big hit of balsamic vinegar at the end is the ingredient that adds pungent sweetness and ties this hearty steak and beans dish together. Don't skip it, and be sure to pour all the pan juices over the dish before serving.

KID FRIENDLY

Spaghetti Squash with Tomatoes and Olives

START TO FINISH 40 min.

½ 2- to 2½-lb. spaghetti squash
2 Tbsp. olive oil
4 cloves garlic, minced
2 14½-oz. cans diced tomatoes with basil, garlic, and oregano (undrained)
4 oz. dried whole grain spaghetti
½ cup pimiento-stuffed green olives, coarsely chopped
⅓ cup golden raisins
¼ cup snipped fresh basil
2 oz. feta cheese, crumbled (½ cup)

1. Wash spaghetti squash, cut in half lengthwise, and remove strings and seeds. Place cut side down in a 2-quart square baking dish. Add 2 Tbsp. water. Cover with vented clear plastic wrap. Microwave, covered, on 100 percent power (high) for 10 to 12 minutes or until squash pierces easily with a fork. Cool slightly.
2. Meanwhile, in a large saucepan heat oil over medium heat. Add garlic; cook 1 minute. Add tomatoes; bring to boiling. Boil gently, uncovered, for 15 minutes or until slightly thickened, stirring occasionally.
3. While the tomatoes cook, in a large pot cook pasta according to package directions; drain and return to the pot.
4. When the squash has cooled slightly, hold in one hand with a hot pad. Using a fork in the other hand, scrape the pulp from the squash into strands. Add squash, tomato sauce, olives, raisins, and basil to pasta in the pot. Season to taste with ground black pepper. Serve topped with feta cheese and additional snipped fresh basil, if desired. Makes 4 servings.

EACH SERVING *362 cal, 14 g fat, 13 mg chol, 987 mg sodium, 54 g carb, 9 g fiber, 9 g pro.*

FLAVOR SECRET

Mild-flavor spaghetti squash is an ideal base for hearty sauces, plus it's a tasty way to get kids to eat veggies.

Dinner on a Dollar

Turn on the oven and cozy up to this warm salad—a deliciously toasty twist on a BLT.

KID FRIENDLY | **LOW FAT** | **FAST**

Roasted BLT Salad

Quick-roasting crunchy greens, such as romaine, lightly chars the edges while softening the inner leaves, resulting in a velvety texture that retains some crunch.

PREP **15 min.** BAKE **15 min.**
OVEN **400°F** COST **$1.37 per serving**

- 4 slices bacon
- 1 cup cherry tomatoes
- 6 tsp. olive oil
- ½ baguette, cut into 1½-inch cubes
- 1 head romaine lettuce, quartered lengthwise
- ¼ tsp. salt
- ¼ tsp. ground black pepper

1. Preheat oven to 400°F. In a large skillet cook bacon until crisp; drain on paper towels. Break into large pieces; set aside.

2. Meanwhile, line a 15×10×1-inch baking pan with foil. Add cherry tomatoes; toss with 2 tsp. of the olive oil. Bake, uncovered, for 10 minutes. Transfer tomatoes and their juices to a medium bowl. Place bread cubes and romaine quarters on the baking pan. Drizzle romaine with 2 tsp. of the olive oil, toss gently to coat. Return pan to oven; bake 5 minutes or until bread is golden and romaine is browned at edges.

3. Add bread to the medium bowl with the tomatoes. Toss gently to combine. Let stand 5 minutes to allow bread to absorb some tomato juices. Transfer tomatoes, bread, romaine, and bacon to a serving platter. Drizzle with remaining 2 tsp. olive oil. Sprinkle with salt and pepper. Makes 4 servings.

EACH SERVING *258 cal, 10 g fat, 9 mg chol, 647 mg sodium, 31 g carb, 2 g fiber, 8 g pro.*

**FUDGY CHERRY AND
PORT BROWNIES**

february

SWEET INDULGENCE Dorie Greenspan shares her recipes for petite chocolate desserts that will make you swoon. Add them to a heartwarming no-fuss buffet for friends and family.

37

53

55

Little Bites of Wonderful

These meant-to-be-shared surprises from baker extraordinaire Dorie Greenspan are not your ordinary box of chocolates.

Smoky Chocolate Crackers

"We have cookies at Beurre & Sel (Dorie and son Joshua's small batch cookie shop in New York City) that we call the cocktail collection," Dorie says. "They're made like shortbread but just tip over to the savory side—perfect paired with wine or champagne. These cookies, which get their smokiness from smoked paprika, have a healthy amount of salt and just enough sugar to bring out the chocolate flavor. They'd be incredible with port and a slice of cheese."

PREP **35 min.** FREEZE **45 min.**
BAKE **6 min. per batch** OVEN **350°F**

1¾ cups all-purpose flour
½ cup unsweetened cocoa powder
1½ tsp. smoked paprika
1 tsp. salt
¾ cup unsalted butter, softened
⅓ cup powdered sugar, sifted
3 Tbsp. granulated sugar
2 egg whites
½ cup finely chopped toasted almonds, (see tip, page 35)

1. In a medium bowl sift together the flour, cocoa powder, smoked paprika, and salt; set aside.
2. In a large mixing bowl beat the butter with an electric mixer on medium speed until smooth and creamy, about 2 minutes. Add powdered and granulated sugars; beat 2 minutes more to blend. Add egg whites; beat on medium speed 1 minute. Reduce speed to low; beat about 1 minute more. (The egg whites will curdle the batter, but the dough will come together when the flour mixture is added.) Still on low speed, add the flour mixture; mix only until it disappears into the dough. You should have a thick, smooth dough. Using a spatula, stir in chopped almonds.
3. Turn the dough out onto a work surface. Divide in half; shape each half into a disk. Place each disk between two sheets of parchment or waxed paper; roll to ¼-inch thickness. Freeze rolled-out dough at least 30 minutes.
4. Position an oven rack in the center of the oven; preheat to 350°F. Line two baking sheets with parchment paper or silicone baking mats.
5. Working with half the dough at a time, use a 2-inch heart-shape cookie cutter to cut as many cookies as you can. Save the scraps of dough. Place hearts about 1 inch apart on the prepared baking sheet.
6. Bake 6 to 8 minutes or just until slightly firm to the touch, rotating baking sheet at the halfway point. Remove from oven; cool 5 minutes. Transfer to a wire rack; cool to room temperature.
7. Cut out remaining dough, always placing cutouts on a cool baking sheet. Combine dough scraps. Shape into a disk, roll, and freeze 15 minutes or until firm. Cut and bake as above. Makes about 50 crackers.
Store Crackers will keep in an airtight container at room temperature up to 1 week.

EACH CRACKER *55 cal, 3 g fat, 7 mg chol, 49 mg sodium, 6 g carb, 1 g fiber, 1 g pro.*

WORKING WITH CHOCOLATE
"You need to pay very close attention to chocolate," Dorie says. "You have to babysit it, especially when you're melting it." There are a number of ways to melt chocolate, including in a double boiler (above) or in the microwave. According to Dorie, chocolate has two enemies: heat and liquid. "When you melt chocolate, you never want to use really high heat—always slow and gentle," she says. "You also want to be sure to keep it away from water, which will cause the chocolate to seize and firm up." This is also why chocolate shouldn't be stored in the refrigerator. "The condensation in the fridge can ruin chocolate," Dorie says. "It's best kept in a cool, dark, dry place."

KID FRIENDLY

Chocolate Puffs with Mascarpone Cream

"Cream puffs are so lovely because they're not particularly sweet, so when you add cocoa, you really taste the chocolate," Dorie says. "The touch of rose in the light, creamy filling is subtle. It's as much about fragrance as it is taste. I'd much rather be given these than a bouquet of roses."

PREP 45 min. BAKE 25 min.
OVEN 425°F/375°F

Cream Puffs
- 2 eggs
- ½ cup all-purpose flour
- 2 Tbsp. unsweetened cocoa powder
- ⅓ cup water
- ¼ cup whole milk
- ¼ cup unsalted butter, cut into chunks
- 2 Tbsp. sugar
- ¼ tsp. salt

Filling
- ½ cup mascarpone cheese
- ½ cup whipping cream
- 2 Tbsp. sugar
- 2 tsp. rose syrup or rose extract, or a drop or two of rosewater to taste (optional)
  Red food coloring (optional)
  Bittersweet or semisweet chocolate, melted (optional)

1. Let eggs stand at room temperature 30 minutes. Position oven racks to divide oven into thirds; preheat to 425°F. Line two baking sheets with parchment paper; set aside.
2. For cream puffs, in a medium bowl sift together flour and cocoa powder. In a medium saucepan combine the water, milk, butter, sugar, and salt; bring to boiling over medium-high heat. Add flour and cocoa mixture all at once; lower heat slightly. Using a wooden spoon or sturdy heatproof spatula, stir vigorously. The mixture will come together in a ball and there will be a film on the bottom of the pan, but do not

stop stirring; give it another minute of vigorous stirring. Transfer hot dough to a mixing bowl; let rest for 2 minutes.
3. Using a whisk (or a stand mixer fitted with the paddle attachment), beat dough 1 minute. Add eggs, one at a time, beating very well after each. You'll have a smooth, shiny dough.
4. Using a small cookie scoop or small spoon, place eight mounds of dough on each of the prepared baking sheets, leaving at least 1 inch of space between mounds.
5. Transfer baking sheets to oven; immediately reduce heat to 375°F. Bake for 25 to 27 minutes or until the puffs feel hollow and lift easily off the paper, rotating the baking sheets from top to bottom and front to back at the halfway point. Cool to room temperature before filling.
6. For filling, in a medium bowl gently stir mascarpone with a spatula to loosen. Beating makes mascarpone turn grainy, so go easy. Set aside.
7. In a medium bowl beat whipping cream just until it starts to thicken. Beat in sugar and rose syrup, if desired. Continue to whip until the cream holds medium peaks. Add a drop of red food coloring (if desired), mix, then add additional drops of coloring. Continue to whip until the cream holds peaks that stand up nicely and just start to fold over at the top. Stir a spoonful of the cream into the mascarpone to lighten. Gently fold in the remaining cream.
8. To assemble, cut cream puffs in half. Using a pastry bag fitted with a large round tip, pipe filling over one half; top with remaining half. To serve, drizzle with melted chocolate, if desired. Makes 16 cream puffs.
Store Unfilled cream puffs will keep in an airtight container in the refrigerator up to 3 days or in the freezer up to 2 weeks. Filling will keep in an airtight container in the refrigerator up to 3 days. Fill puffs just before serving.
EACH CREAM PUFF *130 cal, 10 g fat, 51 mg chol, 54 mg sodium, 8 g carb, 0 g fiber, 2 g pro.*

PERFECT WHIPPED CREAM
"The key to whipped cream is keeping everything cold," Dorie says. Always start with cold cream, and chill the bowl and the beater. Then start beating gently. "People think you need to beat the cream to death, but you want to start slow," she says. When the cream just starts to thicken, that's when you add the sugar. "Watch closely as you continue to whip," Dorie says. "You don't want peaks that stand up and salute you. They should start a bit droopy and then get just firm enough to stand up. It's always better to underwhip than to overwhip."

These will be your most beloved brownies, thanks to port-soaked cherries and so much chocolate that they absolutely ooze decadence. Irresistible warm, they're also unexpectedly spectacular chilled.

Fudgy Cherry and Port Brownies

"I love the richness of port," Dorie says. "When the cherries are soaked, they take on an extra dimension of sweet-tart flavor that balances the fudgy brownie."

PREP 30 min. BAKE 35 min.
OVEN 325°F

- 2 Tbsp. port or water
- 2 Tbsp. water
- ½ cup dried cherries
- 5 Tbsp. unsalted butter, cut into pieces
- 6 oz. semisweet chocolate, coarsely chopped
- ¾ cup sugar
- 2 large eggs, cold
- ¼ tsp. salt
- ⅓ cup all-purpose flour
- 4½ oz. semisweet chocolate, chopped, or ¾ cup semisweet chocolate pieces
  Fresh raspberries (optional)

1. Position oven rack in the center of the oven; preheat oven to 325°F. Line an 8×8×2-inch pan with foil. Butter foil; set aside.
2. In a small saucepan bring the port and water to boiling. Add dried cherries; cook and stir over low heat until fruit is soft and plump and liquid evaporates. Using a spatula, scrape cherries into a bowl; set aside to cool.

3. Set a heatproof bowl over a saucepan of barely simmering water (be sure that the water doesn't touch the bottom of the bowl). Place butter in the bowl; scatter the 6 oz. chocolate over butter. Heat until the chocolate is almost melted (do not heat the mixture so much that the butter and chocolate separate). Remove bowl from heat. Stir until butter and chocolate are smooth.
4. Whisk in the sugar until fully incorporated. Add eggs, one at a time, stirring until batter is smooth and glossy. Whisk in the salt. Gently whisk in the flour, stirring only until it disappears into the batter. Using a spatula, stir in the port-soaked cherries (and any accumulated liquid) and the 4½ oz. chopped chocolate. Scrape batter into prepared pan, smoothing the top as much as possible.
5. Bake 35 minutes. Transfer pan to a wire rack; cool to room temperature. Invert brownies onto a cutting board; gently peel away the foil. Turn brownies over. Cut into 36 squares. Serve with fresh raspberries, if desired. Makes 36 brownies.
Store Keep in an airtight container at room temperature for up to 3 days or in the freezer for up to 3 months.
EACH BROWNIE *85 cal, 4 g fat, 15 mg chol, 22 mg sodium, 12 g carb, 1 g fiber, 1 g pro.*

PAN PREP
For most brownies or bar cookies, Dorie recommends lining the pan with buttered foil. It's an easy way to remove the brownie block from the pan after baking. Tear off a large piece of foil, turn the pan upside down, and mold the foil over the pan. Turn the pan right side up and press the foil into place. Using a pastry brush, slather the foil with softened butter.

KID FRIENDLY

Cocoa Crunch Meringue Sandwiches

"Meringues have a tendency to be one-note," Dorie says. "They're all about the crunch. But when it comes to flavor, all you taste is sweet. Adding cocoa cuts the sweetness, as do finely chopped nuts, which add a little extra crunch. And it's all balanced by the soft, rich chocolaty filling."

PREP 40 min. BAKE 1 hr. 30 min.
STAND 2 hr. CHILL 30 min.
OVEN 250°F

Cookies
¼ cup powdered sugar
2 Tbsp. unsweetened cocoa powder
¼ cup walnuts or blanched almonds, toasted and finely chopped*
2 egg whites, at room temperature
2 Tbsp. granulated sugar

Filling
¼ cup whipping cream
1 Tbsp. unsalted butter
2 oz. semisweet or bittersweet chocolate, finely chopped

1. For cookies, position oven racks to divide oven into thirds; preheat to 250°F. Using a pencil, draw twenty 1½-inch-diameter circles on each of two sheets of parchment paper. Flip over the sheets of parchment and use them to line two baking sheets.
2. In a small bowl sift together powdered sugar and cocoa powder. Add chopped nuts; toss to coat.
3. In a large mixing bowl beat together egg whites and a pinch of salt with an electric mixer on medium speed until egg whites just begin to turn opaque. Increase the speed and add sugar little by little, beating until the meringue holds stiff peaks.
4. Using a flexible spatula, gently fold half of the powdered sugar mixture into the egg white mixture. Mix just until combined. Fold in remaining powdered sugar mixture.

5. Using the penciled circles as a guide, spoon the meringue into 1½-inch rounds on the prepared baking sheets. Use the back of the spoon to spread the meringue evenly. (Or, using a pastry bag fitted with a large round tip, pipe the meringue into rounds on the baking sheets.)
6. Bake 1½ hours. Turn off oven. Keeping the door closed, allow cookies to remain in the oven 1 hour more. Remove baking sheets from oven; cool to room temperature.
7. For filling, in a small saucepan bring cream and butter to boiling. In a heatproof bowl place the chopped chocolate. Pour the hot cream mixture over the chocolate; let stand 5 minutes. Using a small spatula or whisk and starting in the center of the bowl, stir together the cream mixture and chocolate in gradually increasing concentric circles. Stir gently until filling is smooth and glossy. Let stand at room temperature about 1 hour, stirring occasionally. (The filling has to thicken before you can use it to sandwich the cookies.)
8. To assemble, using a small offset spatula or a spoon, top half the cookies with 2 tsp. filling. Spread the filling almost to the edges of the cookies; top with remaining cookies. Chill at least 30 minutes (or up to 1 day). Serve chilled. Makes 20 cookie sandwiches.
*Tip To toast whole nuts or large pieces, spread them in a shallow pan. Bake them in a 350°F oven for 5 to 10 minutes, shaking the pan once or twice. Toast coconut in the same way, but watch it closely to avoid burning it. Toast finely chopped or ground nuts or sesame seeds in a dry skillet over medium heat. Stir often so they don't burn.

EACH COOKIE SANDWICH *53 cal, 4 g fat, 6 mg chol, 14 mg sodium, 5 g carb, 0 g fiber, 1 g pro.*

THE MAGIC OF MERINGUE
As with whipped cream, start slowly when making meringue, Dorie says. "You'll see the mixture go from clear to foamy and then just start to turn opaque," she says. "When you see that change, that's the time to add the sugar and turn up the speed. Add the sugar gradually and keep a watchful eye. When you think it needs a minute more, it doesn't. Once it holds stand-up stiff peaks (no folding over at the top), stop. The meringue should always have a shine. If it starts to lose its sheen, you've gone too far."

MINI CHOCOLATE AND
YOGURT PARFAITS

Mini Chocolate and Yogurt Parfaits

"These creamy parfaits win the gold star for most surprising," Dorie says. "A sweet, tangy combination of yogurt and goat cheese gets an unexpected pop from pink peppercorns."
PREP 30 min. CHILL 3 hrs.

    2 cups plain Greek yogurt
    2 oz. goat cheese (chèvre) (¼ cup)
    ¼ cup honey
    ¼ tsp. freshly ground pink
       peppercorns
    ⅛ tsp. salt
    3 Tbsp. unsweetened cocoa powder
    ¼ cup cherry jam
       Whole pink peppercorns

1. In a food processor combine yogurt, goat cheese, honey, ground pink peppercorns, and salt. Cover and process for 60 to 90 seconds (don't skimp on the time—it takes at least a minute to blend the ingredients until they're creamy and velvety smooth).
2. Reserve 1 cup of the yogurt mixture. Add cocoa powder to remaining mixture; whisk until smooth.
3. Layer one-fourth of the cocoa mixture in 4 small cordial glasses. Spoon one-fourth of the plain reserved yogurt mixture over chocolate. Top with one-fourth of the cocoa mixture. Layer some of the plain yogurt mixture in 4 more small cordial glasses. Spoon remaining cocoa mixture over plain yogurt. Top with remaining half of the plain yogurt. Chill at least 3 hours.
4. In a small saucepan heat jam just until melted; spoon over parfaits. Top with pink peppercorns. Makes 8 parfaits.
EACH PARFAIT *117 cal, 2 g fat, 3 mg chol, 93 mg sodium, 19 g carb, 1 g fiber, 8 g pro.*

VALENTINE'S DAY CHOCOLATE TRAIL MIX

Valentine's Day Chocolate Trail Mix

"This mix is everything you want in a snack," Dorie says. "Sweet, salty, chewy, crunchy—every bite is different. Maybe that's why you can't stop eating it."
PREP 20 min. STAND 1 hr.

    1   cup granola
    1   cup salted pretzel sticks, coarsely
        crushed
    1   cup semisweet chocolate pieces
    1½ cups dried cranberries
    1   cup cocoa-covered almonds
    1   cup dried cherries
    ½   cup freeze-dried raspberries

1. Line two baking sheets with waxed paper; set aside. In a small bowl place granola; in another small bowl place pretzels.
2. In a 2-cup glass measuring cup place ⅔ cup of the chocolate pieces. Microwave on 100 percent power (high) for 30 seconds. Stir chocolate. Continue heating on high for 20 to 30 seconds, stirring every 10 seconds, until chocolate is melted. Stir until smooth. Add remaining ⅓ cup chocolate pieces to the mixture; stir until chocolate is smooth again.
3. Pour half the melted chocolate over the granola; pour remaining half over the pretzels. Stir each until evenly coated. Turn out the contents of each bowl out onto the prepared baking sheets. Separate the chocolate-coated pieces into small chunks. Let stand at room temperature 1 to 2 hours or until set. (If necessary, chill for 15 minutes until chocolate is set.)
4. Break or chop the chocolate-coated granola and pretzels into bite-size morsels (evenness does not count here). Transfer pieces to a large bowl. Add dried cranberries, almonds, and dried cherries. Stir in dried raspberries just before serving. Makes 6 cups.
Store Keep in an airtight container at room temperature up to 3 days.
EACH ¼-CUP SERVING *138 cal, 6 g fat, 0 mg chol, 74 mg sodium, 23 g carb, 2 g fiber, 1 g pro.*

KID FRIENDLY

Triple-Chocolate Cake Balls

"Any time you can play with your food, it's all the more fun," Dorie says of these dainty treats. "Dress them up and they're an elegant treat for adults. Let the kids make them and they're the perfect activity for a Valentine's Day party."

PREP **1 hr. 15 min.** CHILL **2 hrs.** FREEZE **50 min.**

- 1 recipe Best-Ever Chocolate Cake*
- 1 8-oz. package cream cheese, softened
- ¼ cup unsalted butter, softened
- 1½ cups powdered sugar
- ¼ cup unsweetened cocoa powder
- 2 Tbsp. milk
- 6 chocolate graham crackers, coarsely crushed (optional)
- 24 oz. semisweet chocolate pieces, for coating
- ¼ cup shortening
  Unsweetened cocoa powder

1. In a medium bowl beat cream cheese and butter with an electric mixer on medium to high speed for 30 seconds. Add powdered sugar, cocoa powder, and milk; beat together until smooth and creamy.
2. Scrape cream cheese mixture into the crumbled cake. Using a large spoon, mix until blended (at some point it gets hard to mix with a spoon, so just reach into the bowl and use your hands).

Mix in the crushed graham crackers, if desired. Press a piece of plastic wrap against the surface of the dough; chill at least 2 hours (or up to 2 days).
3. In a large bowl finely crumble the cake (it is easiest to cut the cake into quarters and work with one quarter at a time). To form the cake balls, line a few baking sheets with parchment or waxed paper. Using a medium-size cookie scoop or 2 level tablespoons, scoop out mounds of dough and shape into balls between your palms. As you fill a baking sheet, transfer it to the freezer and continue working with the dough. It is easier to coat the balls if they are very cold, so keep them in the freezer at least 30 minutes.
4. To coat the cake balls, line another baking sheet with parchment or waxed paper; set aside. Set a heatproof bowl over a saucepan of barely simmering water (be sure the water doesn't touch the bottom of the bowl). Add the chocolate pieces and shortening. Melt over gentle heat, stirring until smooth.
5. Drop the cake balls into the chocolate one at a time, lifting each out and placing on the prepared baking sheet when coated. If desired, place a small heart shaped candy on the chocolate.
6. When all cake balls are coated, transfer to the freezer for about 20 minutes to harden the chocolate. To serve, coat with cocoa powder. Serve chilled. Pass small skewers or lollipop sticks, if desired. Makes 52 to 60 cake balls.
***Tip** Use a two-layer chocolate cake mix to make about 40 cake balls.
EACH CAKE BALL *191 cal, 11 g fat, 26 mg chol, 76 mg sodium, 25 g carb, 1 g fiber, 2 g pro.*

KID FRIENDLY

Best-Ever Chocolate Cake

PREP **30 min.** STAND **30 min.** BAKE **40 min.** OVEN **350°F**

- ¾ cup unsalted butter
- 3 eggs
- 2 cups all-purpose flour
- ¾ cup unsweetened cocoa powder
- 1 tsp. baking soda
- ¾ tsp. baking powder
- ½ tsp. salt
- 2 cups sugar
- 2 tsp. vanilla
- 1½ cups milk

1. Let butter and eggs stand at room temperature for 30 minutes. Meanwhile, lightly grease and flour a 13×9×2-inch baking pan; set aside.
2. Preheat oven to 350°F. In a large bowl stir together flour, cocoa powder, baking soda, baking powder, and salt; set aside.
3. In a large mixing bowl beat butter with an electric mixer on medium to high speed for 30 seconds. Gradually add sugar, about ¼ cup at a time, beating on medium speed until well combined (3 to 4 minutes). Scrape sides of bowl; continue beating on medium speed for 2 minutes. Add eggs, one at a time, beating after each addition (about 1 minute total). Beat in vanilla.
4. Alternately add flour mixture and milk to beaten mixture, beating on low speed just until combined after each addition. Beat on medium to high speed for 20 seconds more. Spread batter evenly into the prepared pan.
5. Bake 40 to 45 minutes, or until a wooden toothpick inserted in the center comes out clean. Cool cake in pan on a wire rack. Remove cake from pan. Makes 12 servings.
EACH SERVING *355 cal, 14 g fat, 79 mg chol, 260 mg sodium, 54 g carb, 2 g fiber, 6 g pro.*

TRIPLE-CHOCOLATE
CAKE BALLS

All-purpose indulgence. Breakup, makeup, or friends' catch-up, these bite-size wonders will do the trick—with or without a little strawberry ice cream.

KID FRIENDLY | **LOW FAT**

Peanutty Fruit and Chocolate Chip Cookies

"This is the kind of cookie you'll make for Valentine's Day and then make over and over again," Dorie says. "Throw them in the lunch box, set them out with espresso—they're on the border between treats for kids and grown-up indulgence."

PREP 35 min. CHILL 1 hr.
BAKE 6 min. per batch OVEN 350°F

1½ cups regular rolled oats
½ cup all-purpose flour
¼ cup unsweetened cocoa powder
½ tsp. baking soda
⅛ tsp. salt
½ cup unsalted butter, softened
½ cup peanut butter
⅓ cup granulated sugar
½ cup packed light brown sugar
1 egg
3 oz. semisweet chocolate, chopped, or ½ cup semisweet chocolate pieces
½ cup dried cranberries
Strawberry ice cream (optional)

1. In a medium bowl combine oats, flour, cocoa powder, baking soda, and salt; set aside.
2. In a large mixing bowl beat butter and peanut butter with an electric mixer on medium speed until smooth. Add granulated and brown sugars; beat 2 minutes more until mixture is smooth. Add egg; beat for 1 minute. Reduce mixer speed to low; blend in the oat mixture, mixing only until it disappears into the dough. Using a sturdy spatula, stir in chocolate and dried cranberries.
3. Divide dough in half; wrap each half in plastic wrap. Refrigerate at least 1 hour (or up to 2 days).
4. Position oven racks to divide oven into thirds; preheat to 350°F. Line two baking sheets with parchment paper or silicone baking mats.
5. Working with half the dough at a time, shape dough into ¾-inch balls. Place balls about 1 inch apart on the prepared baking sheets, pressing down gently into rounds.
6. Bake 6 to 8 minutes just until firm around the edges, rotating the baking sheets from top to bottom and front to back at the halfway point. Remove baking sheets from oven; let rest for 2 minutes. Carefully transfer cookies to a wire rack. They will firm as they cool. Repeat with remaining dough, always starting with a cool baking sheet.
7. Serve with strawberry ice cream, if desired. Makes about 120 bite-size cookies.

For standard-size cookies Shape dough into 1- to 1¼-inch balls. Place balls about 2 inches apart on prepared baking sheets, pressing down gently into rounds. Bake at 350°F oven for 9 to 11 minutes or just until firm around the edges. Cool as directed. Makes about 45 cookies.

EACH BITE-SIZE COOKIE *31 cal, 2 g fat, 4 mg chol, 14 mg sodium, 4 g carb, 0 g fiber, 1 g pro.*

MEET DORIE
James Beard award-winning author Dorie Greenspan has written 10 cookbooks. For her, baking isn't just about the tasty results, it's about enjoying the process. "When we set aside the time to bake, it's special," Dorie says. "There's something very personal about a treat you've handcrafted. There's no better gift for Valentine's Day. It's a way of giving of yourself."

Home Cooking

FREEZER TO DINNER Yes, you can cook meat, poultry, and fish from a frozen state. Just follow the tips to learn which cuts to buy, how to freeze them, and how best to cook them.

Orange-Simmered Pork Chops with Mango Relish

Bright citrus wakes up this hearty, wintry pork dish. Tropical pineapple and mango add sweetness to balance the heavy hit of spice.

START TO FINISH **30 min.**

- 1 mango, halved, seeded, peeled, and sliced or chopped
- 1 cup pineapple chunks
- 1 small orange or clementine, peeled and segmented
- ¼ cup orange juice
- ¼ cup chopped red onion
- 1 small banana pepper, sliced (optional)
- 1 tsp. finely shredded orange peel
- ⅛ tsp. cayenne pepper
- 4 4-oz. frozen bone-in loin chops, about ¼ inch thick
- ½ tsp. chili powder
- ½ tsp. salt
- ¼ tsp. ground black pepper
- 1 Tbsp. olive oil
- ½ cup orange juice
- 2 tsp. honey
  Fresh cilantro

1. For mango relish, in a medium bowl stir together mango, pineapple, orange segments, the ¼ cup orange juice, red onion, banana pepper (if desired), orange peel, and cayenne pepper; set aside.
2. Sprinkle pork chops with chili powder, salt, and pepper. In a large skillet heat oil over medium-high heat. Add two pork chops; brown 3 minutes each side. Remove from skillet. Add remaining pork chops to skillet; brown 3 minutes each side. Return first two pork chops to skillet.
3. In a small bowl whisk together the ½ cup orange juice and honey; add to skillet. Add ½ cup water. Reduce heat to low. Simmer, covered, 5 minutes or until pork is done (145°F). Spoon mango relish over pork. Cover; simmer 1 minute more. Remove pork and relish; cover to keep warm.
4. Return pan to medium-high heat. Simmer juices, uncovered, 5 minutes or until reduced by half. Drizzle over pork. Sprinkle with cilantro. Makes 4 servings.

To use fresh or thawed chops
Reduce browning time to 1½ minutes each side. Add oil and chops to skillet. Bring to a simmer; immediately add mango relish. Simmer only 1 minute. Proceed as above.

EACH SERVING *360 cal, 16 g fat, 66 mg chol, 368 mg sodium, 30 g carb, 2 g fiber, 24 g pro.*

FREEZE IT RIGHT
Remove pork chops from their original packaging. Freeze in a single layer on a baking sheet until firm, then transfer to a freezer container or bag. If storing meat for several months, wrap each individual piece in vapor- and moisture-proof plastic wrap, heavy-duty foil, or freezer paper before transferring to the freezer bag or container. Store up to 6 months.

PORK CHOPS tenderize and defrost when simmered in liquid—almost any liquid will do. Look for thin chops (often labeled "breakfast pork chops") about ¼ inch thick for the best results.

CHICKEN TENDERS brown on the stove and finish with a quick braise in the oven. If you prefer to buy boneless chicken breast halves, slice horizontally and freeze—thinner cuts cook more evenly.

Lemon-Braised Chicken Tenders and Cauliflower

A salty-sweet mix of chopped green olives, dates, and pistachios gives this simple dish vibrant taste and a little crunch.

PREP 20 min. COOK 10 min.
BAKE 10 min. OVEN 375°F

- 2 Tbsp. olive oil
- 1 lb. frozen chicken breast tenderloins (8 to 10 pieces)
- 1 small onion, chopped
- ½ cauliflower, cut into florets (about 2 cups)
- 5 cloves garlic, slivered
- 1 tsp. snipped fresh thyme
- ¼ cup lemon juice
- ¾ cup reduced-sodium chicken broth
- 1 tsp. finely shredded lemon peel
- 2 cups packaged fresh baby spinach
- ¼ cup bias-sliced green onion
- ⅓ cup pimiento-stuffed green olives, coarsely chopped
- ¼ cup pitted dates, coarsely chopped
- ¼ cup pistachio nuts, coarsely chopped
  Cooked brown rice (optional)
  Lemon peel (optional)

1. Preheat oven to 375°F. In a Dutch oven heat oil over medium-high heat. Add frozen chicken tenders. Cook 3 to 4 minutes on each side or until golden brown. Transfer to a plate.
2. To the same Dutch oven add onion and cauliflower. Cook 2 minutes, until lightly browned. Add garlic, thyme, and ¼ tsp. each salt and cracked black pepper; cook 30 seconds more. Add lemon juice. Stir, scraping up brown bits in bottom of pan. Return chicken to Dutch oven. Add chicken broth and lemon peel. Bring to boiling; cover and transfer to oven.
3. Bake 10 minutes or until chicken is no longer pink (170°F). Add spinach and green onion; cover and let stand 2 minutes to slightly wilt spinach.
4. In a small bowl combine olives, dates, and pistachios. Spoon chicken mixture over cooked rice, if desired. Top with olive mixture and additional lemon peel, if desired. Makes 4 servings.

To use fresh or thawed chicken
Brown chicken except don't return it to the Dutch oven in Step 2. Proceed as above, baking for 10 to 12 minutes. Return chicken to the Dutch oven when you add the spinach and green onion.

EACH SERVING *321 cal, 15 g fat, 73 mg chol, 585 mg sodium, 19 g carb, 4 g fiber, 29 g pro.*

FREEZE IT RIGHT
For ease, use bulk chicken tenders sold in bags in the freezer section. If you're freezing fresh chicken tenders, remove them from their original packaging. Spread in a single layer on a waxed paper-lined baking sheet and freeze until firm. Once frozen, transfer to a freezer container or bag. Store up to 9 months.

SALMON can go straight from the freezer to the oven without sacrificing flavor or texture. Make sure fillets are similar in shape and thickness for even cooking.

Herb-Crusted Salmon with Roasted Tomatoes

Golden raisins lend an unexpected taste of sweetness. A quick soak before adding them to the baking sheet keeps them plump, even when roasted.

PREP **15 min.** ROAST **28 min.**
OVEN **400°F**

- 2 Tbsp. golden raisins
- 1 cup grape or cherry tomatoes
- 2 Tbsp. capers, drained
- 4 Tbsp. olive oil
- ¾ cup packed parsley leaves
- 1 clove garlic
- ¼ tsp. salt
- ¼ tsp. crushed red pepper
- 4 4-oz. frozen salmon fillets, about 1 inch thick
  Fresh parsley leaves (optional)

1. Preheat oven to 400°F. Line a 15×10×1-inch baking pan with foil; set aside.
2. In a small bowl soak raisins in hot water until softened and plump, about 10 minutes. Drain; set aside. To another small bowl add tomatoes and capers. Drizzle with 2 Tbsp. of the olive oil; toss gently to coat.

3. Meanwhile, in a food processor combine parsley, the remaining 2 Tbsp. olive oil, garlic, salt, and crushed red pepper. Cover; process until smooth.
4. Remove salmon from freezer; place on the prepared pan. Spoon parsley mixture over each salmon fillet, spreading to cover. Spoon tomato mixture around salmon on the baking pan.
5. Roast, uncovered, for 14 to 15 minutes. Remove pan from oven. Add raisins, stirring into tomato mixture. Return pan to oven; roast 14 to 15 minutes more or until fish flakes easily with a fork.
6. Transfer salmon to a platter; spoon over tomatoes, capers, raisins, and any remaining pan juices. Sprinkle with fresh parsley leaves, if desired. Makes 4 servings.

To use fresh or thawed fillets Start by roasting tomato mixture 18 minutes. Then add salmon to the baking pan, along with the raisins. Roast 10 to 12 minutes more.

EACH SERVING *310 cal, 21 g fat, 62 mg chol, 332 mg sodium, 7 g carb, 1 g fiber, 24 g pro.*

FREEZE IT RIGHT
Flash-frozen fish is processed and frozen immediately after it's caught. Look for deals on bags of individually vacuum-sealed salmon fillets. Fresh fish should be frozen within 2 days of purchase. Wrap tightly in moisture- and vapor-proof wrap such as plastic wrap, heavy-duty foil, or freezer paper and store in a freezer container or bag up to 3 months.

SHRIMP are freezer-friendly. The quality is often better than what you'll find fresh at stores (most of which has been frozen and thawed). Toss into soups, stews, and stir-fries—they cook in just minutes.

LOW FAT

Shrimp Soup with Chili Tortilla Strips

Comforting, brothy soup gets its zip from poblano pepper and crushed red pepper.

START TO FINISH 45 min.

- 1 large poblano pepper, seeded and chopped (about 1 cup) (see tip, page 11)
- 1 medium onion, chopped (½ cup)
- 2 cloves garlic, minced
- 1 Tbsp. vegetable or olive oil
- 1 qt. reduced-sodium chicken broth
- ¼ tsp. salt
- ¼ tsp. crushed red pepper
- 1 12-oz. package frozen shrimp, peeled and deveined
- 1 cup frozen corn
- 1 15-oz. can cannellini beans (white kidney beans), rinsed and drained
- ¼ cup snipped fresh cilantro
- 2 Tbsp. lime juice
- 1 small avocado, halved, seeded, peeled, and thinly sliced or chopped
- 1 recipe Chili Tortilla Strips

1. In a 4- to 5-quart Dutch oven cook poblano pepper, onion, and garlic in hot oil just until tender. Add broth, salt, and crushed red pepper. Bring to boiling. Add frozen shrimp, corn, and drained beans; return to boiling.

2. Simmer, uncovered, about 2 minutes or until shrimp are opaque. Stir in cilantro and lime juice. Serve in shallow bowls topped with avocado and Chili Tortilla Strips. Makes 6 servings.

Chili Tortilla Strips Preheat oven to 350°F. Brush one side of two 8- to 9-inch flour tortillas with 1 Tbsp. vegetable oil; sprinkle with ½ tsp. chili powder. Using a pizza wheel, cut into strips or wedges. Place in a single layer on an extra large baking sheet. Bake 12 to 15 minutes or until crisp.

EACH SERVING *248 cal, 9 g fat, 83 mg chol, 832 mg sodium, 30 g carb, 5 g fiber, 19 g pro.*

FREEZE IT RIGHT
Look for frozen peeled and deveined shrimp in the freezer section. Go for the big bags when they're on sale, and divide into portions for weeknight ease. Store up to 6 months.

Love Potions

No-fuss fruity drinks + a sweet treat = easy buffet

KID FRIENDLY

Triple-Chocolate Cake with Malted Crunch

PREP 45 minutes   BAKE 25 minutes
COOL 25 minutes   OVEN 350°F

Cake
  2 cups all-purpose flour
  ½ cup unsweetened cocoa powder
  1 tsp. baking powder
  ½ tsp. baking soda
  ½ tsp. salt
  ⅔ cup butter, softened
1¾ cups granulated sugar
  3 eggs
  4 oz. unsweetened chocolate, melted and cooled
  2 tsp. vanilla
1½ cups milk
  ⅓ cup malted milk balls, chopped

Chocolate Buttercream
  6 Tbsp. butter, softened
4½ cups powdered sugar
  6 Tbsp. unsweetened cocoa powder
  5 Tbsp. milk
1½ tsp. vanilla

Chocolate Ganache
  ½ cup whipping cream
  6 oz. semisweet chocolate, chopped
  ½ cup malted milk balls, chopped

1. Line two 9×1½ inch round cake pans with parchment paper. Grease pans; set aside.
2. In a medium bowl stir together the flour, ½ cup cocoa powder, baking powder, baking soda, and salt. Set aside.
3. Preheat oven to 350°F. In a large mixing bowl beat butter with electric mixer on medium-high speed for 30 seconds. Add granulated sugar; beat until combined. Add eggs, one at a time; beat 30 seconds after each. Beat in melted unsweetened chocolate and vanilla. Alternately add flour mixture and 1½ cups milk, beating on low speed after each addition until combined.
4. Divide batter between prepared pans. Bake for 25 to 30 minutes or until a toothpick inserted near centers comes out clean. Cool in pans on wire rack 10 minutes; remove from pans. Cool completely on rack.
5. Meanwhile, for Chocolate Buttercream, in a mixing bowl beat 6 tablespoons butter with electric mixer on medium speed until fluffy. Gradually add 1½ cups powdered sugar and 6 tablespoons unsweetened cocoa powder, beating well. Beat in milk and vanilla. Beat in enough remaining powdered sugar to reach desired consistency.
6. For Chocolate Ganache, in a saucepan bring whipping cream just to boiling over medium-high heat. Remove from heat. Add semisweet chocolate (do not stir). Let stand 5 minutes. Stir until smooth. Cool 15 minutes.
7. Place one layer on serving plate. Spread buttercream. Add cake layer, press ⅓ cup chopped malted milk balls into sides of buttercream. Pour warm Ganache over top. Sprinkle with ½ cup chopped malted milk balls. Makes 16 servings.
PER SERVING *555 cal., 25 g fat, 79 mg chol., 282 mg sodium, 85 g carb., 4 g fiber, 6 g pro.*

Minty Lime Refresher

PREP 5 minutes

  2 parts fresh lime juice
  2 parts simple syrup
  1 part white rum
  1 part club soda, chilled
     Small splash of green-color creme de menthe
     Fresh mint sprig

1. Stir together lime juice, simple syrup, rum, club soda, and a small splash of creme de menthe. Serve over ice with mint.

Sweet-Tart Tropical Punch

PREP 5 minutes

  1 part white rum
  1 part pineapple juice
  1 part bottled tangerine juice
     Fresh pineapple slices or wedges

1. Combine rum and juices. Pour over ice and garnish with fresh pineapple.

Coconut-Banana Creme

PREP 5 minutes

  1 part refrigerated coconut milk
  ½ part rum
  ¼ part orange juice
  ¼ medium banana for every 2 ounces
     of coconut milk
     Vanilla bean paste to taste
     Toasted coconut (see tip, page 35)

1. In a blender combine coconut milk, rum, orange juice, banana, and vanilla bean paste. Cover and blend until smooth. Pour over ice; garnish with toasted coconut.

Blushing Lemonade

PREP 5 minutes

  2 parts vodka
  2 parts pink lemonade
     Splash of limoncello
     Simple syrup, to taste
     Lemon

1. Combine all ingredients and pour over ice. Garnish with a lemon twist.

Delicious Every Day
Fresh and easy ideas for dinner.

CHERRY-CHICKEN
SPIRALS

GNOCCHI WITH MUSHROOMS AND TUNA

Cherry-Chicken Spirals

PREP 30 min. BAKE 25 min.
OVEN 375°F

4 skinless, boneless chicken breast halves (about 1½ lbs. total)
6 slices turkey bacon, halved
⅔ cup snipped dried cherries
3 Tbsp. honey mustard
1 cup whole wheat panko (Japanese-style bread crumbs)
1 Tbsp. snipped fresh thyme
½ tsp. ground black pepper

1. Preheat oven to 375°F. Lightly coat a 13×9×2-inch baking pan with nonstick cooking spray; set aside. Place each chicken breast half between two pieces of plastic wrap. Using the flat side of a meat mallet, pound chicken lightly into a rectangular shape ¼ to ½ inch thick. Discard plastic wrap.
2. In a large skillet cook turkey bacon over medium heat for 2 to 3 minutes per side or just until lightly browned but not crisp. Place on pounded chicken.
3. In a small bowl combine cherries and half the honey mustard. Divide cherry mixture evenly among the pounded chicken. Fold in a short sides; roll up from long edge. Brush rolls with remaining honey mustard. In a shallow dish combine panko, thyme, and pepper. Roll chicken in panko mixture to coat evenly; place, seam sides down, in prepared pan. Lightly coat with nonstick cooking spray.
4. Bake, uncovered, for 25 to 30 minutes or until chicken is no longer pink (170°F). Serve with sautéed greens such as bok choy, if desired. Makes 4 servings.

EACH SERVING *392 cal, 7 g fat, 124 mg chol, 494 mg sodium, 37 g carb, 3 g fiber, 43 g pro.*

FLAVOR SECRET

Honey mustard gives these chicken breasts plenty of zing and a hint of sweetness without any added fat.

Gnocchi with Mushrooms and Tuna

PREP 15 min. BAKE 12 min.
STAND 5 min. OVEN 425°F

1 16-oz. package shelf-stable potato gnocchi
4 cups assorted small and/or sliced mushrooms, such as shiitake or cremini
2 cloves garlic, minced
1 Tbsp. olive oil
1 cup half-and-half
2 5-oz. cans solid light tuna packed in olive oil, drained and broken into chunks
2 oz. Parmesan cheese, shaved Fresh basil leaves (optional)
¼ tsp. crushed red pepper

1. Preheat oven to 425°F. Lightly grease a 1½-quart gratin dish; set aside.
2. In a large pot cook gnocchi in lightly salted water according to package directions; drain.
3. Meanwhile, in a large skillet cook mushrooms and garlic in hot oil over medium heat until tender. Stir in half-and-half. Simmer, uncovered, for 5 to 7 minutes or until liquid begins to thicken. Fold in gnocchi and tuna. Transfer to prepared dish.
4. Bake, uncovered, for 12 to 15 minutes or until lightly browned. Sprinkle with Parmesan cheese. Let stand 5 minutes. Top with basil leaves, if desired, and crushed red pepper. Makes 4 servings.
Make ahead Prepare the casserole through Step 3. Cover and chill up to 48 hours. Bake, covered, for 25 minutes. Uncover; bake 10 to 12 minutes more or until lightly browned and heated through.

EACH SERVING *556 cal, 23 g fat, 115 mg chol, 775 mg sodium, 50 g carb, 3 g fiber, 32 g pro.*

FLAVOR SECRET

Tuna packed in olive oil is a bit pricier, but opt for it over tuna packed in water. It has a wonderful moist, flaky texture, and it gives the casserole a rich boost of flavor.

KID FRIENDLY | FAST

Turkey and Apricot Bread Salad

PREP **10 min.** BAKE **10 min.**
OVEN **350°F**

- 2 cups torn hearty whole grain bread
- 1 Tbsp. extra-virgin olive oil
- 6 cups baby spinach
- 2 cups cooked turkey or chicken, torn into pieces
- ¼ cup dried apricots, cut in thin slivers
- ¼ cup dried cranberries (optional)
- ¼ red onion, thinly sliced
- ⅓ cup white wine vinegar
- ¼ cup extra-virgin olive oil
- 1 Tbsp. Dijon-style mustard
- 2 tsp. snipped fresh rosemary
- ¼ tsp. salt
- ¼ tsp. black pepper
- 2 oz. crumbled blue cheese
- ¼ cup toasted walnuts (see tip, page 35)
  Cracked black pepper (optional)

1. Preheat oven to 350°F. In a medium bowl toss bread with the 1 Tbsp. olive oil; spread in a 15×10×1-inch baking pan. Bake for 10 to 15 minutes or until lightly toasted, stirring twice.
2. Meanwhile, in a large salad bowl toss together spinach, turkey, dried apricots, dried cranberries (if desired), and red onion; set aside.

3. For dressing, in a medium bowl whisk together white wine vinegar, the ¼ cup olive oil, mustard, rosemary, salt, and pepper.
4. Toss the warm bread pieces with the dressing. Add bread and dressing to the spinach mixture; toss to combine. Serve immediately, topped with blue cheese, walnuts, and cracked black pepper (if desired). Makes 6 servings.
EACH SERVING *317 cal, 20 g fat, 44 mg chol, 462 mg sodium, 13 g carb, 3 g fiber, 20 g pro.*

FLAVOR SECRET
Tossing the chunks of bread with the dressing before adding them to the salad allows them to absorb the bright herbal dressing. When you bite in the bread is slightly softened and bursting with flavor.

Dinner on a Dollar

Spice up a casual night at home with classic pub fare. The dish is baked crisp—with a kick!

Spicy Oven-Baked Fish and Sweet Potato Chips

PREP 20 min. BAKE 20 min.
OVEN 425°F COST $1.44 per serving

- 1 lb. fresh or frozen whitefish fillets, about ½ inch thick
- 1 lb. sweet potatoes, cut into ¼- to ½-inch sticks
- 1 Tbsp. olive oil
- 1 tsp. Old Bay seasoning or seafood seasoning
- ½ tsp. chili powder
- ⅓ cup milk
- ⅓ cup all-purpose flour
- ⅓ cup fine dry bread crumbs
- 2 tsp. chili powder
- 1 tsp. paprika
- 2 Tbsp. butter, melted

1. Thaw fish, if frozen. Cut into 3×2-inch pieces. Rinse fish; pat dry with paper towels. Cover and chill until needed.
2. Preheat oven to 425°F. Line a large baking sheet with foil. Lightly coat with nonstick spray; set aside.
3. For chips, pat potatoes dry with paper towels; place in a large bowl. Add olive oil, Old Bay seasoning, ½ tsp. chili powder, and ½ tsp. salt. Toss to coat. Arrange potatoes in a single layer on half of the prepared baking sheet. Bake 10 minutes.
4. Meanwhile, for fish, place milk in a shallow dish. Place flour in another shallow dish. In a third shallow dish combine bread crumbs, 2 tsp. chili powder, paprika, and ¼ tsp. each salt and pepper. Add melted butter; stir until combined.
5. Dip fish pieces in milk; coat with flour. Dip again in milk, then in bread crumb mixture. Remove baking sheet from oven. Using a spatula, carefully turn potatoes. Place fish on the opposite half of hot baking sheet; return to oven. Bake 10 to 15 minutes or until potatoes are golden brown and fish flakes easily with a fork. Serve with lemon wedges and parsley, if desired. Makes 4 servings.
EACH SERVING *419 cal, 17 g fat, 85 mg chol, 859 mg sodium, 39 g carb, 5 g fiber, 27 g pro.*

CRUNCHY GRAIN
CAKES WITH
STRAWBERRY
SALAD

march

SPRING Springtime beckons something fresh and fabulous! Add quinoa, millet, farro—and a few others—to your recipe repertoire. And jams, jellies, and marmalades pair perfectly with baking favorites.

78

81

88

Waves of Grain

A bumper crop of whole grains has popped up in supermarkets. And every pick is ripe with nutrition and flavor. These eight spring-fresh recipes—plus tips and ideas—make it easy to go with the grain.

Red Quinoa Salad with Raspberries and Beets

"Grains like red quinoa have a subtle sweetness to them, so they're a lot of fun paired with fruit," Robin says. If you don't have red quinoa, you can swap golden or black."

PREP 30 min. COOK 15 min.
STAND 5 min.

- 1 cup red quinoa, rinsed and drained
- 1⅓ cups fresh raspberries
- 1 small red Fresno or red jalapeño chile, halved and seeded (see tip, page 11)
- 2 Tbsp. chopped shallots
- 1 Tbsp. sugar
- ½ tsp. salt
- ¼ cup white wine vinegar
- ⅓ cup extra-virgin olive oil
- 4 cups torn red leaf lettuce
- 4 small beets, cooked* and sliced (about 1 lb.)
- 4 large red radishes, sliced
- ½ cup roasted pistachio nuts, coarsely chopped (see tip, page 35)
- ½ cup fresh cilantro

1. In a small saucepan bring 1½ cups of water to boiling. Add quinoa; return to boiling. Reduce heat to low; cover tightly. Simmer about 15 minutes or until liquid is absorbed. Remove from heat. Let stand, covered, for 5 minutes. Transfer to a large bowl; cool to room temperature.
2. For dressing, in the bowl of a food processor combine ⅓ cup of the raspberries, the chile, shallots, sugar, and salt. Cover and process until pureed. Scrape down sides. Add vinegar; process until combined. With food processor running, slowly add oil in a thin steady stream (dressing will thicken as oil is added).
3. In a large bowl gently combine cooked quinoa, lettuce, beets, and radishes. Drizzle dressing over salad; toss gently to mix. Transfer mixture to a serving dish. Top with remaining raspberries, pistachios, and cilantro. Makes 6 servings.

*Cooking beets Place unpeeled beets in a large saucepan. Add enough water to cover. Bring to boiling; reduce heat. Cook, covered, 30 to 35 minutes or until tender. Drain and cool. Slip skins off beets.

Grain changeup Substitute cooked bulgur or red rice for the quinoa. Omit Step 1; begin with Step 2.

EACH SERVING 349 cal, 19 g fat, 0 mg chol, 262 mg sodium, 39 g carb, 9 g fiber, 8 g pro.

QUINOA FACTS

This protein-packed grain has exploded in popularity. In red, white, and black varieties, quinoa—technically a seed—cooks up soft and fluffy, bringing dishes a mild, nutty undertone. All colors taste basically the same, making varieties interchangeable.

MEET ROBIN

Chef and cookbook author Robin Asbell is devoted to creating easy, delicious recipes from healthful ingredients. She loves the ease of cooking with grains—and the many health benefits they offer. "Studies are continually touting the health reasons for choosing whole grains," Robin says. They are an excellent source of nutrients, including fiber, vitamin B, and iron, and they have been found to reduce risks of stroke, type 2 diabetes, and heart disease. Additionally, grains can be a helpful tool for maintaining healthy weight.

WHEAT BERRIES This quintessential whole grain (unprocessed wheat kernels), these big juicy "berries" pop when you eat them, lending hearty, chewy texture.

Wheat Berry Gazpacho Salad

"What fun to combine a grain salad and a classic gazpacho soup," Robin says. "This dish is all about contrast and texture—savory and sweet, crunchy and creamy. Soaking the wheat berries cuts down on the cooking time. If you want to get ahead, do both the soaking and cooking the night before. Cooked wheat berries can be stored in the fridge up to 3 days."

PREP **20 min.** SOAK **1 hr.**
COOK **1 hr.** BAKE **22 min.** OVEN **300°F**

- 1 cup wheat berries
- 6 ½-inch-thick slices whole grain crusty country bread
- 1 Tbsp. extra-virgin olive oil
- 1 tsp. snipped fresh oregano
- 1 tsp. snipped fresh tarragon
- ¼ tsp. salt
- 3 oz. Manchego or Parmesan cheese, shaved or grated
- 1 15-oz. can chickpeas, rinsed and drained (optional)
- 1 cup chopped fresh tomatoes
- 1 cup seedless green grapes, halved
- ½ cup sliced or chopped English cucumber
- ¼ cup seeded and chopped yellow sweet pepper
- ¼ cup extra-virgin olive oil
- 2 Tbsp. chopped red onion
- 2 Tbsp. red wine vinegar
- 1 Tbsp. snipped fresh oregano
- 2 tsp. snipped fresh tarragon
- ½ tsp. salt
   Cracked black pepper

1. In a medium bowl combine wheat berries and 3 cups water. Let soak 1 hour; drain. Transfer to a medium saucepan. Add water to cover by 2 inches; place over high heat. Bring to boiling; reduce heat. Simmer, covered, for 45 minutes to 1 hour, or until wheat berries are tender and some of the grains are splitting open at the tip. Pour into a fine-mesh strainer; drain. Transfer to a large bowl. Let cool completely.
2. Preheat oven to 300°F. Place bread slices on a baking sheet. In a small bowl combine 1 Tbsp. olive oil, 1 tsp. oregano, and 1 tsp. tarragon. Brush olive oil mixture on bread slices. Sprinkle with ¼ tsp. salt. Bake 20 minutes or until bread is crisp. Sprinkle with cheese; bake 2 minutes more.
3. Meanwhile, in a large bowl combine chickpeas (if using), tomatoes, grapes, cucumber, sweet pepper, ¼ cup olive oil, red onion, red wine vinegar, 1 Tbsp. oregano, 2 tsp. tarragon, and ½ tsp. salt. Toss to combine. Add wheat berries; toss to mix well.
4. To serve, spoon wheat berry mixture over bread slices. Sprinkle with black pepper. Makes 6 servings.
Grain changeup Substitute 2¼ cups cooked farro or rye berries for the cooked wheat berries. Omit Step 1; begin with Step 2.
EACH SERVING *364 cal, 16 g fat, 10 mg chol, 685 mg sodium, 43 g carb, 6 g fiber, 14 g pro.*

STORING GRAINS
Follow these tips get the most out of grains.

● Keep uncooked grains in their unopened packages or transfer to an airtight container and store in a cool, dark, dry place. If storing longer than 1 month, Robin recommends keeping them in the fridge or freezer. Like nuts, grains contain natural oils so they can become rancid and spoil. Be sure to check the "use-by" date on the package.

● "Grains are a fantastic food to make ahead," Robin says. "Cook up a batch, then store in the fridge or freezer. When you're ready to use, just add a little water and reheat gently to allow the starches to release again." Cooked grains will keep in the refrigerator up to 3 days or in the freezer up to 1 month.

Bulgur Salad with Chickpeas, Feta, and Mint

"Bulgur is such a great grain because it's one of the quickest to cook," Robin says. "Chewy bulgur is offset by bright, salty feta and an unexpected zing of lime."

PREP 35 min. COOK 10 min. STAND 10 min.

- 1 cup bulgur
- 1 tsp. salt
- 2 Tbsp. olive oil
- 8 cloves garlic, thinly sliced
- ¼ cup red wine vinegar
- ¼ cup olive oil
- 1 tsp. finely shredded lime peel
- 3 Tbsp. lime juice
- 1 tsp. cracked black pepper
- 3 cups shredded purchased roasted chicken
- 1 15-oz. can chickpeas or cannellini beans (white kidney beans), rinsed and drained
- 1 cup chopped orange, red, and/or yellow sweet pepper
- 4 oz. feta cheese, cubed (about 1 cup)
- 1 cup coarsely chopped fresh flat-leaf Italian parsley
- 1 cup coarsely chopped fresh mint

1. In a medium saucepan bring 1½ cups water to boiling. Add bulgur and ½ tsp. of the salt. Return to boiling; reduce heat. Simmer, covered, for 10 minutes. Remove from heat; let stand 10 minutes or until water is absorbed and bulgur is tender. Transfer to a large bowl.
2. Meanwhile, in a small saucepan heat 2 Tbsp. olive oil over high heat. Add garlic; reduce heat to medium high. Cook and stir 30 to 45 seconds until garlic starts to turn golden around the edges. Remove from heat. Stir garlic and oil into bulgur.
3. For dressing, in a screw-top jar combine red wine vinegar, ¼ cup olive oil, lime peel, lime juice, remaining ½ tsp. salt, and pepper. Cover and shake well. Stir dressing into bulgur. Add chicken, cannellini beans, sweet pepper, feta cheese, ¾ cup of the parsley, and ¾ cup of the mint to bulgur mixture; toss to mix well. To serve, top with remaining parsley and mint. Makes 6 servings.
Grain changeup Substitute 2½ cups cooked brown rice or quinoa for the cooked bulgur. Omit Step 1; begin with Step 2.

EACH SERVING 467 cal, 24 g fat, 79 mg chol, 826 mg sodium, 33 g carb, 9 g fiber, 31 g pro.

Black Rice Salad with Snap Peas, Carrots, and Almonds

"Ebony-black rice is so beautiful—it almost has a purple sheen," Robin says. "The grain has a mild, sweet flavor that has mass appeal, and the Marcona almonds (a Spanish variety that's slightly sweeter and rounder than typical California almonds) bring out the nuttiness of the grain."

PREP 20 min. COOK 30 min. COOL 1 hr.

- 2 cups black rice
- 4 cups microgreens and/or shredded cabbage
- 4 small carrots, sliced and/or coarsely chopped
- 8 oz. sugar snap peas, trimmed, halved lengthwise, and coarsely chopped
- 4 green onions, diagonally sliced
- ¼ cup fresh lime juice
- ¼ cup honey
- ⅓ cup tamari sauce
- ⅓ cup canola oil
- 2 tsp. wasabi paste
- ½ cup Marcona almonds

1. In a 2- to 3-quart saucepan bring 3½ cups water to boiling; add rice. Reduce heat to low; cover tightly. Cook 30 minutes or until all the water is absorbed. Cool completely. Transfer to a large bowl. Add microgreens, carrots, snap peas, and green onions; toss to combine.

2. For dressing, in a medium bowl whisk together lime juice, honey, tamari, canola oil, and wasabi paste. Pour dressing over rice and vegetables; toss to combine. Sprinkle with Marcona almonds. Makes 8 servings.

Grain changeup Substitute cooked farro or wheat berries for the black rice. Omit Step 1; begin with Step 2.

EACH SERVING *352 cal, 15 g fat, 0 mg chol, 716 mg sodium, 50 g carb, 5 g fiber, 9 g pro.*

BLACK RICE This Chinese variety of medium-grain rice carries all the whole grain goodness of brown, but with gorgeous color and sweeter flavor. Its dramatic look calls for a dramatic treatment— such as this salad, with sweet, sour, and spicy wasabi-spiked dressing; crisp vegetables; and the surprise of Marcona almonds.

FARRO Also known as emmer, this ancient wheat variety, is a staple in food-loving Italy. It seems to keep that al dente texture no matter how much you cook it, making it perfect for baked dishes.

Farro, Cherry Tomato, and Asparagus Casserole

"This recipe is a terrific way to introduce someone to whole grains," Robin says. "Farro is a classic old Italian grain. This comforting, Italian-style preparation—packed with fresh spring veggies and topped with a little cheese—is a fun spin."

PREP 20 min. COOK 30 min.
BAKE 20 min. STAND 10 min.
OVEN 400°F

- 2 Tbsp. extra-virgin olive oil
- 3 large shallots, chopped
- 1⅓ cups pearled farro or farro (see Farro Facts, right), rinsed and drained
- 3 cups reduced-sodium chicken stock or broth
- ½ tsp. salt
- ¼ tsp. ground black pepper
- 1 cup shredded carrots
- 1 cup cherry tomatoes, halved
- ⅓ cup fresh basil, shredded
- 4 eggs, lightly beaten
- 1½ cups half-and-half or light cream
- ½ cup grated Asiago cheese
- ⅓ cup whole wheat bread crumbs
- 2 Tbsp. coarsely chopped fresh Italian parsley
- 6 to 8 oz. fresh asparagus spears, trimmed
   Fresh basil leaves

1. Grease or oil a 2-quart gratin or baking dish; set aside. In a medium saucepan heat oil over medium heat. Add shallots; reduce heat to medium-low. Cook 5 minutes or until tender. Add farro; stir to coat. Add stock, salt, and pepper. Return to boiling; Reduce heat. Simmer, uncovered, for 20 to 25 minutes for pearled farro (or 45 to 50 minutes for regular farro) or until tender.
2. Remove farro from heat. Stir in carrots, tomatoes, and ⅓ cup basil. Cover; let stand 5 minutes.
3. Preheat oven to 400°F. Scrape farro mixture into prepared casserole dish; spread into a thin layer. In a medium bowl whisk together eggs, half-and-half, and cheese. Pour egg mixture over farro mixture; stir to combine.
4. In a small bowl combine bread crumbs and parsley; sprinkle over casserole. Place asparagus spears in a crisscross pattern on the breadcrumbs. Lightly coat the asparagus and crumb mixture with olive oil cooking spray.

5. Bake, uncovered, for 20 to 25 minutes or until a knife inserted near center comes out clean. Let stand 10 minutes. To serve, sprinkle with fresh basil. Makes 4 servings.
EACH SERVING *586 cal, 24 g fat, 223 mg chol, 744 mg sodium, 63 g carb, 7 g fiber, 27 g pro.*

FARRO FACTS
Farro comes either whole or partially pearled, a process that scrapes off the bran layer, and makes the farro cook faster but removes some of the nutrition. Like wheat berries, whole farro can take an hour to cook. Soak for at least 3 hours or overnight to reduce cooking time.

MIXED-RICE BLENDS There's no need to choose when you can find whole grain rice blends—black, red, brown, and wild—all in one package. Try them anywhere you use rice.

KID FRIENDLY

Crunchy Grain Cakes with Strawberry Salad

"Grain blends are a wonderful way to sample whole grains and make a tasty pilaf," Robin says. "These grain cakes have a golden, crispy crust that everyone will love. The crunchy, hearty rice cakes are perfectly paired with sweet strawberries and crunchy bok choy."

PREP 25 min. COOK 13 min.
OVEN 200°F

Grain Cakes
- 1 cup mixed whole grain rice
- ¼ cup Greek yogurt
- 1 egg, lightly beaten
- 2 Tbsp. fine dry whole wheat bread crumbs
- 1 tsp. paprika
- ½ tsp. salt
- ¼ tsp. cracked black pepper
- ½ to 1 tsp. cumin seeds
- 2 to 3 Tbsp. extra-virgin olive oil
- ⅓ cup chopped red onion

Strawberry Salad
- 2 to 3 bunches baby bok choy, separated into leaves (or 8 cups coarsely chopped regular bok choy)
- 1 lb. strawberries, sliced
- ⅓ cup thinly sliced red onion
- ¼ cup walnut oil or extra-virgin olive oil
- 2 Tbsp. fresh lemon juice
- 1 Tbsp. honey
- 1 tsp. Dijon-style mustard
- 1 clove garlic, minced
- ½ tsp. salt
- ¼ tsp. cracked black pepper

1. For Grain Cakes, preheat oven to 200°F. Grease a large baking sheet; set aside. In a large saucepan cook rice according to package directions for the minimum time suggested, omitting any fat or seasoning packets; drain well.
2. Meanwhile, in a large bowl whisk together yogurt, egg, bread crumbs, paprika, salt, and pepper. Add rice to yogurt mixture; stir to combine.

3. In a large nonstick skillet cook and stir cumin seeds in 1 Tbsp. of the hot oil for 2 minutes. Add red onion; cook 3 to 5 minutes more or until onion is tender. Stir cumin seeds and onion into rice mixture; cool slightly. Form mixture into 3-inch patties. In the same skillet, heat remaining oil over medium heat. Cook patties, half at a time, about 2 minutes each side or until crisp. Place in a single layer on the prepared baking sheet. Transfer to oven to keep warm.
4. For Strawberry Salad, in a large bowl combine bok choy, strawberries, and red onion; toss to combine. For dressing, in a small screw-top jar combine walnut oil, lemon juice, honey, mustard, garlic, salt, and pepper. Cover and shake well to combine. Pour dressing over salad; toss to combine. Serve with Grain Cakes. Makes 4 servings.
EACH SERVING 468 cal, 24 g fat, 47 mg chol, 766 mg sodium, 56 g carb, 7 g fiber, 12 g pro.

BLACK BARLEY Hefty and a little spicy, black barley is at home with other big assertive flavors. It's a hull-less variety, meaning the whole grain is intact for even more fiber, robust flavor, and chewy texture.

Short Ribs with Black Barley and Mushrooms

"Black barley, sometimes labeled purple barley, has a toothsome texture that stands up to rich, velvety short ribs," Robin says.

PREP **25 min.** STAND **3 hrs.**
COOK **2 hrs.**

- 1 cup black or purple barley
- 6 beef short ribs
- 2 Tbsp. extra-virgin olive oil
- 1 medium onion, cut in thin wedges
- 8 oz. shiitake mushrooms, trimmed and halved
- 3½ cups reduced-sodium beef broth
- 2 star anise
- ¼ tsp. salt
- ½ tsp. cracked black pepper
- 2 Tbsp. coarsely chopped fresh Italian parsley
- 2 garlic cloves, minced
- 2 tsp. shredded lemon peel
  Freshly ground black pepper

1. In a large heatproof bowl combine barley and enough boiling water to cover completely. Let stand at least 3 hours or up to 24 hours; drain.
2. Trim any surface fat from ribs; season with salt and ground black pepper. In a 4-quart Dutch oven brown ribs on all sides, half at a time, in hot oil, over medium-high heat. Remove ribs; set aside. Discard all but 1 Tbsp. drippings in Dutch oven; reduce heat to medium. Add onion and mushrooms. Cook and stir about 5 minutes or until onion is tender.
3. Return ribs to pan. Add barley, broth, star anise, salt, and cracked black pepper. Bring to boiling; reduce heat. Simmer, covered, for 2 hours or until ribs and barley are tender. Remove ribs; set aside. Simmer barley mixture, uncovered, until the broth is thickened (some liquid will remain). Remove and discard star anise.

4. In a small bowl combine parsley, garlic, and lemon peel. To serve, spoon barley mixture over beef ribs. Sprinkle with parsley mixture and freshly ground black pepper. Makes 4 servings.
Grain changeup Substitute cooked regular pearled barley for the black barley. Omit Step 1; begin with Step 2.
EACH SERVING *561 cal, 21 g fat, 92 mg chol, 755 mg sodium, 48 g carb, 14 g fiber, 43 g pro.*

MILLET This magical grain is so small and tender that you can turn it into a light side dish or salad. Or make it vanish completely with a whirl in the blender or food processor. Pureed, it lends velvety texture to vegetable mashes and soups.

Creamy Carrot and Millet Soup with Grilled Cheese Croutons

"Millet is an underappreciated grain," Robin says. "It cooks quickly and has a mild sweet flavor. In this soup it acts as a natural whole grain thickener that's also gluten-free."

PREP **15 min.** COOK **45 min.**

2 Tbsp. butter
1 medium onion, chopped
1 lb. carrots, peeled and chopped (about 3 cups)
½ cup millet
2½ cups reduced-sodium chicken or vegetable stock or broth
½ tsp. salt
1¼ cups milk
½ cup crème fraîche or sour cream
1 recipe Grilled Cheese Croutons (optional)
3 green onions, sliced
2 Tbsp. chopped fresh dillweed Paprika and coarse salt (optional)

1. For soup, in a 3- to 4-quart pot melt butter over medium heat. Add onion; cook for 10 minutes, until tender. Add the carrots, millet, stock, and salt. Bring to boiling over high heat. Reduce heat to low. Cook, covered, for 35 minutes until millet and carrots are very tender. Cool slightly.
2. Transfer soup to a food processor.* Cover and process until completely smooth, scraping down sides as necessary. Add milk and crème fraîche. Cover and process until smooth.
3. Return soup to the pot; cook and stir over low heat until heated through. For a thinner texture, stir in additional milk. To serve, top with Grilled Cheese Croutons, if desired. Sprinkle with green onions and dillweed, as well as paprika and coarse salt, if desired. Makes 4 servings.

Grilled Cheese Croutons Cut a 6 oz. French baguette into ¼-inch-thick slices. Brush one side of each slice with olive oil. Sandwich 2 oz. shredded Gruyère or Swiss cheese between each of 2 baguette slices, oiled side out. In a large nonstick skillet toast sandwiches over medium heat about 2 to 3 minutes per side or until golden. Cool slightly; cut into croutons.
* If using a blender, place a folded kitchen towel over the lid of the appliance and hold it down as you turn on machine and blend.
EACH SERVING *352 cal, 20 g fat, 61 mg chol, 816 mg sodium, 36 g carb, 6 g fiber, 9 g pro.*

Home Cooking

JAM SESSION Classic fruit flavors from jam, jelly, marmalade, and preserves give these easy spring baking favorites—cake, muffins, quick bread, and cookies—a fresh-from-the-jar twist.

A pocket of blueberry preserves is the luscious surprise tucked inside citrusy blueberry muffins.

Citrus-Topped Double-Blueberry Muffins

A sprinkle of lemon-orange sugar lends both bright flavor and a little crunch to the muffin tops. For even more crunch, try coarse raw (turbinado) sugar.

PREP 15 min. BAKE 20 min.
COOL 15 min. OVEN 375°F

- 2 cups all-purpose flour
- ¾ cup sugar
- 2½ tsp. baking powder
- ¼ tsp. salt
- 2 eggs
- ¾ cup buttermilk or milk
- 6 Tbsp. butter, melted
- 1 cup fresh or frozen blueberries
- ½ cup blueberry preserves
- 1 tsp. finely shredded orange peel
- 1 tsp. finely shredded lemon peel
- 2 Tbsp. sugar
- 2 Tbsp. butter, melted

1. Preheat oven to 375°F. Line twelve 2½-inch muffin cups with paper liners. Set aside.
2. Stir together flour, the ¾ cup sugar, baking powder, and salt in a medium mixing bowl. Make a well in the center of flour mixture; set aside.
3. Whisk together eggs, buttermilk, and 6 Tbsp. melted butter; add all at once to the flour mixture. Stir just until moistened (batter should be lumpy). Fold in blueberries. Remove 1 cup of batter.
4. Spoon remaining batter into prepared muffin cups, filling about half full. Spoon 2 tsp. of blueberry preserves into the center of each muffin. Top with remaining batter to cover the preserves, filling muffin cups about two-thirds full. Bake 20 minutes or until golden.
5. Meanwhile, stir together orange peel, lemon peel, and the 2 Tbsp. sugar. Remove muffins from oven; brush with 2 Tbsp. melted butter. Sprinkle citrus-sugar mixture on top. Cool in muffin cups on wire rack for 15 minutes. Serve warm. Makes 12 servings.
EACH SERVING *263 cal, 9 g fat, 52 mg chol, 225 mg sodium, 43 g carb, 1 g fiber, 4 g pro.*

FILL 'EM UP
Use the back of the preserve-filled spoon to press a divot into the center of the batter, then use another spoon to push in the preserves.

BAKING WITH LYNN
"Each of these baked goods can act as a base for your own favorite fruit flavors," says *Better Homes and Gardens*® Test Kitchen Director Lynn Blanchard, who developed these recipes. "Don't love grape? Swap in strawberry. Don't have lime marmalade? Orange would be equally delightful. These treats adapt easily."

Layers of raspberry jelly and raspberry cream elevate humble sponge cake to a lovely company-worthy treat.

Raspberry and Vanilla Stack Cake

To easily cut sponge cake into layers, cover the cake with plastic wrap and freeze 2 hours before slicing.

PREP 40 min. BAKE 30 min.
COOL 15 min. OVEN 350°F

1½   cups all-purpose flour
1½   tsp. baking powder
 ½   tsp. salt
  3   eggs, room temperature
1½   cups sugar
 ¾   cup milk
  3   Tbsp. butter
  2   tsp. vanilla bean paste or vanilla extract
1¼   cups whipping cream
 ⅔   cup raspberry or cherry jelly

1. Grease and flour a 13×9×2-inch baking pan. Line the bottom of pan with waxed paper; set aside. In a small bowl stir together flour, baking powder, and salt; set aside.

2. Preheat oven to 350°F. In a medium mixing bowl beat eggs with an electric mixer on high speed about 4 minutes or until thick. Gradually add sugar, beating on medium speed 4 to 5 minutes or until light and fluffy. Add flour mixture; beat on low to medium speed just until combined.

3. In a small saucepan heat and stir milk and butter until butter is melted. Add to batter along with the vanilla paste; beat until combined. Pour batter into prepared pan.

4. Bake 30 to 35 minutes or until a wooden toothpick inserted near center comes out clean. Cool cake in pan on a wire rack for 15 minutes. Remove cake from pan; peel off waxed paper. Place cake on a baking sheet. Cover with plastic wrap; cool completely.

5. In a large chilled bowl beat whipping cream with an electric mixer on medium speed until soft peaks form. Gradually add ⅓ cup of the jelly. Beat until combined; set aside.

6. Using a serrated knife, trim cake edges to create straight sides. Cut cake lengthwise in half. Cut each half into seven 4¼ ×1¾ inch pieces. (You should have 14 mini cakes.) Split cakes horizontally into 3 layers. For each individual cake, spread a thin layer of jelly on the bottom cake layer; top with 1 Tbsp. whipped cream mixture. Add second cake layer; repeat jelly and whipped cream steps. Finish with top cake layer. Sprinkle with powdered sugar. Makes 14 cakes.

EACH CAKE *295 cal, 12 g fat, 77 mg chol, 179 mg sodium, 45 g carb, 1 g fiber, 4 g pro.*

SPREAD SWEETNESS
Jelly spreads best when it's been heated. Heat 1 to 1½ minutes on 100 percent power, stirring every 30 seconds until jelly is a spreadable consistency. Cool slightly then use a table knife or small offset spatula to spread the raspberry jelly in an even layer.

A swirl of lime marmalade infuses coconut bread with zesty citrus; a quick brush over the top adds even more zing.

Coconut-Lime Bread

A tumble of barely browned coconut enhances the loveliness of this simple quick bread.

PREP **25 min.** BAKE **55 min.**
COOL **10 min.** STAND **overnight**
OVEN **350°F**

- 2 cups all-purpose flour
- 1 cup sugar
- 2 tsp. baking powder
- ½ tsp. salt
- 1 egg
- 1 cup coconut milk or milk
- ⅓ cup butter, melted
- 1 cup flaked coconut, toasted
- ¾ cup lime marmalade, melted*
- 1 Tbsp. lime marmalade, melted
- ¼ cup chip or flake coconut, toasted (see tip, page 35)

1. Preheat oven to 350°F. Grease and flour the bottom and ½ inch up the sides of a 9×5×3-inch loaf pan; set aside.
2. In a large bowl stir together flour, sugar, baking powder, and salt. In a medium bowl beat egg with a fork; stir in coconut milk and melted butter. Add egg mixture all at once to flour mixture. Stir just until moistened (batter should be lumpy). Fold in 1 cup of toasted flaked coconut.

3. Spoon one-third of the batter into prepared pan. Spoon half of the ¾ cup marmalade over batter. Repeat with remaining batter and marmalade, ending with batter. Using a thin metal spatula or table knife, swirl the marmalade through the bread.
4. Bake 55 to 60 minutes or until a wooden toothpick inserted near center comes out clean. Cool in pan on a wire rack 10 minutes. Remove from pan. Cool completely on wire rack. Wrap with plastic wrap; store at room temperature overnight before slicing.
5. Before slicing, brush top of loaf with 1 Tbsp. melted marmalade. Sprinkle with ¼ cup toasted coconut. Makes 14 servings.
*Melting marmalade Spoon marmalade into a 2-cup microwave-safe measuring cup. Heat 1 to 1½ minutes on 100 percent power, stirring every 30 seconds until marmalade is a spoonable consistency. (To soften only 1 to 2 Tbsp. of marmalade, heat just 20 to 30 seconds.)

EACH SERVING *292 cal, 12 g fat, 25 mg chol, 214 mg sodium, 45 g carb, 1 g fiber, 3 g pro.*

SIMPLY SWIRL
Using a thin metal spatula or table knife, cut down through batter. Working from one side of the pan to the other, move the knife in a fluid zigzag motion to whirl the marmalade through the bread. Take just one pass through—you don't want to overmix the batter.

Silky grape jam was made for crunchy, nutty shortbread. With delicate almond flavor and melt-in-your-mouth texture, this just might be one of our best cookies ever.

KID FRIENDLY

Grape-Glazed Almond Butter Shortbread

Natural almond or peanut butter has a tendency to separate, so when you open the jar you might notice a layer of oil on the surface. Be sure to stir to evenly incorporate oil and butter before measuring.

PREP **20 min.** BAKE **14 min.**
OVEN **325°F**

    1 cup butter, softened
    ½ cup natural almond butter or
       natural peanut butter*
    ½ cup packed brown sugar
    ½ tsp. salt
    2 cups all-purpose flour
    ⅔ cup Concord grape jam
       Sliced almonds and small round
       candies (optional)
       Sea salt (optional)

1. Preheat oven to 325°F. Line a cookie sheet with parchment paper; set aside.
2. In a large mixing bowl combine butter, almond butter, brown sugar, and salt. Beat with an electric mixer on medium speed until combined. Gradually beat in half the flour. Stir in remaining flour with a spatula or wooden spoon.

3. On a piece of waxed paper pat dough into an 8×6 inch rectangle; cut into 48 equal pieces (about 1-inch squares). Roll pieces into balls; place 2 inches apart on the prepared cookie sheet. Using a flat-bottom measuring cup dipped in flour, flatten dough balls to ¼-inch thickness.
4. Bake 12 minutes or until lightly browned and tops of cookies are set. Remove cookie sheet from oven. Stir jam to a spreadable consistency. Top each cookie with a generous ½ tsp. jam, spreading jam nearly to edges. Return to oven; bake 2 minutes more. While cookies are warm, top if desired, with sliced almonds and candies or sea salt. Makes 48 cookies.
*If you use regular peanut butter, the dough will be a bit softer. Cover and chill dough for 30 to 60 minutes until firm enough to shape and cut.
Store Place cookies in a single layer in an airtight container. Refrigerate up to 3 days or freeze up to 1 month. Thaw before serving.
EACH COOKIE *90 cal, 5 g fat, 10 mg chol, 66 mg sodium, 10 g carb, 0 g fiber, 1 g pro.*

GLAZE OVER
The warmth of the cookies will slightly melt the jam, making it easier to spread. Use the back of a spoon to spread the jam.

Pause for Passover

Set the Seder table with one of these bright, seasonally inspired roasts from cookbook author and Jewish cooking expert Joan Nathan.

Brisket with Ginger, Orange Peel, and Tomato

"French Jews tend to use a breast of veal, but for this version, inspired by Chef Daniel Rose of Spring restaurant in Paris, a beef or veal brisket can be used," Joan says.

PREP 35 min. COOK 2 hrs. 45 min. OVEN 325°F/275°F

1 3- to 5-lb. beef or veal brisket
2 Tbsp. vegetable oil
12 cipollini onions, trimmed and halved, or 2 medium onions, thickly sliced
6 carrots
8 cloves garlic, peeled
1 Tbsp. cider vinegar
1 cup dry white wine
3 cups veal, beef, or chicken stock
3 small tomatoes, halved
2 thyme sprigs or ½ tsp. dried thyme
1 bay leaf
5 parsley sprigs
1 ½-inch slice of fresh ginger
  Green tops from 1 leek
2 lemons
2 oranges

1. Preheat oven to 325°F. Season brisket with salt and freshly ground black pepper.
2. Place an 8-quart Dutch oven or large pot over medium heat; add oil. Brown brisket 4 minutes per side. Remove; set aside. Add onions, carrots, and garlic cloves to Dutch oven; cook just until soft, adding more oil if necessary. Add vinegar, stirring with a wooden spoon to scrape up any bits in bottom of pan. Increase heat to high. Add white wine; cook and stir 3 minutes, allowing liquid to reduce slightly.
3. Return brisket to Dutch oven. Add stock. Bring to a simmer; add tomatoes, thyme, bay leaf, parsley, ginger, and tops from leek. Stir in grated peel of 1 lemon and 1 orange. Cover; transfer to oven. Bake for 45 minutes. Reduce heat to 275°F; bake 2 to 2½ hours more or until meat is tender. Remove Dutch oven from oven; uncover.
4. Transfer meat to a cutting board; slice meat on the bias. Using a slotted spoon, remove carrots, onions, garlic, and tomatoes; set aside and keep warm. For sauce, strain remaining juices; discard solids. Return sauce to Dutch oven. Bring to boiling; reduce heat. Simmer, uncovered, until slightly thickened or to desired consistency.
5. Arrange meat on a serving platter with vegetables. Remove zest of remaining lemon and orange; scatter on top. Top with coarsely chopped fresh parsley and garnish with additional bay leaves, if desired. Serve sauce with meat. Serves 6 to 8.

EACH SERVING *502 cal, 26 g fat, 150 mg chol, 667 mg sodium, 13 g carb, 3 g fiber, 49 g pro.*

"If you prepare the same Passover dishes year after year, but have an itch for something new, these are the recipes to try," Joan Nathan says.

Garlicky Roasted Lamb with Potatoes

The shoulder roast is often cut into stew meat and not labeled as such. Ask for the cut at your meat or specialty market.

PREP 30 min. COOK 1 hr. 20 min.
OVEN 450°F/350°F

- 1 3-lb. boneless lamb leg or shoulder roast
- 3 anchovy fillets, cut in 3 pieces each
- 6 cloves garlic, peeled and cut in slivers
- 8 small potatoes
- 2 Tbsp. olive oil
- 1 lb. zucchini, cut into chunks
- 3 sprigs each fresh rosemary, thyme, and sage, coarsely chopped*
  Juice and finely grated peel of 1 orange (juiced and peeled)
  White pepper

1. Preheat oven to 450°F. Using a sharp knife, pierce lamb and insert the anchovy pieces and garlic slivers in the slits; season with salt and black pepper. Transfer to a small roasting pan filled with 1 cup water.

2. In a medium bowl toss potatoes with 1 Tbsp. of the olive oil; scatter around lamb. In the same bowl toss zucchini with remaining olive oil; set aside. Roast lamb and potatoes for 20 minutes. Remove pan from oven; add zucchini and herbs to roasting pan. Reduce heat to 350°F. Return pan to oven; cook 1 to 1½ hours more, spooning over pan juices occasionally, until temperature reaches 135°F when tested with an instant-read thermometer. Remove pan from oven. Cover; let rest 10 minutes.

3. Transfer lamb and vegetables to a serving platter. Meanwhile, add orange juice and peel to juices in roasting pan. Cook and stir over medium heat 3 to 4 minutes until liquid is reduced by half (about ½ cup). Sprinkle with white pepper to taste. Serve with sauce and orange wedges, if desired. Makes 6 to 8 servings.

* Remove and discard any rigid stems.

EACH SERVING *586 cal, 38 g fat, 129 mg chol, 367 mg sodium, 25 g carb, 4 g fiber, 36 g pro.*

MEET JOAN

Joan is the author of 10 cookbooks including the James Beard Award-winning *Jewish Cooking in America* and *The New American Cooking*. Her most recent book is *Quiches, Kugels, and Couscous: My Search for Jewish Cooking in France* (Knopf; $39.95). Joan has also hosted cooking shows and produced a documentary on Jewish culinary traditions for PBS.

Delicious Every Day

Fresh and easy ideas for dinner.

LOW FAT **FAST**

Stout, Beef, and Cabbage Stir-Fry

START TO FINISH 30 min.

12 oz. extra-stout beer
2 to 3 Tbsp. honey
2 Tbsp. tomato paste
1 Tbsp. brown mustard
1 tsp. caraway seeds, crushed
8 1-inch wedges cabbage
1 cup peeled baby carrots, halved or cut into ½-inch chunks
2 Tbsp. olive oil
1 lb. beef top sirloin steak, cut into ¾-inch-thick slices
1 small onion, halved and thinly sliced
1 Tbsp. all-purpose flour
Fresh flat-leaf Italian parsley leaves (optional)

1. In a medium bowl whisk together beer, honey, tomato paste, mustard, caraway seeds, and ½ tsp. each salt and cracked black pepper; set aside.
2. Place cabbage and carrots in a 2-quart microwave-safe baking dish; add 2 Tbsp. water. Microwave, covered, on 100 percent power (high) for 8 to 10 minutes or until crisp-tender, stirring once. Set aside and keep warm.
3. Meanwhile, in a very large nonstick skillet heat olive oil over medium-high heat. Add beef. Cook, stirring frequently, 3 to 4 minutes or just until slightly pink in the center. Remove beef from skillet; keep warm.
4. Add onion to skillet. Cook, stirring occasionally, 4 to 5 minutes or until tender. Pour beer mixture into skillet. In a small bowl stir together 2 Tbsp. water and the flour; stir into onion and beer mixture. Return beef to skillet; cook and stir 3 minutes or until bubbly.

5. Serve beef mixture with cabbage wedges and carrots. Sprinkle with parsley leaves, if desired. Makes 4 servings.
EACH SERVING *365 cal, 12 g fat, 68 mg chol, 532 mg sodium, 30 g carb, 6 g fiber, 29 g pro.*

FLAVOR SECRET
Hearty stout beer lends robust flavor to this stir-fry spin on classic Irish fare. Honey cuts the bitterness in the beer; taste the sauce and add a little more honey if needed to reach the right balance for you.

ROOT VEGETABLE
SOUP WITH
PARSLEY PESTO

Root Vegetable Soup with Parsley Pesto

PREP 25 min. COOK 30 min.

- 2 Tbsp. butter
- 8 cloves garlic, peeled
- 5 cups peeled and coarsely chopped root vegetables such as golden beets, Yukon gold potatoes, rutabagas, celery roots, parsnips, and/or carrots
- 1 cup chopped onion
- 2 14½-oz. cans reduced-sodium beef broth
- 2 to 3 tsp. prepared horseradish
- 1 recipe Parsley Pesto or purchased pesto
- 4 ciabatta rolls, split and toasted

1. In a Dutch oven melt butter over medium-high heat. Add garlic, chopped root vegetables, onion, and ½ tsp. each salt and pepper. Cook about 10 minutes or until vegetables are golden brown, stirring occasionally. Add broth; cover and simmer 10 minutes.
2. Stir in horseradish. Cook, uncovered, 10 minutes more. Season to taste with salt and pepper.
3. Meanwhile, spread a small spoonful of Parsley Pesto on the cut sides of the toasted ciabatta roll halves. Place rolls on a baking sheet, cut sides up. Broil 4 to 5 inches from heat about 1 minute or until pesto is heated through. Drizzle any remaining pesto into the soup. Makes 4 servings.
Parsley Pesto In a food processor combine 1 cup coarsely chopped fresh flat-leaf Italian parsley, ¼ cup toasted pine nuts (see tip, page 35), ¼ cup grated Parmesan cheese, and 1 clove garlic. Process until finely chopped. Gradually add 2 to 3 Tbsp. olive oil until desired consistency.
EACH SERVING 437 cal, 21 g fat, 20 mg chol, 1,207 mg sodium, 53 g carb, 10 g fiber, 12 g pro.

FLAVOR SECRET

The subtle sweetness of barely caramelized root vegetables gets a spicy punch from horseradish. This condiment brings pungency to everyday dishes and is high in vitamin C.

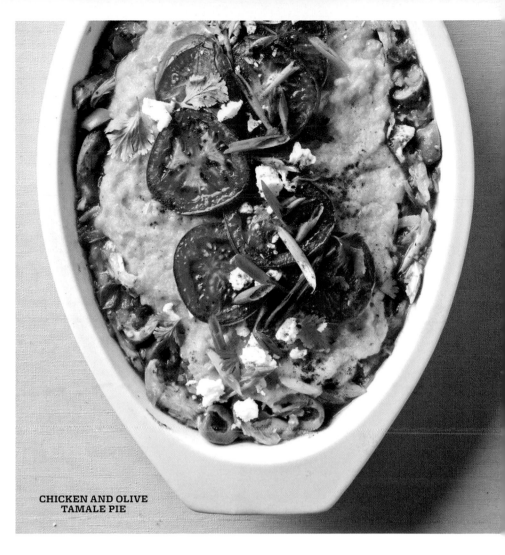

CHICKEN AND OLIVE TAMALE PIE

LOW FAT

Chicken and Olive Tamale Pie

PREP 10 min. COOK 15 min.
BAKE 20 min. OVEN 400°F

- ½ cup cornmeal
- 1 14¾-oz. can cream-style corn
- 1 lb. shredded cooked chicken* (about 3 cups)
- 1 16-oz. jar mild or medium green salsa
- ⅓ cup pimiento-stuffed green olives, chopped
- 1 tomato, thinly sliced
- ⅓ cup crumbled queso fresco or feta cheese
  Snipped cilantro, green onion, and/or chili powder (optional)

1. Preheat oven to 400°F. In a large saucepan bring 1¼ cups water to boiling. Gradually whisk in cornmeal; reduce heat. Cook, whisking constantly, 3 minutes. Stir in corn; return to boiling. Reduce heat to medium-low. Cook, stirring frequently, for 10 minutes.
2. Meanwhile, in a 1½-quart gratin or 2-quart rectangular baking dish combine shredded chicken, salsa, and olives. Spoon cornmeal mixture over chicken mixture. Top with tomato slices. Bake, uncovered, for 20 to 25 minutes or until pie is heated through.
3. Top with crumbled cheese. Sprinkle with cilantro, green onion, and chili powder, if desired. Makes 4 servings.
*Cooked rotisserie chicken from the grocery store is convenient for weeknight meals. Shred the meat and store in the fridge for meals throughout the week.
EACH SERVING 402 cal, 11 g fat, 101 mg chol, 1,204 mg sodium, 41 g carb, 4 g fiber, 38 g pro.

FLAVOR SECRET

Green salsa—salsa verde—is made with tomatillos. Keep a jar in the pantry for a quick enchilada sauce or a base for tortilla soup. If you don't have green salsa on hand, red salsa is equally delicious.

Dinner on a Dollar

Breakfast favorites bacon, eggs, and toast get a tasty dinner makeover in this no-fuss spaghetti dish.

KID FRIENDLY | FAST

Bacon and Egg Spaghetti

Don't skip cooking the eggs in the reserved bacon drippings. Not only does this simple step boost the flavor, it also means there's one less pan to clean.

START TO FINISH **30 min.**

OVEN **350°F** COST **$1.15 per serving**

- 1 slice white or whole grain bread, cut into pieces
- ⅓ cup grated Parmesan cheese
- 1½ tsp. extra-virgin olive oil
- 8 oz. dried spaghetti
- 6 slices bacon
- 3 cloves garlic, minced
- 2 Tbsp. extra-virgin olive oil
- ½ tsp. salt
- ¼ tsp. crushed red pepper
- 4 eggs
  Snipped fresh chives, grated Parmesan cheese, and cracked black pepper (optional)

1. Preheat oven to 350°F. In a food processor combine bread, 1 Tbsp. of the Parmesan, and 1½ tsp. of the oil. Cover and process until coarse crumbs form. Spread in a 15×10×1-inch baking pan. Bake, uncovered, for 10 minutes or until golden. Cool on wire rack.

2. In a large pot cook pasta according to package directions. Drain; reserving ¾ cup water; set aside.

3. Meanwhile, in a large skillet cook bacon over medium heat until crisp; drain well on paper towels. Tear bacon into large pieces; set aside. Keep skillet warm, reserving 1 to 2 Tbsp. drippings in the skillet.

4. In the same large pot used for the pasta cook garlic in the 2 Tbsp. oil over medium-high heat for 1 minute. Add salt and crushed red pepper. Add cooked pasta and remaining Parmesan. Add enough reserved pasta water to reach desired consistency; toss to coat.

5. In the large skillet heat bacon drippings over medium heat. Break eggs into skillet. Reduce heat to low; cook eggs 3 to 4 minutes or until desired doneness.

6. Divide spaghetti among four plates. Top with bacon and toasted bread crumbs. Serve with eggs. Sprinkle with chives, Parmesan, and pepper, if desired. Makes 4 servings.

EACH SERVING *470 cal, 21 g fat, 205 mg chol, 776 mg sodium, 11 g carb, 2 g fiber, 21 g pro.*

**SEARED SHRIMP
SALAD WITH WOK
DRESSING**

april

FAST AND FRESH Introduce bright new flavors to every day recipes with savory and sweet juice blends, and get dinner on the table flash with oh-so-easy stir-fries.

104

107

111

Sizzle and Stir

Spice up weeknight meals with these quick and seasonally delicious one-dish wonders. All you need is a few fresh ingredients and simple turns in a wok or skillet. Dinner is served!

Creamy Peas and Ham

A half-cup of cream gives this take on classic peas and ham its full, rich flavor.
START TO FINISH 35 min.

- 2 ½-inch-thick slices country bread, cut into ½-inch cubes (1 cup)
- 3 Tbsp. peanut or vegetable oil
- 1 Tbsp. minced garlic
- ½ tsp. salt
- ½ tsp. freshly ground pepper
- 4 medium shallots, chopped (½ cup)
- 3 cups sugar snap peas, strings removed (10 oz.)
- 8 oz. cooked ham, diced (1 cup)
- 2 cups frozen peas, thawed and patted dry
- ½ cup whipping cream
- ¾ cup coarsely chopped fresh mint
- 1 Tbsp. butter, sliced

1. In a large bowl toss bread cubes with 2 Tbsp. of the peanut oil, 1 tsp. of the garlic, ¼ tsp. of the salt, and ¼ tsp. of the pepper.
2. Heat a 14-inch flat-bottom wok or 12-inch stainless-steel skillet over high heat. Add the bread cubes; stir-fry 2 to 3 minutes or until toasted. Transfer to a paper-towel-lined plate; set aside.
3. Swirl remaining 1 Tbsp. oil into pan. Add shallots; stir-fry 1 minute. Add remaining 2 tsp. garlic, sugar snap peas, and ham; stir-fry 1 to 2 minutes. Add peas, remaining ¼ tsp. salt, and ¼ tsp. pepper; stir-fry 1 minute. Swirl in whipping cream; stir-fry 1 minute or until sugar snap peas are crisp-tender and cream thickens. Stir in half the mint. Remove pan from heat.
4. To serve, top with butter. Sprinkle with remaining mint and bread cubes. Makes 4 servings.
EACH SERVING *455 cal, 27 g fat, 73 mg chol, 1,293 mg sodium, 36 g carb, 8 g fiber, 19 g pro.*

STIR-FRY KNOW-HOW
To stir-fry simply means to quickly fry small pieces of food in a small amount of oil, over very high heat while constantly stirring—something you can do in either a wok or a stainless-steel skillet. For Grace, stir-frying begins with a well-seasoned 14-inch, flat-bottom carbon steel wok. Wok or skillet—with these recipes, you'll discover techniques and flavors beyond the traditional while celebrating the bounty of spring.

MEET GRACE
Spring is the perfect time to introduce bright, bold new flavors to your cooking. Whether you're trying a new vegetable or adding a dash of heat, get ready to jump-start your kitchen routine. These recipes will encourage you to dust off your trusty wok or take a new look at your skillet and explore the versatility of wok cooking, from stir-fries to braises.

For James Beard award-winning cookbook author Grace Young, a favorite use for the wok is stir-frying. "I consider stir-frying a form of culinary magic in which ingredients are transformed," Grace says. "The stir-fry method is so fast and easy. No matter what budget you're on, this is a way anyone can prepare a good, nutritious weeknight meal."

MARKET
VEGETABLES WITH
PEANUT SAUCE

"It's critical that vegetables are dry to the touch before you add them to the wok," Grace says. "Excess moisture will steam them, turning the dish into a soggy braise."

SMOKY COD WITH
SWEET POTATOES

ZESTY GREEK
CHICKEN WITH MINT

Smoky Cod with Sweet Potatoes

START TO FINISH 35 min.

1 lb. ½- to ¾-inch-thick fresh or frozen cod fillets
1 cup clam juice
½ cup dry white wine
1 tsp. cornstarch
⅓ cup mayonnaise
1 canned chipotle chile pepper in adobo sauce, chopped, about 1 Tbsp.
2 tsp. white wine vinegar
1 tsp. Dijon-style mustard
¾ tsp. salt
¼ tsp. freshly ground black pepper
2 Tbsp. all-purpose flour
3 Tbsp. peanut oil or vegetable oil
1 medium sweet potato, peeled, halved lengthwise, and very thinly sliced (2 cups)
1 large onion, cut in thin wedges (1 cup)
1½ cups fresh sweet corn kernels (3 ears)
¼ cup chopped parsley

1. Thaw fish, if frozen. Rinse and pat dry; set aside. In a bowl combine clam juice, white wine, and cornstarch; set aside. For chipotle aïoli, in another bowl combine mayonnaise, chipotle pepper, vinegar, and mustard. Cover and chill. **2.** Sprinkle cod pieces with ¼ tsp. of the salt and the pepper. Lightly coat with flour, shaking off excess. Heat a 14-inch flat-bottom wok or 12-inch stainless-steel skillet over medium-high heat until a bead of water vaporizes within 2 seconds. Add 2 Tbsp. of the peanut oil. Add cod pieces; cook, undisturbed, 2 minutes, or until opaque and browned on the bottom. Turn fillets over; cook 2 to 3 minutes until opaque and browned. Transfer to a plate. Break cod into chunks; set aside. **3.** Swirl remaining 1 Tbsp. peanut oil into pan over medium-high heat. Add sweet potato and onion; stir-fry 4 minutes. Add corn and remaining ½ tsp. salt; stir-fry 1 minute. Swirl clam juice mixture into pan; bring to boiling. Boil gently, uncovered, for 2 minutes. Return cod to pan. Cover and reduce heat to medium. Cook 1 to 2 minutes or until cod is just cooked through and sweet potatoes are tender. Serve with chipotle aïoli and sprinkle with chopped parsley. Makes 4 servings.

EACH SERVING *461 cal, 27 g fat, 56 mg chol, 1,082 mg sodium, 28 g carb, 3 g fiber, 28 g pro.*

Zesty Greek Chicken with Mint

START TO FINISH 45 min.

¼ cup snipped fresh mint
2 tsp. finely shredded lemon peel
4 tsp. lemon juice
2 Tbsp. olive oil
1 tsp. salt
¼ tsp. freshly ground pepper
1 medium cucumber
1 6-oz. container plain, nonfat Greek yogurt
1 Tbsp. minced garlic
1 lb. chicken breast tenderloins, ¼ inch thick
1 tsp. cornstarch
3 Tbsp. dry sherry
2 Tbsp. peanut or vegetable oil
⅔ cup dried orzo
4 roma tomatoes, quartered (2 cups)

1. In a bowl combine mint, lemon peel, 2 tsp. of the lemon juice, olive oil, ¼ tsp. of the salt, and ⅛ tsp. of the pepper; set aside. In a medium saucepan bring 4 cups salted water to boiling. **2.** For tzatziki, peel and grate half of the cucumber. Cut the remaining cucumber into bite-size chunks; set aside. Squeeze grated cucumber to remove excess water. In a bowl combine grated cucumber, yogurt, remaining 2 tsp. lemon juice, 1 tsp. of the garlic, and ¼ tsp. of the salt; set aside. **3.** Halve any large chicken tenders. In a shallow bowl combine chicken, cornstarch, 1 Tbsp. of dry sherry, remaining 2 tsp. garlic, remaining ½ tsp. salt, and remaining ⅛ tsp. pepper. Stir until cornstarch is no longer visible. Stir in 1 Tbsp. of the peanut oil; set aside. **4.** Heat a 14-inch flat-bottom wok or 12-inch stainless-steel skillet over high heat until a bead of water vaporizes within 2 seconds. Add orzo; cook and stir 1 to 2 minutes. Remove orzo from pan; transfer to boiling water in saucepan. Cook for 9 minutes or until tender. Drain; set aside. **5.** Meanwhile, add remaining 1 Tbsp. of peanut oil to pan. Add chicken; spread evenly in a single layer. Cook, undisturbed, 1 minute, until chicken

begins to sear. Stir-fry 1 minute or just until chicken is opaque. Swirl in remaining 2 Tbsp. dry sherry; stir-fry 1 to 2 minutes or until chicken is cooked through. Add tomato wedges; stir-fry 30 seconds. Remove pan from heat. Stir in cooked orzo and reserved cucumber. **6.** Drizzle with the mint mixture. Serve with tzatziki. Makes 4 servings.

EACH SERVING *432 cal, 17 g fat, 73 mg chol, 740 mg sodium, 32 g carb, 3 g fiber, 34 g pro.*

FAST

Market Vegetables with Peanut Sauce

START TO FINISH 24 min.

⅓ cup crunchy peanut butter
2 Tbsp. brown sugar
3 Tbsp. soy sauce
2 Tbsp. lime juice
⅛ tsp. crushed red pepper
¼ cup dry sherry, or apple or orange juice
2 Tbsp. peanut or vegetable oil
2 Tbsp. peeled and minced ginger
4 medium carrots, chopped
8 oz. green beans, trimmed (1 cup)
3 cups coarsely chopped napa cabbage
2 hard-cooked eggs, chopped

1. In a bowl combine peanut butter, brown sugar, 2 Tbsp. of the soy sauce, lime juice, and crushed red pepper. Stir to combine. In another bowl combine sherry and remaining 1 Tbsp. soy sauce. **2.** Heat a 14-inch flat-bottom wok or 12-inch stainless-steel skillet over high heat until a bead of water vaporizes within 2 seconds. Swirl in the peanut oil. Add ginger; stir-fry 10 seconds. Add carrots; stir-fry 1 minute. Add green beans; stir-fry 1 minute. Swirl in sherry mixture; stir-fry 2 minutes or until vegetables are crisp-tender and most of the liquid is absorbed. Add cabbage; cook 30 seconds or until slightly wilted. **3.** To serve, drizzle with peanut butter mixture. Top with chopped eggs. Makes 4 servings.

EACH SERVING *335 cal, 21 g fat, 93 mg chol, 954 mg sodium, 26 g carb, 5 g fiber, 12 g pro.*

Spicy Jerk Pork with Pepper Fried Rice

"One of the keys to making a delicious fried rice is starting with cold rice," Grace says. "For best results, cook the rice (in salted water) the day before. Fluff it, then cover and chill it overnight."

START TO FINISH 30 min.

- 2 to 3 tsp. curry powder
- ½ tsp. salt
- ¼ tsp. cayenne pepper
- ¼ tsp. ground ginger
- 1 Tbsp. soy sauce
- 1 Tbsp. white wine or dry sherry
- 12 oz. pork tenderloin, thinly sliced, crosswise
- 3 Tbsp. peanut or vegetable oil
- 2 red, orange, and/or yellow sweet peppers, cut into bite-size pieces (about 2 cups)
- 1 banana pepper, sliced crosswise and seeded
- 3 cups cold cooked long-grain rice
  Fresh flat-leaf Italian parsley
  Lime wedges

1. In a small bowl combine curry powder, salt, cayenne, and ginger. In a separate small bowl combine soy sauce and white wine; set aside.
2. Place pork and spice mixture in a resealable plastic bag. Seal bag; toss to coat.
3. Heat a 14-inch flat-bottom wok or 12-inch stainless-steel skillet over high heat until a bead of water vaporizes within 2 seconds. Swirl 1 Tbsp. of the peanut oil into pan and add pork; stir-fry 2 minutes or until pork is no longer pink. Remove pork from pan. Swirl in another 1 Tbsp. of oil. Add peppers; stir-fry 2 to 3 minutes. Remove peppers from pan. Add remaining 1 Tbsp. of oil and rice; stir-fry 2 minutes, breaking up rice with a spatula until heated through. Swirl in soy sauce mixture. Return pork and peppers to pan; stir-fry 1 minute until cooked through. To serve, sprinkle with parsley. Pass lime wedges. Makes 4 servings.
EACH SERVING 368 cal, 13 g fat, 55 mg chol, 600 mg sodium, 39 g carb, 3 g fiber, 22 g pro.

Skillet Bucatini with Spring Vegetables

If you use a skillet, Grace suggests caramelizing lemon slices in oil and tossing them with pasta.

START TO FINISH 35 min.

- 4 oz. dried bucatini pasta or thick spaghetti
- 2 Tbsp. peanut or vegetable oil
- 12 oz. asparagus, ends trimmed and cut into 2-inch pieces (2½ cups; 14 spears)
- 6 cloves garlic, sliced
- 3 cups red and yellow cherry tomatoes, halved
- ¾ tsp. salt
- ¾ cup chopped fresh basil
- ½ cup chopped pitted Kalamata olives
- ¼ tsp. freshly ground pepper
- ½ cup grated Parmesan cheese
  Lemon wedges (optional)

1. In a large pot cook pasta according to package directions. Drain; reserve ½ cup pasta water. Return pasta to pot. Add 1 Tbsp. of the peanut oil. Toss until well combined; set aside.
2. Heat a 14-inch flat-bottom wok or 12-inch stainless-steel skillet over high heat until a bead of water vaporizes within 2 seconds. Swirl in remaining 1 Tbsp. peanut oil.
3. Add asparagus; stir-fry 2 minutes. Add garlic; stir-fry 10 seconds. Add cherry tomatoes and ½ tsp. of the salt; stir-fry 30 seconds. Add basil and olives; stir-fry 30 seconds. Remove pan from heat. Add pepper, remaining ¼ tsp. salt and pasta. Add enough reserved pasta water for desired consistency. To serve, sprinkle with Parmesan cheese. Pass lemon wedges, if desired. Makes 4 servings.
EACH SERVING 278 cal, 13 g fat, 9 mg chol, 785 mg sodium, 33 g carb, 5 g fiber, 11 g pro.

Sizzling Steak with Lime Basil Sauce

"We forget about pan-searing a steak in a wok, but it's an ideal pan for cooking steak to perfection," Grace says.

START TO FINISH 30 min.

- ¼ cup snipped fresh basil
- ¼ cup finely chopped red sweet pepper
- 3 Tbsp. lime juice (1 lime)
- 2 Tbsp. fish sauce
- 1 Tbsp. rice vinegar
- 1 Tbsp. sugar
- 2 9-oz. ½-inch-thick ribeye or beef shoulder petite tender steaks, trimmed and cut into 4 pieces
  Salt
- 2 Tbsp. peanut or vegetable oil
- 1 cup sliced green onion
- 1 medium zucchini, halved lengthwise and cut into ¼-inch-thick slices
- 1 medium yellow squash, halved lengthwise and cut into ¼-inch-thick slices
- 2 cups baby spinach
- ¾ cup loosely packed basil leaves

1. For dressing, in bowl combine basil, red pepper, lime juice, 3 Tbsp. warm water, fish sauce, rice vinegar, and sugar. Stir until sugar is dissolved; set aside. Sprinkle both sides of steaks with salt.
2. Heat a 14-inch flat-bottom wok or 12-inch stainless-steel skillet over medium-high heat until a bead of water vaporizes within 2 seconds. Swirl in 1 Tbsp. of the peanut oil. Add steaks; pan-fry 3 to 5 minutes until medium-rare, turning halfway through cooking. Remove steaks to platter; set aside.
3. Swirl remaining 1 Tbsp. peanut oil into pan over high heat. Add green onions; stir-fry 30 seconds or until softened. Add zucchini and yellow squash; stir-fry 1 minute. Transfer to a bowl. Add spinach to pan; cook 15 seconds. Stir into vegetables. Stir in basil. To serve, spoon vegetables over steaks. Drizzle with dressing. Makes 4 servings.
EACH SERVING 411 cal, 28 g fat, 87 mg chol, 1,099 mg sodium, 14 g carb, 3 g fiber, 29 g pro.

SPICY JERK PORK
WITH PEPPER
FRIED RICE

"Once you
understand
stir-fry techniques,
you can have fun
and improvise,"
Grace says.

SKILLET BUCATINI
WITH SPRING
VEGETABLES

SIZZLING STEAK
WITH LIME BASIL
SAUCE

Salad for dinner? Yes, please!
Warm up spring's best butter lettuce with stir-fried
shrimp, zippy vegetables, and a hard-to-resist
drizzle of dressing.

KID FRIENDLY | **FAST**

Seared Shrimp Salad with Wok Dressing

"When you open a can of coconut milk, there's a layer of cream that rises to the top," Grace says. "Be sure to stir before measuring."

START TO FINISH **25 min.**

- 2 Tbsp. peanut or vegetable oil
- 1 Tbsp. toasted sesame oil
- 1 Tbsp. minced garlic
- 1½ tsp. Asian chili sauce (such as Sriracha sauce)
- 1 tsp. soy sauce
- ½ tsp. honey
- ½ tsp. salt
- 1 Tbsp. minced fresh ginger
- 1 lb. large shrimp, peeled, deveined, and patted dry
- ¼ cup coconut milk
- 1 head butter lettuce, broken into leaves
- ¼ cup julienned radishes
- 1 avocado, coarsely chopped
- 2 Tbsp. rice vinegar
- ¼ cup coarsely chopped pistachios

1. For dressing, in screw-top jar combine 1 Tbsp. peanut oil, sesame oil, ½ tsp. of garlic, chili sauce, soy sauce, honey, and ¼ tsp. of the salt. Cover; shake well. Set aside.
2. Heat a 14-inch flat-bottom wok or 12-inch stainless-steel skillet over high heat until a bead of water vaporizes within 2 seconds of contact. Swirl in remaining 1 Tbsp. of peanut oil. Add ginger and remaining garlic; stir-fry 10 seconds.
3. Push ginger mixture to sides of pan. Add shrimp to center of pan; spread in one layer. Cook, undisturbed, 1 minute, until shrimp begin to sear. Stir-fry 1 minute or until shrimp begin to turn pink. Add remaining ¼ tsp. salt. Swirl coconut milk down sides of the pan. Stir-fry 1 to 2 minutes more or until shrimp are opaque and most of the liquid has evaporated.
4. To serve, layer lettuce leaves, radishes, and avocado; top with shrimp. Add dressing to hot pan; heat 30 seconds. Drizzle dressing over salad. Splash with rice vinegar. Sprinkle with chopped pistachios. Makes 4 servings.
EACH SERVING *366 cal, 24 g fat, 172 mg chol, 579 mg sodium, 11 g carb, 4 g fiber, 27 g pro.*

PREPPING SHRIMP
Peeling and deveining shrimp is a simple process.

1. Using a paring knife, make a shallow slit along the back from the head to the tail.

2. Peel back the shell, leaving the tail, if preferred.

3. Find the black vein that runs along the center of the back. Use your fingers or the tip of a knife to carefully remove and discard it.

Home Cooking

JUICY SECRETS Have you noticed all those colorful fruit-and-veggie juice blends in grocery produce aisles? Here are four reasons to save some from breakfast and cook with them tonight.

Spring Vegetable Chicken Noodle Soup

Comfort food favorite chicken noodle soup gets a makeover for spring with carrots and sugar snap peas, plus a surprising kick from curry powder and crushed red pepper.

START TO FINISH **30 min.**

- 2 Tbsp. olive oil
- 1 small onion, finely chopped
- 2 cloves garlic, minced
- 1½ tsp. curry powder
- 4 cups refrigerated orange-carrot juice (such as Bolthouse Farms Orange + Carrot or Naked Orange Carrot)
- 1 14½-oz. can reduced-sodium chicken broth
- 1 cup carrots, diagonally sliced
- 1 cup sliced celery
- 4 oz. dried medium noodles (2 cups)
- 2 cups shredded cooked chicken
- 1 cup sugar snap peas, trimmed
- 2 Tbsp. fresh parsley
- ¼ to ½ tsp. crushed red pepper

1. In a 4- to 5-quart Dutch oven heat olive oil over medium heat. Add onion and garlic; cook and stir 2 minutes. Add curry powder; cook 1 minute more. Carefully stir in orange-carrot juice, chicken broth, 1 cup water, and ½ tsp. salt; add carrots and celery. Bring to boiling; reduce heat. Simmer, covered, 20 minutes.

2. Add noodles; cook 6 minutes, stirring occasionally. Add chicken and sugar snap peas; heat through. Stir in parsley and crushed red pepper. Makes 4 servings.

EACH SERVING *426 cal, 13 g fat, 78 mg chol, 661 mg sodium, 50 g carb, 4 g fiber, 27 g pro.*

ORANGE YOU GLAD
Orange-carrot juice blends lend a little sweetness and bright acidity to dishes. Many contain apple—which, combined with citrus, gives a nicely tart flavor.

KID FRIENDLY | LOW FAT | FAST

Sweet Berry Dressing

This versatile dressing is especially delicious over a salad of fresh spinach, raspberries, mushrooms, and sliced green onion.

START TO FINISH 15 min.

⅔ cup refrigerated berry-vegetable juice blend
¼ cup olive oil
2 Tbsp. lemon juice
1 Tbsp. honey
¼ tsp. salt
Dash pepper
1 to 1½ tsp. poppy seeds

1. In a blender combine juice blend, oil, lemon juice, honey, salt, and pepper; process until well blended. Stir in poppy seeds. Makes 20 (1-Tbsp.) servings.
EACH SERVING *41 cal, 3 g fat, 0 mg chol, 37 mg sodium, 2 g carb, 0 g fiber, 0 g pro.*

BEYOND BERRY

Berry-veggie blends are loaded with the flavor of sweet fruits. You might not even notice the big batch of vegetables, such as beets, carrots, and corn.

Green Pesto Sauce

This twist on traditional pesto gets a mellow sweetness from the green juice blend. Serve with steamed or roasted vegetables, swirl into a tomato-base soup, or toss with pasta.

START TO FINISH **20 min.**

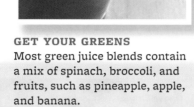

- ½ cup refrigerated green juice blend (such as Naked Green Machine)
- 2 Tbsp. olive oil
- 2 Tbsp. lemon juice
- 1½ cups firmly packed fresh flat-leaf Italian parsley
- ½ cup firmly packed basil leaves
- ½ cup pine nuts, toasted (see tip, page 35)
- ½ cup grated Parmesan cheese
- 3 cloves garlic, sliced
- ½ tsp. salt

1. In a food processor or blender combine all ingredients. Cover and process until almost smooth. Makes 21 (1-Tbsp.) servings.

EACH SERVING *48 cal, 4 g fat, 2 mg chol, 88 mg sodium, 2 g carb, 0 g fiber, 1 g pro.*

GET YOUR GREENS
Most green juice blends contain a mix of spinach, broccoli, and fruits, such as pineapple, apple, and banana.

Mango juice helps a favorite cake become a better-for-you baked good. It's lower in fat, calories, and cholesterol than the traditional spring treat.

Mango-Carrot Cake

Mango juice brings out this cake's sweet carrot flavor and creates a moist texture similar to a cake doughnut.

PREP 40 min. BAKE 25 min. COOL 10 min. OVEN 350°F

- 2 cups all-purpose flour
- 1 Tbsp. baking powder
- ½ tsp. salt
- ¼ tsp. ground nutmeg
- ½ cup butter, softened
- 1 cup granulated sugar
- 2 eggs
- 1¼ cups refrigerated mango juice blend (such as Odwalla Mango Tango or Naked Juice Mighty Mango)
- 3 cups finely shredded carrot
- 1 recipe Cream Cheese Frosting
- 1 recipe Carrot Ribbons

1. Preheat oven to 350°F. Grease and flour two 8×1½-inch round cake pans; set aside. In a medium bowl combine flour, baking powder, salt, and nutmeg; set aside.

2. In a large mixing bowl beat butter on medium-high speed 30 seconds. Gradually add granulated sugar; beat until combined. Beat 2 minutes more. Add eggs, one at a time, beating well after each addition. Alternately add flour mixture and ¾ cup of the mango juice; beat on low after each addition just until combined. Stir in shredded carrots. Pour batter into prepared pans.

3. Bake 25 to 30 minutes or until golden and a wooden pick inserted near center comes out clean. Cool in pans on wire rack 10 minutes. Remove from pans; cool completely. Place remaining ½ cup mango juice blend in a small saucepan; bring to boiling. Boil gently, uncovered, 3 to 4 minutes or until reduced to ¼ cup. Remove from heat; cool. Frost top of one cake layer with Cream Cheese Frosting. Top with remaining cake layer; frost as desired. Drizzle with reduced juice; top with Carrot Ribbons. Makes 12 servings.

Cream Cheese Frosting In a large mixing bowl beat together one 8-oz. package cream cheese and ¼ cup butter until smooth. Beat in 1 tsp. vanilla. Gradually beat in 4 cups powdered sugar.

Carrot Ribbons Using a vegetable peeler, thinly slice 1 carrot lengthwise. Place in a bowl of ice water for at least 30 minutes. Drain well before using.

EACH SERVING *506 cal, 19 g fat, 82 mg chol, 418 mg sodium, 81 g carb, 1 g fiber, 5 g pro.*

MIGHTY MANGO
Most mango juice blends contain a mix of mango, orange, apple, and banana. Also find mango-carrot blends, which work well with this cake.

Good for You

Hearty appetizers come together beautifully around a savory tomato chutney. Make it a meal with a nutritious (and beautiful) salad.

Antipasto Platter with Tomato Chutney

PREP 30 min. COOL 20 min. COOK 30 min.

- 2 lb. roma tomatoes, seeded and coarsely chopped
- 1 medium onion, finely chopped
- 2 cloves garlic, minced
- ½ cup red wine vinegar
- 1 Tbsp. sugar
- ½ tsp. salt
- ½ tsp. paprika
- ⅛ to ¼ tsp. cayenne pepper
- 1 Tbsp. snipped fresh basil
  Assorted antipasti (choose from olive oil-packed tuna sprinkled with capers, blanched asparagus and broccoli, fresh mozzarella, baby sweet peppers, paper-thin slices prosciutto, and whole grain crackers or breads)

1. In a medium saucepan combine tomatoes, onion, garlic, vinegar, sugar, salt, paprika, and cayenne pepper. Bring to boiling; reduce heat. Simmer, uncovered, for 30 minutes or until chutney is thickened and saucelike, stirring occasionally.

2. Remove from heat; cool about 20 minutes. Serve warm, sprinkled with basil and with desired antipasti. Refrigerate any remaining chutney up to 5 days. Bring to room temperature before serving. Makes 20 (2-Tbsp.) servings.

EACH SERVING 29 cal, 0 g fat, 0 mg chol, 122 mg sodium, 6 g carb, 1 g fiber, 1 g pro.

Greens and Barley Salad

A colorful mix of greens, vegetables, and barley gives this nutritious salad unique texture.

START TO FINISH 30 min.

- 4 cups assorted greens, such as baby bok choy, endive, radicchio, and/or butter lettuce
- ½ head cauliflower, sliced ½ inch thick
- 2 carrots, peeled, and then sliced with a peeler into ribbons
- ⅔ cup cooked barley
- ¼ cup lemon or lime juice
- 2 Tbsp. honey
- 1 Tbsp. olive oil
- 1 tsp. paprika
- ⅛ tsp. nutmeg
- ⅛ tsp. cayenne pepper
  Walnuts, chopped and toasted (see tip, page 35) (optional)

1. In a large bowl combine vegetables and barley.

2. For dressing, in a screw-top jar combine lemon or lime juice, honey, olive oil, paprika, nutmeg, and cayenne pepper. Cover and shake well. Drizzle over salad. Sprinkle with toasted walnuts, if desired.

EACH SERVING *138 cal, 4 g fat, 0 mg chol, 51 mg sodium, 26 g carb, 3 pro.*

Delicious Every Day

Fresh and easy ideas for dinner.

Sweet Potato Quesadillas with Cucumber Relish

PREP 20 min. COOK 27 min.

- 1 15- to 16-oz. can navy beans, rinsed and drained
- ⅓ cup snipped fresh cilantro
- 1 Tbsp. lime juice
- 1 small fresh jalapeño pepper, seeded and finely chopped (see tip, page 11)
- 1 tsp. ground ancho chile pepper
- ½ cucumber, quartered and sliced
- 3 to 4 medium radishes, halved and thinly sliced
- 1 large sweet potato, peeled and coarsely chopped (12. oz.)
- ½ tsp. ground cumin
- 4 10-inch whole wheat flour tortillas
- 1½ cups coarsely chopped baby spinach
- 2 green onions, thinly sliced
- ¾ cup shredded Monterey Jack cheese (3 oz.)
  Plain Greek yogurt (optional)
  Paprika (optional)

1. In a medium bowl combine beans, ¼ cup of the cilantro, lime juice, jalapeño, and chile pepper; set aside. For cucumber relish, in another bowl combine cucumber, radishes, and remaining cilantro; set aside.
2. In a medium saucepan cook sweet potato in lightly salted boiling water, covered, for about 15 minutes or until tender. Remove from heat; drain. Return potato to saucepan; coarsely mash. Stir in cumin.
3. Spread sweet potato mixture over half of each tortilla. Top each with bean mixture, spinach, green onions, and cheese. Fold each tortilla in half over the filling, pressing gently.

4. Heat a grill pan or large nonstick skillet over medium-high heat. Cook quesadillas, two at a time, for 6 minutes or until lightly browned, turning once halfway through. Repeat with remaining quesadillas. Cut into wedges. Serve with cucumber relish and Greek yogurt sprinkled with paprika, if desired. Makes 4 servings.
EACH SERVING *461 cal, 12 g fat, 19 mg chol, 1,167 mg sodium, 67 g carb, 29 g fiber, 23 g pro.*

FLAVOR SECRET
Vitamin-packed sweet potatoes get nutty, peppery flavor from cumin and zip from jalapeño and lime. Plenty of fiber in both the sweet potato and beans (also a good source of protein) makes this recipe satisfying enough for a main dish.

Curried Salmon with Tomatoes and Dried Plums

PREP 20 min. BAKE 10 min.
COOK 20 min. OVEN 350°F

- 1 lb. fresh or frozen salmon fillets, cut into 1½-inch cubes
- 1 medium green sweet pepper, chopped (¾ cup)
- 1 small red onion, chopped (½ cup)
- 1 stalk celery, chopped
- 2 cloves garlic, minced
- 1 Tbsp. olive oil
- 2 14½-oz. cans diced tomatoes, undrained
- ½ cup dried plums, coarsely chopped
- 2 tsp. curry powder
- ⅔ cup Israeli couscous*
  Fresh mint

1. Thaw fish, if frozen. Rinse and pat dry; set aside. Preheat oven to 350°F.
2. In a large ovenproof skillet cook and stir sweet pepper, red onion, celery, and garlic in hot oil over medium-high heat for 3 minutes. Add canned tomatoes, dried plums, and curry powder. Cook and stir for 2 minutes; remove from heat.
3. Add salmon to skillet; transfer to oven. Bake, uncovered, for 10 minutes or until salmon just begins to flake.
4. Meanwhile, in a small saucepan bring 1⅓ cups of water to boiling. Stir in couscous; return to boiling. Reduce heat. Simmer, covered, about 12 minutes. Remove from heat; cover and let stand 2 minutes. Drain if necessary.
5. To serve, spoon salmon over couscous. Sprinkle with fresh mint. Makes 4 servings.

*Tip Israeli couscous is an interesting ingredient with its slightly toasted taste and pearl shape, however you can swap in regular couscous, rice, or orzo.

EACH SERVING 392 cal, 11 g fat, 62 mg chol, 418 mg sodium, 45 g carb, 6 g fiber, 28 g pro.

FLAVOR SECRET

Dried plums aren't just for healthful snacking. This pantry favorite—along with canned tomatoes—gives sweet balance to salmon spiked with robust curry powder. For even easier prep look for already chopped packaged prunes at the grocery store.

Dinner on a Dollar

Make dinner fast with shrimp tacos. This version gets a splash of citrus flavor from zesty lime slaw.

KID FRIENDLY | **LOW FAT**

Shrimp Tacos with Lime Slaw

START TO FINISH 35 min.
COST $1.55 per serving

- 1 lb. fresh or frozen medium shrimp, peeled and deveined
- 1 Tbsp. olive oil
- 3 cloves garlic, minced
- 1 tsp. ground cumin
- ½ tsp. chili powder
- ½ tsp. salt
- 1 lime
- 3 cups shredded red cabbage
- ½ cup sour cream
- 1 tsp. finely chopped canned chipotle pepper in adobo sauce
- 12 6-inch corn tortillas
  Fresh cilantro (optional)
  Lime wedges (optional)

1. Thaw shrimp, if frozen. Rinse shrimp; pat dry. In a resealable plastic bag combine olive oil, garlic, cumin, chili powder, and ¼ tsp. of the salt; add shrimp. Seal bag and turn to coat shrimp; chill 30 minutes.
2. Meanwhile, finely shred peel from lime; juice lime. For lime slaw, in a bowl combine the lime peel, lime juice, cabbage, and remaining ¼ tsp. salt; set aside. In a bowl combine sour cream and chipotle pepper. Wrap tortillas in foil.
3. Thread shrimp on 10-inch metal or wooden skewers (see tip, page 111). On a covered grill, grill tortilla packet directly over medium heat for 5 minutes; turning once. Add shrimp to grill; cook 5 to 8 minutes or until opaque, turning halfway through grilling. Remove tortilla packet from grill. Remove shrimp from skewers.
4. To serve, spread tortillas with sour cream mixture. Top with lime slaw and shrimp. Sprinkle with cilantro and pass lime wedges, if desired. Makes 6 servings.
EACH SERVING *135 cal, 4 g fat, 62 mg chol, 198 mg sodium, 15 g carb, 2 g fiber, 9 g pro.*

BEST-EVER
STRAWBERRY
RHUBARB PIE

BETTER COOK Tips and techniques that expand skills beyond chopping and baking will have folks asking how you became such an amazing cook! Plus totable bars for your next potluck.

131

137

139

Delicious Discoveries

Rejuvenate your repertoire with new ingredients, cooking techniques, and recipes to make you a better cook. You're never too old to learn!

KID FRIENDLY

Herbed Chicken with Spring Vegetables

A springy mix of herbs, garlic, and lemon works magic when cooked inside this roasted chicken.

PREP **1 hr.** GRILL **1 hr. 10 min.**
STAND **10 min.**

¼ cup snipped fresh flat-leaf Italian parsley
2 Tbsp. snipped fresh tarragon
2 tsp. finely shredded lemon peel
½ tsp. salt
1 4½- to 5-lb. whole roasting chicken
1 lemon wedge or ½ Meyer lemon
4 cloves garlic, halved and smashed
3 sprigs fresh flat-leaf Italian parsley
2 sprigs fresh tarragon
1 Tbsp. olive oil
1½ lbs. assorted small new potatoes, halved or quartered
2 cloves garlic, minced
2 Tbsp. olive oil
1 lb. asparagus, trimmed and cut into 3-inch pieces
6 thick green onions, tops trimmed
2 small Meyer lemons, halved (optional)
Sea salt

1. In a small bowl combine the ¼ cup parsley, the 2 Tbsp. tarragon, lemon peel, and salt. Reserve 2 Tbsp. of the herb mixture for the vegetables. Cover and set aside.
2. Rinse chicken; pat dry with paper towels. Using your fingers, loosen the skin on the chicken breast and legs. Carefully spoon 2 Tbsp. of the remaining herb mixture under the skin of the chicken.
3. Add lemon wedge, 4 cloves garlic, the 3 sprigs of parsley, and the 2 sprigs tarragon to the cavity of the chicken. Brush the surface of chicken skin with olive oil. Pat remaining herbs onto the surface of chicken; set aside. Place the chicken on a rack in a roasting pan.
4. For a charcoal grill, arrange medium-hot coals around a drip pan. Test for medium heat above pan. (You should be able to hold your hand, palm side down, at the same height as the food that will be grilled for a 4-second count.) Place the roasting pan in the center of the grill; cover and cook for 50 minutes. (For a gas grill, preheat grill. Reduce heat to medium. Adjust for indirect cooking. Place roasting pan on grill rack above the burner that is turned off. Grill as directed.)
5. Meanwhile, place potatoes in a large microwave-safe bowl. Add the 2 cloves minced garlic and 1 Tbsp. of the olive oil; stir to coat. Cover bowl with waxed paper. Microwave on 100 percent power (high) for 8 minutes, stirring twice. Add asparagus, green onions, and, if desired, lemon halves. Drizzle with remaining olive oil. Sprinkle with sea salt. Toss to evenly coat vegetables.
6. Add prepared vegetables to the roasting pan; cover grill and cook for 20 to 25 minutes more or until chicken is no longer pink (170°F in thigh muscle). Remove roasting pan from the grill. Sprinkle the reserved 2 Tbsp. of herb mixture over vegetables. Cover pan with foil; let stand 10 minutes. (The temperature of the chicken will rise to 180°F while standing.)
7. Using tongs and a kitchen fork, lift the chicken out of the roasting pan and transfer to a serving platter. Serve with vegetables. Makes 6 servings.

EACH SERVING *479 cal, 25 g fat, 116 mg chol, 425 mg sodium, 24 g carb, 4 g fiber, 40 g pro.*

Stack cakes are all the rage, especially this apricot version laced with lime and honey. A stovetop griddle makes easy work of it: Just cook the layers like flapjacks.

Apricot Stack Cake

Made from whole raw almonds and packed with protein, almond flour gives this stack cake its subtle hint of nutty flavor. Find it in the baking aisle of most grocery stores.

PREP **25 min.** STAND **15 min.** CHILL **2 hr.**

 2 15-oz. cans apricot halves in light syrup
 1 cup dried apricots, chopped
 2 Tbsp. honey
 2 tsp. finely shredded lime peel
 2 eggs, lightly beaten
 1¼ cups buttermilk
 ¼ cup melted butter
 1 cup all-purpose flour
 ½ cup almond flour
 ⅓ cup granulated sugar
 1 tsp. baking powder
 ¼ tsp. baking soda
 ¼ tsp. salt
   Whipped cream
   Lime peel strips
   Honey
   Fresh or canned apricots, quartered (optional)

1. For apricot filling, drain syrup from the 2 cans of apricot halves in to a small saucepan. Set apricot halves aside. Bring drained syrup to boiling; remove from heat. Add dried apricots. Let stand 15 minutes to soften. Drain and discard syrup. In a food processor or blender combine the drained apricot halves and the softened dried apricots. Cover and process or blend until smooth. Transfer to a bowl. Stir in the honey and lime peel; set aside.

2. In a large bowl whisk together eggs, buttermilk, and melted butter until combined. Add flour, almond flour, sugar, baking powder, baking soda, and salt. Whisk until smooth.

3. Pour about ½ cup batter onto a hot, lightly greased griddle or heavy skillet. Spread batter to a 7½- to 8-inch circle. Cook over medium heat for 1 to 2 minutes, turning cake when surface is bubbly and edges are slightly dry. Cook cake 1 minute more until golden brown.

4. Place cake in an 8-inch springform pan. Top with ⅓ to ½ cup of apricot filling. Repeat with remaining batter and filling, finishing with apricot filling on top. Yields 6 to 7 layers. Cover and chill 2 hours or overnight.

5. To serve, top with whipped cream, apricots, if desired, then sprinkle with lime peel strips, and drizzle with honey. Top with. Makes 8 servings.

EACH SERVING *391 cal, 17 g fat, 84 mg chol, 294 mg sodium, 58 g carb, 4 g fiber, 7 g pro.*

Add intriguing flavor to the simplest foods by sprinkling on a homemade global spice blend. A new trend-setting favorite is dukkah—an aromatic Egyptian mix of hazelnuts and spices.

Spice and Honey Roasted Carrots

Combined with a dusting of fragrant dukkah, carrots take on global flavor. For a delicious and crispy snack, thoroughly wash and dry reserved carrot tops, drizzle with olive oil, and roast alongside the carrots.

PREP 20 min. ROAST 25 min.
OVEN 425°F

1½ lbs. regular or rainbow carrots, scrubbed and peeled, if desired
1 Tbsp. olive oil
½ cup coarsely chopped hazelnuts
1 Tbsp. coriander seeds
1 Tbsp. sesame seeds
1½ tsp. cumin seeds
½ tsp. salt
¼ tsp. ground black pepper
1 Tbsp. honey
Lemon wedges

1. Preheat oven to 425°F. Trim carrots, reserving tops if desired. Halve any large carrots lengthwise.
2. Line a shallow roasting pan with foil. Evenly spread carrots in pan. Drizzle with olive oil. Roast carrots, uncovered, for 20 minutes.
3. Meanwhile, for dukkah, heat a small skillet over medium-high heat. Add hazelnuts; cook and stir 3 minutes or until fragrant and toasted. Transfer to a glass bowl. Add the coriander, sesame, and cumin to the hot skillet. Cook on medium-high heat for 2 minutes or until fragrant and toasted. Remove spices from heat and transfer to another bowl. Cool for 10 minutes.
4. Using a spice grinder, coffee grinder, or mortar and pestle, grind or crush toasted spices just until coarsely ground or desired consistency. Add the hazelnuts, salt, and pepper, crushing nuts slightly. Remove carrots from the oven. Drizzle with honey; toss to evenly coat. Sprinkle carrots with half the dukkah*. Return to the oven; roast 5 to 10 minutes more.
5. Serve carrots with lemon wedges. Makes 6 servings.
* Remaining dukkah can be stored in a tightly sealed container up to 2 weeks.
EACH SERVING 152 cal, 9 g fat, 0 mg chol, 274 mg sodium, 17 g carb, 5 g fiber, 3 g pro.

DUKKAH

Originating from Egypt, dukkah (DOO-kah) is a vibrant mix of nuts and spices that has steadily grown in popularity. There's no exact science to making the perfect dukkah, so customize it to your liking. Swap pistachios for hazelnuts, or use almonds or walnuts. Toasting the nuts and spices is a must to bring out the different flavors in the blend. Try dukkah as a dip with olive oil, use it as a spice rub for meat, or toss it with pasta.

SPRING
VEGETABLE
SOUP

Thai-Style Tuna Burgers

With ginger-laced mayonnaise and a splash of fish sauce, these burgers pay homage to bold savory flavor.

PREP **10 min.** STAND **10 min.**
BAKE **10 min.** OVEN **450°F**

- ⅓ cup mayonnaise with olive oil
- 2 tsp. grated fresh ginger
- 2 eggs, beaten
- 1 cup panko (Japanese-style bread crumbs)
- 1 Tbsp. fish sauce
- 1 tsp. Asian chili sauce (Sriracha)
- 2 5-oz. cans wild albacore tuna*
- ¼ cup celery, very thinly sliced
- ¼ cup chopped green onion
- 4 small ciabatta buns, halved and toasted
- ⅓ cup pea shoots or micro greens
- 4 miniature sweet peppers, thinly sliced

1. Preheat oven to 450°F. In a small bowl combine mayonnaise and ginger; transfer 2 Tbsp. to a large bowl. Cover remaining mayonnaise mixture and chill. To the same large bowl add eggs, panko, fish sauce, and Asian chili sauce. Flake tuna and add to bowl. Add celery and green onion and stir. Let stand 10 minutes.
2. With wet hands, shape tuna mixture into four ¾-inch-thick patties. Place tuna patties on a greased baking sheet. Bake 10 minutes or until done (160°F).
3. To serve, spread ciabatta halves with remaining mayonnaise mixture. Add a tuna patty to bottom half of each bun. Top with pea shoots, sliced peppers, and bun tops. Makes 4 servings.
* If using a brand packed in oil or water, drain tuna.
EACH SERVING *391 cal, 18 g fat, 118 mg chol, 1,066 mg sodium, 25 g carb, 2 g fiber, 28 g pro.*

Spring Vegetable Soup

Use a slow cooker to coax out layers of flavors from this brothy vegetable soup.

PREP **20 min.** SLOW COOK **6 hr.** (low) or **3 hr.** (high)

- 1 cup 100 percent vegetable juice
- 1 cup carrot juice
- 4 cups vegetable broth
- 1 tsp. ground cumin
- ¼ tsp. ground white pepper
- ½ lb. carrot chunks
- 1 cup pearl onions, peeled (about 8 oz.)
- 8 oz. green beans, trimmed
- 8 oz. new potatoes, halved or quartered

1. In a 4-quart slow cooker combine vegetable juice, carrot juice, and vegetable broth. Add cumin and white pepper. Add carrot chunks, pearl onions, green beans, and new potatoes.
2. Cook, covered, on low-heat setting for 6 hours or on high-heat setting for 3 hours.
EACH SERVING *72 cal, 0 g fat, 0 mg chol, 498 mg sodium, 16 g carb, 3 g fiber, 2 g pro*

THAI-STYLE TUNA
BURGERS

CHOCOLATE AND
MANGO YOGURT

Varieties and flavors of yogurt abound in supermarkets, and now yogurt is easier than ever to make at home. Strain it for Greek-style, which takes well to mix-ins.

KID FRIENDLY | **FAST**

Chocolate and Mango Yogurt

Combine fruit, nuts, and chocolate to create a nutrient-dense yogurt sure to give you a burst of energy.
START TO FINISH 5 min.

- 1 cup Homemade Vanilla Yogurt or purchased Greek vanilla yogurt
- 1 mango, chopped, about 1 cup
- ½ cup toasted walnut pieces (see tip, page 35)
- ¼ cup bittersweet or semisweet chocolate, coarsely chopped or grated
- 2 Tbsp. snipped fresh mint leaves
- 2 to 3 tsp. agave nectar or honey

1. In a shallow serving dish combine yogurt, mango, walnuts, chocolate, and mint. Stir together. Sweeten to taste with agave nectar or honey. Makes 4 servings.
EACH SERVING *238 cal, 17 g fat, 8 mg chol, 31 mg sodium, 20 g carb, 3 g fiber, 6 g pro.*

KID FRIENDLY

Homemade Vanilla Yogurt

Making yogurt introduces a world of possibilities for breakfast and beyond. For thick Greek-style yogurt, strain through cheesecloth overnight.
COOK 10 min. COOL 45 min.
STAND 8 hr.

- 4 cups whole milk
- 6 oz. plain whole milk yogurt without added gelatin (¾ cup)
- 1 Tbsp. vanilla bean paste or vanilla extract

1. In a large saucepan, with a thermometer attached, heat milk to 180°F, carefully monitoring the temperature. Maintain 180°F temperature for at least 10 minutes. Remove the saucepan from heat and cool milk to 110°F. (This will take about 45 minutes.)
2. Stir yogurt and vanilla bean paste into milk. Transfer milk mixture to a yogurt maker. Set fermentation time to 8 hours.
3. Serve immediately or cover and store in the refrigerator for 3 to 5 days. Makes 8 servings.
EACH SERVING *107 cal, 6 g fat, 16 mg chol, 59 mg sodium, 7 g carb, 0 g fiber, 5 g pro.*

YOGURT TIPS

From choosing a starter to deciding on consistency, making yogurt comes with many variables. These tips will help you get started.

• Yogurt starter introduces the necessary bacteria to begin the fermentation process. For purchased starters, choose from whole milk yogurt, nonfat dry milk powder, and packaged yogurt culture. Or use homemade yogurt reserved from a previous batch.

• For thick yogurt, use whole milk or a mixture of milk and cream that has been heated to 180°F and held at that temperature for 30 minutes prior to cooling to 110°F. Strain the finished yogurt through three layers of 100-percent-cotton cheesecloth in a fine-mesh strainer set over a bowl. Cover with plastic wrap and refrigerate for 24 hours. Then follow recipe as directed.

Strawberry-rhubarb pie celebrates spring. Thanks to Jamie Oliver's surprising crust technique, it's a cinch to put together.

KID FRIENDLY

Best-Ever Strawberry-Rhubarb Pie

Yummy strawberry-rhubarb pie filling gets a spark of spicy ginger flavor then goes into a remarkably easy slice-and-bake crust.

PREP **45 min.** FREEZE **1 hr.**
STAND **15 min.** BAKE **1 hr. 15 min.**
OVEN **375°F**

Rich Butter Pastry
2¼ cups all-purpose flour
¼ cup granulated sugar
¼ tsp. salt
½ cup shortening
¼ cup cold butter, cut into ½-inch cubes
6 to 7 Tbsp. ice water

Strawberry-Rhubarb Filling
1¼ cups sugar
2½ Tbsp. quick-cooking tapioca
1 Tbsp. grated fresh ginger
¼ tsp. salt
1 lb. fresh rhubarb, cut into 1-inch pieces (3 cups) or one 16-oz. package frozen cut rhubarb
3 cups sliced fresh strawberries

1. For Rich Butter Pastry, in a medium bowl stir together flour, sugar, and salt. Using a pastry blender, cut in shortening and butter cubes until pieces are peasize. Sprinkle 1 Tbsp. of the water over part of the flour mixture; toss with a fork. Push moistened pastry to side of bowl. Repeat moistening flour mixture, using 1 Tbsp. of the water at a time, until all the flour mixture is moistened. Gather flour mixture into a ball, using hands to combine until it holds together. Divide pastry into two portions; one portion with one-third of the dough and one portion with two-thirds of the dough. Shape the small piece of pastry into a 5×1½-inch round log. Shape the large piece of dough into a 7×2-inch round log. Wrap pastry with plastic wrap and freeze for 1 to 2 hours or until firm.
2. Meanwhile, for Strawberry-Rhubarb Filling, in a large bowl stir together sugar, tapioca, ginger, and salt. Add rhubarb and strawberries; gently toss until coated. Let rhubarb mixture stand for 15 minutes, stirring occasionally. (If using frozen rhubarb, let mixture stand 45 minutes.) Meanwhile, remove pastry from freezer and let stand 10 to 15 minutes or until easy to slice.
3. Preheat oven to 375°F. Using a sharp knife with a thin blade, cut the chilled 7-inch dough log into 28 thin slices. Place 16 of the slices around the edge of a 9-inch deep-dish pie plate. Place the remaining slices in the bottom of the pie plate. Using your fingers, press the pieces of the pastry together to fill in the gaps. Flute edge as desired.

4. Stir fruit mixture and transfer to the pastry-lined pie plate. Slice the remaining pastry into 15 to 18 slices. Place slices on top of fruit.
5. To prevent overbrowning, cover edge of pie with foil. Place a foil-lined baking sheet on the rack below the pie in oven. Bake for 60 minutes (75 minutes if using frozen fruit.) Remove foil; bake 15 to 20 minutes more or until filling is bubbly and crust is golden. Cool on a wire rack. Makes 8 servings.
EACH SERVING *481 cal, 19 g fat, 15 mg chol, 201 mg sodium, 74 g carb, 3 g fiber, 5 g pro.*

NO-FAIL CRUST

Rolling out piecrust and transferring it to a pie plate is perhaps one of the most daunting steps in preparing a pie. Jamie Oliver's technique of using sliced dough rounds to line the pie plate makes tears in the dough old news. Rolled into logs and securely wrapped, this Rich Butter Pastry will keep in the freezer up to 1 month. With the perfect crust only a few slices away, any day becomes an occasion for fresh-out-of-the-oven pie.

WALNUT MILK

Skip the stabilizers and preservatives of store-bought and make fresh nut milk at home. With an hour of soaking time and a quick blending with water, sweetener, vanilla, and salt, walnuts became a tasty topping for cereal or a nutritious beverage.

KID FRIENDLY
Walnut Milk

Silky nut milks are a healthful alternative to traditional dairy milks and are surprisingly simple to make. For a smoother milk, strain through cheesecloth.

PREP 15 min. STAND 1 hr.

- 1 cup walnut halves, rinsed (4 oz.)
- 3 cups water
- 1 Tbsp. honey or agave nectar
- 1 tsp. pure vanilla extract
  Pinch of kosher salt

1. Place walnuts in a medium bowl then fill with enough water to cover by 1 inch. Cover and set aside. Soak at room temperature at least 1 hour or up to 12 hours for easy blending.
2. Drain walnuts; rinse thoroughly. In a blender combine walnuts, the fresh water, honey, vanilla, and salt; blend on low speed until very smooth, at least 2 minutes. Serve immediately or store in the refrigerator up to 5 days.

EACH SERVING *182 cal, 16 g fat, 0 mg chol, 37 mg sodium, 8 g carb, 2 g fiber, 4 g pro.*

KID FRIENDLY | FAST
Walnut-Date Smoothie

PREP 5 minutes

- 1 cup Walnut Milk
- 1 cup plain or vanilla yogurt
- ¾ cup medjool dates, pitted and roughly chopped (5 ounces)
- 1 tsp. vanilla extract
- ¼ tsp. ground cinnamon
- 1 cup ice cubes (about 8)

1. In a blender container combine Walnut Milk, yogurt, dates, vanilla, and cinnamon. Blend on high speed until smooth, at least 1 minute.
2. Add ice and blend briefly on high speed just until ice is broken up. Pour into chilled glasses and serve immediately. Makes 3 servings.

PER SERVING *248 cal, 7 g fat, 5 mg chol, 70 mg sodium, 44 g carb, 4 g fiber, 6 g pro.*

VERSATILE NUT MILK
Browse any grocery store and you'll find a selection of nut milks, increasingly popular because of its nutritious benefits and refreshing flavor. Try them in cereal, in your morning coffee, or in this smoothie.

Home Cooking

PASS THE BAR It's potluck time! These four new takes on dessert bars are sure to please. Grab one while you can—these shareable sweets won't stick around for long.

Lemon-Lime Bars

Be sure to pour the lemon filling over the crust immediately after you take it out of the oven to ensure that the lemon layer sets.

PREP **35 min.** BAKE **35 min.**
OVEN **350°F**

- 2 cups all-purpose flour
- ½ cup powdered sugar
- 2 Tbsp. cornstarch
- ¼ tsp. salt
- ¾ cup butter, cut up
- 4 eggs, lightly beaten
- 1½ cups granulated sugar
- ⅓ cup half-and-half
- 3 Tbsp. all-purpose flour
- 1 tsp. finely shredded lemon peel
- ⅓ cup lemon juice
- 1 tsp. finely shredded lime peel
- ⅓ cup lime juice
- 1 drop green food coloring
  Powdered sugar
  Thin strips of lemon and lime peel (optional)

1. Preheat oven to 350°F. Grease a 13×9×2-inch baking pan. Line pan with parchment, pressing the paper onto the bottom and up the sides of the pan; set aside. For crust, in a large bowl combine the 2 cups flour, powdered sugar, cornstarch, and salt. Using a pastry blender, cut in butter until mixture resembles coarse crumbs. Press firmly into bottom of prepared pan. Bake 15 minutes.
2. Meanwhile, in a medium mixing bowl whisk together eggs, granulated sugar, half-and-half, and 3 Tbsp. flour; divide equally between two bowls. To one bowl add lemon peel and lemon juice; to the other bowl add lime peel, lime juice, and green food coloring. Pour lemon filling over hot crust; bake 10 to 12 minutes or until set. Carefully pour lime filling over lemon filling; bake 10 to 12 minutes more or until set. Cool completely in pan on a wire rack.
3. Use paper to lift from the pan. Cut into bars. Sift powdered sugar over bars. Top with lemon and lime peel, if desired. Cover and refrigerate to store. Makes 32 bars.
EACH BAR *129 cal, 5 g fat, 36 mg chol, 67 mg sodium, 19 g carb, 2 g pro.*

CUT AND DRY
Cut the butter into the flour mixture just until it resembles coarse crumbs to create a buttery, flaky crust. The crust will look dry after you prebake it, but no worries! It will have a wonderfully delicate texture.

Cheesecake bars take a walk on the tropical side. Coconut makes an appearance in both the crust and the filling, then mango tops it all off.

Coconut Cheesecake Bars

Find the big, beautiful flakes from raw chip coconut at natural or health food stores. If you prefer, substitute regular unsweetened shredded coconut—just keep an eye on it when toasting; it might brown a bit faster.

PREP **25 min.** BAKE **25 min.**
COOL **15 min.** CHILL **2 hrs.**
OVEN **350°F**

- ½ cup raw chip coconut
- ¾ cup graham cracker crumbs
- 2 Tbsp. granulated sugar
- 1 tsp. finely shredded orange peel
- ¼ cup butter, melted
- 1 8-oz. package cream cheese, softened
- ⅓ cup granulated sugar
- 1 tsp. vanilla
- ¼ cup orange juice
- 1 egg
- 1 mango, halved, seeded, peeled, and chopped

1. Preheat oven to 350°F. Spread coconut in a 9×9×2-inch baking pan. Bake, uncovered, 4 to 5 minutes or until toasted, stirring once. Cool. For crust, place 2 Tbsp. of the toasted coconut in the bowl of a food processor. Transfer remaining coconut to a bowl; cover and set aside. To food processor add graham cracker crumbs, the 2 Tbsp. sugar, and the orange peel. Gradually add melted butter, processing with on-off turns until mixture begins to come together. Press mixture into the bottom of the 9×9×2-inch baking pan. Bake 10 minutes. Cool about 15 minutes on a wire rack, .

2. For filling, in a large mixing bowl beat the cream cheese, the ⅓ cup sugar, and vanilla with an electric mixer until combined. Add orange juice; beat until smooth. Stir in egg. Pour filling over baked crust. Bake about 15 minutes or just until center is set. Cool on wire rack. Cover and chill at least 2 hours.

3. Cut into bars. Spoon on mango and sprinkle with reserved toasted coconut. Makes 16 bars.

EACH BAR *144 cal, 9 g fat, 35 mg chol, 106 mg sodium, 13 g carb, 2 g pro.*

QUICK CRUMBS
A food processor makes easy work of this orange-coconut twist on graham cracker crust. If you have whole graham crackers, process 10½ whole large rectangles of crackers to make the ¾ cup crumbs before combining with other ingredients.

Sweet, rich, buttery goodness— the simplest of ingredients makes these decadent bars irresistible.

Gooey Butter Bars

These bars are a blank canvas for whatever topping you like. We piled on strawberries tossed with a little honey and minced ginger, but you could also try blueberries with a bit of finely shredded lemon peel or a simple glaze made with powdered sugar and tangerine juice. Or skip the topping altogether. These bars are just as good on their own.

PREP 25 min. BAKE 30 min.
OVEN 350°F

1½ cups all-purpose flour
¼ cup granulated sugar
½ cup butter
⅔ cup butter, softened
1¼ cups granulated sugar
¼ cup light-color corn syrup
1 egg
½ tsp. almond extract
1 cup all-purpose flour
⅔ cup half-and-half
3 cups sliced and/or halved fresh strawberries
2 Tbsp. honey
1 tsp. grated fresh ginger

1. Preheat oven to 350°F. Line a 13×9×2-inch baking pan with parchment; set aside. For crust, in a medium bowl combine the 1½ cups flour and ¼ cup sugar. Using a pastry blender, cut in the ½ cup butter until mixture resembles fine crumbs. Pat into prepared pan; set aside.

2. In a large mixing bowl beat softened butter with an electric mixer on medium-high speed for 30 seconds. Gradually beat in the 1¼ cups granulated sugar. Beat in corn syrup, egg, and almond extract just until combined. Alternately add the flour and half-and-half, beating after each addition just until combined (batter may appear slightly curdled). Gently spread into crust-lined baking pan. Bake about 30 minutes or just until center is set. Cool in pan on wire rack. Use parchment to lift from the pan; cut into bars.

3. In a small bowl toss strawberries with honey and ginger. Spoon over bars before serving. Makes 24 bars.

EACH BAR *209 cal, 10 g fat, 34 mg chol, 88 mg sodium, 29 g carb, 2 g pro.*

SPREAD GENTLY
This crust is very delicate (it will look incredibly crumbly even as you press it into the bottom of the pan). Gently spread the second layer with a spatula.

A too-good-to-resist combo—peaches and caramel—becomes even more delicious piled on a dense, chewy crust smeared with a whisper of white chocolate.

KID FRIENDLY

Peach Caramel Blondie Bars

Look for dulce de leche in the Mexican section of your grocery store or in Mexican markets. You could also use caramel-flavor ice cream topping—it will be delicious, just not as thick.

PREP 20 min. BAKE 20 min.
OVEN 325°F

- ¾ cup all-purpose flour
- ½ tsp. baking powder
- ¼ tsp. salt
- ¼ cup butter, softened
- ⅔ cup sugar
- 1 egg
- 2 oz. white baking chocolate, chopped
- ½ cup dulce de leche or thick caramel-flavor ice cream topping
- 2 small fresh peaches, peeled, pitted, and sliced
- ⅓ cup pistachio nuts, coarsely chopped

1. Preheat oven to 325°F. Line a 9×9×2-inch baking pan with foil. Grease foil; set aside.
2. For crust, in a medium bowl stir together flour, baking powder, and salt. Set aside. In a large mixing bowl beat butter with an electric mixer on medium to high speed 30 seconds. Add sugar; beat 5 minutes, scraping bowl occasionally. Add egg, beating well. Gradually add flour mixture, beating on low speed until combined. Spread evenly in prepared pan. Bake 20 minutes or until crust is lightly browned and feels nearly firm in the center. Cool slightly on a wire rack.
3. In a small saucepan melt white chocolate over low heat. Spread evenly over the crust; let stand until completely set (chill briefly if needed).
4. Use foil to lift from pan. Spread with dulce de leche. Cut into bars. Top with peaches; sprinkle with pistachios. Makes 16 bars.
EACH BAR *155 cal, 6 g fat, 23 mg chol, 97 mg sodium, 23 g carb, 1 g fiber, 3 g pro.*

THE THICK OF IT
Use a spatula to spread the blondie crust batter into an even layer—it will be thick! Lining the pan with buttered foil makes removing the bars from the pan a cinch.

Delicious Every Day

Fresh and easy ideas for dinner.

CURRIED PORK BURGERS

GRILLED CHICKEN WITH LEMON-CUCUMBER RELISH

Curried Pork Burgers

PREP 15 min. GRILL 14 min.

¼ cup light mayonnaise
¼ tsp. curry powder
1½ lbs. ground pork
¼ cup finely chopped red onion
3 cloves garlic, minced
1 tsp. curry powder
1 tsp. Worcestershire sauce
½ tsp. salt
½ tsp. ground black pepper
¼ tsp. crushed red pepper
2 ½-inch-thick slices red onion
2 tsp. olive oil
4 slices Texas toast
4 red cabbage leaves

1. In a small bowl combine mayonnaise and the ¼ tsp. curry powder; set aside. In a large bowl combine pork, chopped red onion, garlic, 1 tsp. curry powder, Worcestershire sauce, salt, black pepper, and crushed red pepper. Shape into four ¾-inch-thick patties. Lightly brush red onion slices with olive oil.
2. Grill patties on the rack of a covered grill directly over medium heat for 14 to 18 minutes or until done (160°F), turning once halfway through grilling. Add red onion slices the last 8 minutes of grilling, turning once. Grill Texas toast slices 1 to 2 minutes per side or until toasted.
3. Place a cabbage leaf on each slice of Texas toast. Spread with mayonnaise mixture. Top with pork patties and some of the red onion. Makes 4 servings.
EACH SERVING 647 cal, 45 g fat, 128 mg chol, 711 mg sodium, 28 g carb, 3 g fiber, 33 g pro.

FLAVOR SECRET

Try swapping beef for pork on your next burger night. These rich, juicy patties get extra-bold flavor from Worcestershire sauce and a bit of heat from curry powder.

Grilled Chicken with Lemon-Cucumber Relish

PREP 18 min. GRILL 12 min.

4 skinless, boneless chicken breast halves
1 to 2 Tbsp. olive oil
2 tsp. ground cumin
½ tsp. salt
¼ tsp. cracked black pepper
1 medium seedless cucumber, chopped (2½ cups)
1 large tomato, chopped (1 cup)
¼ cup finely chopped onion
½ tsp. finely shredded lemon peel
2 Tbsp. lemon juice
2 cloves garlic, minced
⅓ cup nonfat plain Greek yogurt
1 Tbsp. honey
1 Tbsp. milk

1. Brush chicken breast halves with oil; sprinkle with ground cumin, salt, and pepper. Grill on a covered grill directly over medium heat for 12 to 15 minutes until done (170°F), turning once.
2. Meanwhile, for Lemon-Cucumber Relish, in a medium bowl combine cucumber, tomato, onion, lemon peel, lemon juice, and garlic; stir to combine. In a small bowl combine yogurt, honey, and milk; stir to combine.
3. To serve, top chicken with Lemon-Cucumber Relish. Drizzle with yogurt sauce. Makes 4 servings.
EACH SERVING 283 cal, 8 g fat, 109 mg chol, 503 mg sodium, 12 g carb, 1 g fiber, 40 g pro.

FLAVOR SECRET

The go-to seasoning of the moment? Cumin. It lends big flavor to lean chicken breasts, while the cool Lemon-Cucumber Relish makes a bright, crisp accompaniment. The simple, slightly sweet sauce made with Greek yogurt pulls it all together.

Artichoke and Tomato Pasta

START TO FINISH **25 min.**

- 8 oz. dried bucatini, fettuccine, or whole grain spaghetti
- ¼ cup grated Parmesan cheese
- ½ cup chopped sweet onion
- ¼ cup olive oil
- 2 cloves garlic, minced
- 1 28-oz. can crushed or diced tomatoes
- 1 6-oz. jar marinated artichoke hearts, drained and coarsely chopped
- ¼ tsp. salt
- ¼ tsp. freshly ground black pepper
  Fresh basil leaves
  Grated Parmesan cheese (optional)

1. In a Dutch oven cook pasta according to package directions. Drain, reserving ¼ cup pasta water. Return pasta to the pot. Add Parmesan cheese; toss to combine. Add enough of the reserved pasta water to evenly coat pasta with cheese.

2. Meanwhile, in a large saucepan cook onion in hot oil over medium heat until tender, about 5 minutes. Add garlic; cook 30 seconds more. Add undrained tomatoes, artichoke hearts, salt, and pepper. Cook and stir until slightly thickened. Mash slightly with a wooden spoon.

3. To serve, top pasta with tomato mixture and basil leaves. Sprinkle with additional grated Parmesan cheese, if desired. Makes 4 servings.

EACH SERVING *478 cal, 21 g fat, 4 mg chol, 586 mg sodium, 61 g carb, 6 g fiber, 13 g pro.*

FLAVOR SECRET

Dried spaghetti can almost always be found in the pantry, but think about adding a few more pastas to your weeknight arsenal. Bucatini, a long strand pasta with a hollow center, is a fun change-up. It's slightly thicker than spaghetti, perfect for a robust, chunky sauce made with the pantry staples, canned tomatoes and jarred artichoke hearts.

Dinner on a Dollar

Freezer-favorite edamame makes its springtime debut in this easy veggie-packed fried rice.

KID FRIENDLY | LOW FAT | FAST

Spring Green Fried Rice

The trick to flavorful fried rice is beating the soy sauce and eggs together before adding them to the skillet. Nutty toasted sesame oil packs a guaranteed punch of flavor in every bite.

PREP 15 min. COOK 12 min.

COST 64¢ per serving

- 2 eggs
- 1 tsp. soy sauce
- 1 tsp. toasted sesame oil
- 1 Tbsp. vegetable oil
- 1 clove garlic, minced
- 1 tsp. minced fresh ginger
- 2 cups shredded green cabbage
- ¾ cup shelled frozen edamame, thawed
- ½ cup frozen peas, thawed
- 2 cups cooked brown rice, chilled
- 2 Tbsp. soy sauce
- ¼ cup sliced green onion
  Crushed red pepper (optional)

1. In a small bowl beat eggs and 1 tsp. soy sauce; set aside. In a wok or large skillet heat toasted sesame oil over medium heat. Add egg mixture; stir gently until set. Remove egg; cool slightly. Using your hands, roll the cooked egg into a log. Using a sharp knife, slice the egg into strips; set aside.
2. In the same skillet heat vegetable oil over medium-high heat. Add garlic and ginger; cook for 30 seconds. Add cabbage; cook and stir for 2 minutes. Add edamame and peas; cook for 2 minutes. Add rice and 2 Tbsp. soy sauce; cook and stir 2 to 4 minutes or until heated through. Add egg mixture and green onion; cook and stir about 1 minute or until heated through. Top with crushed red pepper, if desired. Makes 4 servings.

EACH SERVING 251 cal, 9 g fat, 93 mg chol, 669 mg sodium, 3 g carb, 5 g fiber, 11 g pro.

STRAWBERRY AND ARUGULA SALAD WITH MANCHEGO FRICOS

CELEBRATE SUMMER Now's the time to eat your way though a rainbow of produce, mix up a bright cocktail, and try something new on the grill. See how delicious this season can be.

150

160

163

GRILLED CORN WITH
SMOKY LIME BUTTER

Easy Does It

Gather family and friends for a laid-back soiree featuring summer favorites, old and new. With make-ahead tips you won't get stuck behind the grill.

WATERMELON-MINT COOLERS

KID FRIENDLY | **FAST**

Grilled Corn with Smoky Lime Butter

For more pronounced grill marks, peel back the husks and silks from the grilled corn, slather on butter, and return to the grill for 5 minutes.
PREP **10 min.** GRILL **20 min.**

- 8 ears fresh sweet corn with husks
- ½ cup butter, softened (1 stick)
- 1 lime
- 2 Tbsp. minced fresh cilantro or parsley
- ½ tsp. salt
- ½ tsp. smoked paprika
- ¼ tsp. ground black pepper

1. Heat a charcoal or gas grill to medium-high. Grill corn 20 minutes, turning every 5 minutes.
2. Meanwhile, for Smoky Lime Butter, in a small bowl combine butter, zest from half the lime, and juice of whole lime. Stir in cilantro, salt, smoked paprika, and pepper. Transfer butter mixture to a serving bowl.
3. Remove husks and silks from corn and serve with Smoky Lime Butter. Makes 8 servings.
Make ahead To keep grilled corn warm, cover with foil and let stand up to 20 minutes. Store prepared Smoky Lime Butter, covered, in refrigerator up to 1 week. Let stand at room temperature 1 hour before serving.
EACH SERVING *181 cal, 13 g fat, 31 mg chol, 260 mg sodium, 17 g carb, 2 g fiber, 3 g pro.*

LOW FAT | **FAST**

Watermelon-Mint Coolers

To turn this drink into a mojito-style cocktail, add 2 cups of white rum to the watermelon mixture. Top with club soda before serving.
START TO FINISH **25 min.**

- 5 cups chopped seedless watermelon (3¼ lb.)
- ¼ cup packed fresh mint leaves
- ½ cup sugar
- ½ cup water
- ½ cup fresh lime juice
- ¾ tsp. aromatic bitters
- 4 to 5 cups ginger ale, chilled

1. In a blender container place watermelon; puree until smooth. In a small heatproof bowl use a wooden spoon to mash mint leaves and ¼ cup of the sugar; add ¼ cup of the water. Microwave on high until fragrant, 1 to 2 minutes. Using a slotted spoon, transfer mint leaves to blender, leaving sugar in bowl. Blend until mint is chopped.
2. To bowl of sugar mixture add remaining ¼ cup sugar and ¼ cup water. Microwave 1 to 2 minutes or until sugar dissolves into a syrup. Cover and chill.
3. To serve, strain watermelon mixture into an iced-filled pitcher or jar; stir in syrup, lime juice, and bitters. Divide watermelon coolers among ice-filled glasses; top with ginger ale. Garnish with mint sprigs. Makes 8 servings.
Make ahead Cover and chill watermelon coolers up to 8 hours.
EACH SERVING *125 cal, 0 g fat, 0 g chol, 12 mg sodium, 32 g carb, 1 g fiber, 1 g pro.*

Slice just before serving, then let guests choose between vinegary herb-packed Chimichurri Sauce and velvety cocoa-laced Mole BBQ Sauce—both made ahead so you'll be back mingling with the crowd, drink in hand, in no time.

KID FRIENDLY

Grilled Steak

If you can't find flank steak, use boneless top blade steak and remove the center line of gristle before slicing and serving.

PREP 15 min. STAND 20 min.
GRILL 16 min.

- 3 lbs. beef flank steak
- 2 tsp. kosher salt
- 2 tsp. smoked paprika
- 1 tsp. packed brown sugar
- ½ tsp. ground ancho chile pepper
- ½ tsp. ground black pepper
- 1 recipe Chimichurri Sauce (optional)
- 1 recipe Mole BBQ Sauce (optional)

1. Rinse steak; pat dry with paper towels. For rub, in a bowl combine the remaining ingredients except sauces. Sprinkle rub over steak; pat evenly. Let steak stand 20 minutes at room temperature before grilling.
2. Heat a charcoal or gas grill to medium. Scrape grill clean; coat with oil. Grill steak, covered, 8 to 10 minutes per side until medium-rare (145°F).
3. Remove steaks from grill; let rest 5 minutes. Slice crosswise into ⅛-inch-thick slices. Serve with Chimichurri Sauce or Mole BBQ Sauce. Makes 8 servings.
Make ahead Cover and chill seasoned, uncooked steak up to 8 hours before grilling.
EACH SERVING 386 cal, 23 g fat, 111 mg chol, 741 mg sodium, 6 g carb, 2 g fiber, 37 g pro.

KID FRIENDLY | FAST

Chimichurri Sauce

Stirring in the vinegar right before serving keeps this sauce a brilliant bright green.

START TO FINISH 10 min.

- 2 cups packed fresh parsley leaves and small stems
- 1 cup packed fresh cilantro leaves and small stems
- ½ cup extra-virgin olive oil
- ⅓ cup red sweet pepper, coarsely chopped
- 2 Tbsp. onion, coarsely chopped
- 3 cloves garlic, coarsely chopped
- ¾ tsp. kosher salt
- ½ tsp. dried oregano, crushed
- ⅛ to ¼ tsp. red pepper, crushed
- ⅛ tsp. ground black pepper
- ⅛ tsp. sugar
- 2½ Tbsp. sherry vinegar

1. In blender container or food processor combine all ingredients except vinegar with ¼ cup water. Cover; blend until finely chopped, stopping to scrape down sides. Transfer to bowl; stir in vinegar before serving. Makes 10 servings.
Make ahead Prepare sauce without vinegar. Chill in an airtight container up to 2 days or freeze for longer storage. Bring to room temperature; stir in vinegar just before serving.
EACH SERVING 104 cal, 11 g fat, 0 g chol, 156 mg sodium, 2 g carb, 1 g fiber, 1 g pro.

KID FRIENDLY | FAST

Mole BBQ Sauce

"The undercurrent of cocoa gives this sauce its deep earthy flavor," David says. "Try it on anything from pork to chicken."

PREP 10 min. COOK 2 min.

- ¾ cup ketchup
- 2 Tbsp. butter, chopped
- 1 Tbsp. packed dark brown sugar
- 1 Tbsp. unsweetened cocoa powder (not Dutch-process)
- 1 Tbsp. cider vinegar
- 1 Tbsp. molasses
- 1½ tsp. yellow mustard
- 1½ tsp. Worcestershire sauce
- ¾ tsp. smoked paprika
- ¾ tsp. ground ancho chile pepper
- ½ tsp. kosher salt
- ½ tsp. dried oregano, crushed
- ¼ tsp. garlic powder
- ¼ tsp. onion powder
- ¼ tsp. ground cinnamon
- ⅛ tsp. ground black pepper

1. In a small heatproof bowl combine all ingredients and 1 Tbsp. water. Microwave on 100 percent power (high) 2 to 3 minutes or until hot and bubbly, stopping once to stir. Cool and serve. Makes 8 servings.
Make ahead Chill sauce up to 1 week. Bring to room temperature before serving.
EACH SERVING 71 cal, 3 g fat, 8 mg chol, 375 mg sodium, 10 g carb, 0 g fiber, 1 g pro.

GRILLED STEAK WITH
CHIMICHURRI SAUCE AND
MOLE BBQ SAUCE

HERBED POTATO SALAD

GRILLED VEGETABLES WITH SUMMER HOLLANDAISE

The grill makes short work of Broccolini and asparagus, leaving the veggies crisp-tender with a flicker of smoky flavor. Prepare vegetables earlier in the day, or grill while the steak rests.

KID FRIENDLY | FAST
Herbed Potato Salad

Olive oil and vinegar thin the dressing in this creamy potato salad. Garnish with your favorite fresh herbs to add even more flavor.

PREP 15 min. COOK 15 min.

3 lbs. small red potatoes, unpeeled, and cut into 1½-inch chunks
3 Tbsp. extra-virgin olive oil
2 Tbsp. cider vinegar
1 Tbsp. fresh herbs (such as snipped tarragon, dillweed, or parsley)
2 Tbsp. sour cream
2 Tbsp. mayonnaise
2 tsp. Dijon-style mustard
1 green onion, chopped
1 tsp. salt
½ tsp. ground black pepper
¼ tsp. celery seeds (optional)

1. For potatoes, place steamer basket in large saucepan. Add water to reach just below bottom of basket; heat until simmering. Add potatoes to basket. Cover; reduce to medium heat. Steam 15 to 18 minutes or until potatoes are fork-tender. Remove from heat. Cool slightly.
2. Meanwhile, in a large bowl combine remaining ingredients. Add potatoes; toss gently to combine. Serve potato salad warm or cool. Makes 8 servings.
Make ahead Cover; chill up to 4 hours. Let stand 20 minutes at room temperature before serving.
EACH SERVING 195 cal, 8 g fat, 3 mg chol, 375 mg sodium, 27 g carb, 3 g fiber, 3 g pro.

KID FRIENDLY | FAST
Grilled Vegetables

"Grilling Broccolini and asparagus over dry heat concentrates their sweetness and adds a delectable smoky flavor," David says.

PREP 10 min. GRILL 3 min.

3 lbs. fresh asparagus spears and/or Broccolini, trimmed
2 Tbsp. olive oil
½ tsp. salt
¼ tsp. ground black pepper
1 recipe Summer Hollandaise

1. Heat a charcoal or gas grill to medium. Snap off and discard woody bases from asparagus. Spread asparagus and/or Broccolini on 2 large baking pans. Drizzle with oil. Sprinkle with salt and pepper. Turn to coat.
2. Place vegetables on grill perpendicular to bars of grill grate. Cook just until tender, 3 to 5 minutes, turning once. Transfer to a platter. Serve with Summer Hollandaise. Makes 8 servings.
Oven method Preheat oven to 400°F. Transfer roasting pan with coated vegetables to oven. Roast, uncovered, about 15 minutes or until crisp-tender, turning once.
Make ahead Vegetables can be grilled ahead, covered, and chilled. Serve at room temperature.
EACH SERVING 200 cal, 17 g fat, 100 mg chol, 425 mg sodium, 10 g carb, 4 g fiber, 5 g pro.

KID FRIENDLY | FAST
Summer Hollandaise

"Making this sauce in a blender means there's no fear of it separating," David says.

START TO FINISH 10 min.

3 pasteurized egg yolks
½ lemon, juiced
½ tsp. salt
Pinch of mustard powder
Pinch of ground white pepper (optional)
½ cup butter, melted
1 tsp. snipped fresh tarragon leaves

1. In a blender or small food processor combine egg yolks, lemon juice, salt, mustard powder, and, if desired, white pepper. Cover; blend or process until smooth. With machine running, drizzle in melted butter until thickened. Add tarragon; blend just until chopped. Transfer to a small saucepan and gently heat over low heat, 2 to 4 minutes, until warm. Serve with Grilled Vegetables. Makes 8 servings.
Make ahead Chill sauce up to 8 hours; gently reheat before serving.
EACH SERVING 124 cal, 13 g fat, 100 mg chol, 250 mg sodium, 1 g carb, 0 g fiber, 1 g pro.

FRESH VEGETABLE CHIPS WITH CARAMELIZED ONION DIP

golden, 15 to 20 minutes. Remove from heat; cool. Stir in garlic.

2. In a medium bowl combine the cooled onion mixture, sour cream, mayonnaise, remaining ½ tsp. salt, and pepper. Cover; chill 1 hour to blend flavors.

3. Transfer to a serving bowl; stir. Serve dip with Fresh Vegetable Chips. Makes 8 servings.

Make ahead Cover; chill up to 24 hours before serving. Let stand 20 minutes at room temperature before serving.

EACH SERVING *147 cal, 12 g fat, 16 mg chol, 467 mg sodium, 10 g carb, 1 g fiber, 1 g pro.*

FAST

Cucumber-Honeydew Salad with Feta

"Rinsing onions tames their raw taste," David says. "Serve this salad as is or over a bed of arugula."

START TO FINISH **20 min.**

- 2 Tbsp. lemon juice
- ¼ cup extra-virgin olive oil
- 1 tsp. honey
- ¼ tsp. salt
- ⅛ tsp. ground black pepper
- ¼ tsp. poppy seeds (optional)
- 5 cups seeded and cubed honeydew melon (1 medium)
- 2 cups unpeeled and cubed cucumber (1)
- ⅓ cup finely chopped red onion, briefly rinsed and patted dry
- 3 Tbsp. chopped fresh dillweed
- 1 cup feta cheese, crumbled (4 oz.)

1. In a large bowl pour lemon juice. Whisk in olive oil in a slow, steady stream until incorporated. Whisk in honey, salt, pepper, and, if desired, poppy seeds. Add melon, cucumber, onion, and dillweed. Toss to combine. Just before serving top with feta cheese. Makes 10 servings.

Make ahead Cover; chill up to 8 hours. Let stand 20 minutes before serving.

EACH SERVING *118 cal, 8 g fat, 10 mg chol, 202 mg sodium, 11 g carb, 1 g fiber, 2 g pro.*

KID FRIENDLY | **LOW FAT** | **FAST**

Fresh Vegetable Chips

"These chips are a fresh and playful take on the traditional chips you see at parties," David says.

START TO FINISH **30 min.**

- 1 bunch large red radishes, trimmed (12 oz.)
- 1 small jicama, peeled
- 1 large daikon, peeled
- 1 tsp. smoked paprika
- 1¼ tsp. salt
- ¼ tsp. sugar
- ¼ tsp. ground black pepper
- 4 tsp. finely shredded lime peel
- 1 recipe Caramelized Onion Dip (optional)

1. Slice radishes, jicama, and daikon about ¼ inch thick. Halve large slices of jicama. Transfer vegetables to platter.
2. In a small bowl combine smoked paprika, salt, sugar, pepper, and lime peel.
3. To serve, sprinkle paprika mixture over vegetables. Serve with Caramelized Onion Dip, if desired. Makes 8 servings.

Make ahead Cover chips; chill up to 8 hours.

EACH SERVING *37 cal, 0 g fat, 0 g chol, 389 mg sodium, 8 g carb, 4 g fiber, 1 g pro.*

KID FRIENDLY

Caramelized Onion Dip

"If things get sticky, add a small amount of water to the onions while they cook," David says.

PREP **20 min.**   COOK **15 min.**
CHILL **1 hr.**

- 2 Tbsp. olive oil
- 2 cups chopped onions, chopped (2 large)
- 2 tsp. sugar
- 1 tsp. salt
- 4 cloves garlic, minced
- 1½ cups light sour cream
- ⅔ cup light mayonnaise
- ¼ tsp. ground black pepper

1. In a large skillet heat oil over medium heat. Add onions, sugar, and ½ tsp. of the salt; toss. Reduce heat to medium-low. Cook and stir onions until

CUCUMBER-
HONEYDEW
SALAD WITH FETA

Give glazed doughnuts a turn on the grill. They'll be deliciously puffy and lightly charred in seconds. Pile these glistening confections high and serve with big bowls of Strawberry Basil Dip or Mint Julep Dip made the day before.

KID FRIENDLY | FAST
Grilled Doughnuts

For more flavor, dust doughnuts with cinnamon, nutmeg, or cardamom just before grilling.
START TO FINISH **10 min.**

  8 glazed doughnuts
  1 recipe Strawberry Basil Dip
  1 recipe Mint Julep Dip

1. Heat a charcoal or gas grill to medium-low. Coat doughnuts with nonstick cooking spray. Grill doughnuts, covered, until lightly browned, 30 seconds to 1 minute on each side. Watch closely to avoid burning. Serve grilled doughnuts with Mint Julep Dip and Strawberry Basil Dip. Makes 8 servings.
EACH SERVING *283 cal, 15 g fat, 18 mg chol, 215 mg sodium, 32 g carb, 1 g fiber, 4 g pro.*

KID FRIENDLY | FAST
Strawberry Basil Dip

Fragrant basil combines with strawberry and honey for a dip that's good enough to eat by the spoonful.
START TO FINISH **10 min.**

  6 oz. fresh strawberries, hulled
     (1¼ cup)
  4 oz. cream cheese, softened (¼ cup)
  3 Tbsp. honey
  1 Tbsp. packed fresh basil leaves

1. In a blender container or food processor combine strawberries, cream cheese, and honey. Cover; blend or process until smooth, stopping to scrape down sides as necessary. Add basil; pulse just until chopped. Serve immediately. Makes 12 servings.
Make ahead Chill dip up to 8 hours. Serve at room temperature.
EACH 2-TBSP. SERVING *52 cal, 4 g fat, 10 mg chol, 30 mg sodium, 6 g carb, 0 g fiber, 1 g pro.*

FAST
Mint Julep Dip

Reminiscent of a summery cocktail, this dip is a crowd-pleasing accompaniment to warm grilled doughnuts.
START TO FINISH **10 min.**

  6 Tbsp. sugar
  1 Tbsp. packed fresh mint leaves
  6 oz. cream cheese, softened (¾ cup)
  ¼ cup milk
  2 Tbsp. bourbon

1. In a small bowl combine sugar and mint leaves. Using a wooden spoon, mash mint and sugar until fragrant, 30 seconds to 1 minute.
2. In a blender container or food processor combine sugar mixture, cream cheese, milk, and bourbon. Cover; blend or process until smooth, stopping to scrape down sides as necessary. Serve immediately. Makes 10 servings.
Make ahead Chill dip up to 8 hours. Serve at room temperature.
EACH 2-TBSP. SERVING *96 cal, 6 g fat, 20 mg chol, 58 mg sodium, 8 g carb, 0 g fiber, 2 g pro.*

MEET DAVE
David Joachim is a grilling expert and author of *Fire It Up: 400 Recipes for Grilling Everything.* He says throwing a party can feel overwhelming, but his mantra is to keep it simple. "Making as much as you can ahead of time allows you to be a guest at your own party," David says. "Don't overburden yourself with things to grill while your guests arrive." Whipping up blender-friendly sauces and big batches of drinks the day before keeps the party breezy and carefree for guests and host alike.

GRILLED
DOUGHNUTS

STRAWBERRY
BASIL DIP

MINT JULEP DIP

Home Cooking

FRESH PICKS Produce at its peak not only tastes better—it's better for you. These big summer salads from *Better Homes and Gardens® Fresh* cookbook are brimming with the best the season has to offer.

STRAWBERRY AND ARUGULA SALAD WITH MANCHEGO FRICOS

**GRILLED ZUCCHINI
SALAD WITH
MOZZARELLA AND DILL**

Strawberry and Arugula Salad with Manchego Fricos

Italian for "little trifles," fricos are lacy wafers of crispy fried cheese. They're made by cooking little piles of finely shredded cheese in a skillet until the cheese starts to bubble and brown slightly around the edges. Sometimes a bit of flour or herbs is mixed in. They are absolutely delicious to garnish salads or soups. Here they're made with Manchego, Spanish sheep milk cheese. Make them with Parmesan or cheddar as well.

PREP **15 min.** COOK **9 min.**

- 1 cup shredded Manchego cheese (4 oz.)
- 3 Tbsp. olive oil
- 3 Tbsp. balsamic vinegar
- ¼ tsp. kosher salt
- ¼ tsp. freshly ground black pepper
- 3 cups strawberries, halved and/or quartered
- 4 cups baby arugula

1. For each frico, heat a medium nonstick skillet over medium heat. Sprinkle one-third of the cheese on the bottom of the skillet, shaking the skillet so cheese is in an even layer. Cook for 2 to 3 minutes or until cheese browns around the edges. Remove skillet from heat for 30 to 40 seconds or until cheese is set. Using a spatula and fork, carefully turn frico over, return to heat, and cook for 1 to 2 minutes more or until underside is golden. Slide frico out of pan onto a wire rack.
2. For salad, in a large bowl combine olive oil, balsamic vinegar, salt, and pepper. Add strawberries and arugula; toss to coat. Transfer salad to six serving plates or a large platter.
3. Break fricos into pieces and serve with salad. Makes 6 servings.
EACH SERVING *165 cal, 13 g fat, 17 mg chol, 192 mg sodium, 8 g carb, 2 g fiber, 6 g pro.*

Grilled Zucchini Salad with Mozzarella and Dill

This rustic salad couldn't be any simpler. Slices of grilled zucchini are arranged on a serving platter with fresh mozzarella, then sprinkled with aromatic fresh dill and crushed red pepper and drizzled with lemon juice and olive oil. Just season to taste with salt and black pepper, if you like, and serve with slices of toasted bread.
PREP **10 min.** GRILL **8 min.**

- 3 medium zucchini, sliced lengthwise into ¼-inch planks
- 3 Tbsp. extra-virgin olive oil Salt and ground black pepper
- 1 8-oz. fresh mozzarella ball, pulled into large pieces
- 2 Tbsp. coarsely snipped fresh dill
- ¼ tsp. crushed red pepper
- 1 Tbsp. lemon juice

1. On a baking sheet arrange zucchini in a single layer. Drizzle with 1 Tbsp. of the olive oil; sprinkle with salt and black pepper.
2. For a charcoal or gas grill, place zucchini on the rack of a covered grill directly over medium heat. Grill about 8 minutes or until tender, turning once.
3. On a serving platter arrange warm zucchini and the mozzarella. Sprinkle with dill and crushed red pepper. Drizzle with lemon juice and the remaining 2 Tbsp. olive oil. Makes 4 servings.
Stove Top Method To cook zucchini indoors, prepare zucchini as directed in Step 1. Preheat a grill pan over medium heat. Add zucchini to grill pan. Cook for 6 to 8 minutes or until tender, turning once. Continue as directed.
EACH SERVING *265 cal, 22 g fat, 40 mg chol, 323 mg sodium, 3 g carb, 1 g fiber, 11 g pro.*

When you're at the farmer's market, talk to farmers about how they like to prepare the produce you're buying. They often have easy recipes and tips.

Grilled Romaine Salad with Tomato and Corn Tumble

Hearts of romaine are the inner leaves of the elongated head of lettuce. They are smaller, sweeter, and lighter green—tending to yellow—than the outer leaves. Despite their delicate nature, they're still sturdy enough to stand up to grilling.

PREP **20 min.** SOAK **1 hr.**
GRILL **27 min.**

- 2 to 3 ears fresh sweet corn (husks intact)
- 4 Tbsp. extra-virgin olive oil
- 2 Tbsp. sherry vinegar or red wine vinegar
- 1 Tbsp. Dijon mustard
- 1 Tbsp. snipped garlic chives*
- 2 hearts of romaine lettuce, halved lengthwise
- 1 cup grape and/or pear tomatoes (red, yellow, and/or green), halved
- ¼ cup crumbled ricotta salata or feta cheese (1 oz.)

1. Place corn with husks and silks intact in a large bowl. Add enough cold water to cover. Soak 1 hour.
2. Meanwhile, for garlic-chive vinaigrette, in a screw-top jar combine 3 Tbsp. of the olive oil, the vinegar, mustard, and garlic chives. Cover and shake well; set aside.
3. Brush the romaine with the remaining 1 Tbsp. olive oil; set aside. For a charcoal or gas grill, place corn on the rack of a covered grill directly over medium heat. Grill for 25 to 30 minutes or until kernels are tender, turning once and rearranging ears occasionally. Grill romaine, cut sides down, directly over medium heat for 2 to 3 minutes or until slightly charred and wilted.
4. Place a romaine heart half on each of four salad plates. Remove corn husks and silks from ears. Cut kernels from cobs. In a medium bowl combine corn kernels and tomatoes. Drizzle with some of the vinaigrette; toss to coat. Drizzle romaine with the remaining vinaigrette. Spoon the corn and tomato mixture over romaine halves. Season with sea salt and freshly ground black pepper. Top with cheese. Makes 4 servings.
***Tip** For the garlic chives, you can substitute 1 Tbsp. snipped fresh chives and 1 clove garlic, minced.
EACH SERVING *200 cal, 16 g fat, 6 mg chol, 255 mg sodium, 13 g carb, 3 g fiber, 4 g pro.*

Joining a CSA (Community Supported Agriculture) is a convenient way to get fresh, local food. Every week each member receives seasonal produce directly from a farmer's crop.

Succotash Salad with Buttermilk Avocado Dressing

There are many versions of succotash—that most Southern of summer side dishes. Some are simply lima beans and corn and others include chopped sweet pepper as well. This hearty salad expands on that theme with butterhead lettuce, blue cheese, chicken, and bacon. Lima beans have a short growing season and are seldom available fresh. If you can find them, by all means use them. Otherwise, frozen lima beans—like frozen peas—are high quality.

PREP 25 min. COOK 20 min.

- 2 ears fresh sweet corn
- ½ cup fresh or frozen lima beans
- ¾ cup buttermilk
- ½ avocado, halved, seeded, and peeled
- 1 Tbsp. snipped fresh Italian flat-leaf parsley
- ¼ tsp. salt
- ¼ tsp. onion powder
- ¼ tsp. dry mustard
- ¼ tsp. ground black pepper
- 1 clove garlic, minced
- 1 large head butterhead (Boston) lettuce, torn
- 2 cups sliced grilled chicken breast* (8 oz.)
- 6 slices bacon, crisp-cooked, drained, and crumbled
- ½ cup finely chopped red onion
- ½ cup crumbled blue or feta cheese (2 oz.)

1. Cut corn kernels from cobs; set kernels aside. In a small saucepan bring 1 cup of lightly salted water to boiling. Add lima beans; simmer about 15 minutes or until tender. Remove with a slotted spoon; set aside. Add corn to saucepan. Simmer for 3 minutes or until tender; drain and set aside.

2. For dressing, in a blender combine buttermilk, avocado, parsley, salt, onion powder, dry mustard, pepper, and garlic. Cover and blend until smooth. Pour into a small pitcher.

3. Line a large platter or four serving plates with the lettuce. Arrange chicken, crumbled bacon, corn, lima beans, onion, and cheese in rows on lettuce. Serve with dressing. Makes 4 servings.

* Tip For grilled chicken, lightly season 12 oz. skinless, boneless chicken breast halves with salt and ground black pepper. For a charcoal or gas grill, place chicken on the rack of a covered grill directly over medium heat. Grill for 12 to 15 minutes or until chicken is no longer pink (170°F), turning once halfway through grilling.

EACH SERVING *375 cal, 15 g fat, 87 mg chol, 692 mg sodium, 24 g carb, 5 g fiber, 36 g pro.*

MORE FROM FRESH

Discover how rewarding it can be to cook with fresh ingredients at their peak—all year round. *Better Homes and Gardens® Fresh* (Houghton Mifflin Harcourt, $29.99) presents 300 appealing recipes for seasonal produce, plus an illustrated guide to help you eat in season. Fresh is available wherever books are sold. hmhbooks.com/freshcookbook

Delicious Every Day

Fresh and easy ideas for dinner.

Crab Cakes with Apricot Sauce

PREP 20 min. COOK 6 min.
BAKE 10 min. OVEN 350°F

- 2 eggs, lightly beaten
- 1½ cups panko (Japanese-style bread crumbs)
- ¼ cup sliced green onion
- 2 Tbsp. mayonnaise
- 2 tsp. Worcestershire sauce
    Hot pepper sauce
- 2 6-oz. cans cooked crabmeat, drained, flaked, and cartilage removed
- 2 Tbsp. olive oil
- 1 Tbsp. butter
- ⅓ cup apricot fruit spread
- 1 tsp. Chinese-style hot mustard
- ¼ tsp. ground ginger
    Sliced heirloom tomatoes (optional)
    Fresh dill (optional)

1. Preheat oven to 350°F. For crab cakes, in a large bowl combine eggs, 1 cup of the panko, green onion, mayonnaise, Worcestershire, and hot pepper sauce to taste. Fold in crabmeat. Shape into four cakes about 1¼ inches thick. Place remaining panko in a shallow bowl. Add crab cakes; lightly coat on both sides.
2. In an extra-large nonstick oven-safe skillet heat olive oil and butter over medium-high heat. Add crab cakes. Cook for 6 to 8 minutes or until golden on both sides, turning once. Transfer skillet to the oven; bake for 10 to 15 minutes or until cakes reach 160°F on an instant-read thermometer.
3. Meanwhile, for Apricot Sauce, in a small microwave-safe bowl stir together apricot fruit spread, mustard, and ground ginger. Microwave on 100 percent power (high) for 20 to 30 seconds or until heated through.

4. Spoon Apricot Sauce over crab cakes. Serve with sliced tomatoes and sprinkle with fresh dill, if desired. Makes 4 servings.
EACH SERVING *383 cal, 19 g fat, 148 mg chol, 1,126 mg sodium, 29 g carb, 1 g fiber, 22 g pro.*

FLAVOR SECRET
You might think of crab cakes as special-occasion fare, but they are surprisingly simple—especially with a few cans of crabmeat tucked away in the pantry. Also look for packaged crabmeat in the refrigerated section of grocery stores.

Brats with Cucumber-Blueberry Slaw

PREP 15 min. COOK 12 min.
GRILL 5 min.

6 uncooked bratwurst links
1½ cups apple juice
3 cups shredded savoy cabbage
½ cup thinly sliced cucumber
⅓ cup fresh blueberries
3 Tbsp. sliced green onion
⅓ cup buttermilk
2 Tbsp. light mayonnaise
1 Tbsp. snipped fresh parsley
1 Tbsp. snipped fresh dill
1 small clove garlic, minced
⅛ tsp. salt
⅛ tsp. ground black pepper
6 bratwurst buns, split and toasted

1. In a large saucepan combine bratwurst and apple juice; bring to boiling. Reduce heat and simmer, covered, for 12 minutes, rearranging once, until sausages reach 160°F on an instant-read thermometer.
2. Meanwhile, for Cucumber-Blueberry Slaw, in a medium bowl combine cabbage, cucumber, blueberries, and green onion. In a small bowl stir together buttermilk, mayonnaise, parsley, dill, garlic, salt, and pepper. Add buttermilk mixture to slaw; toss gently to coat.
3. For a charcoal or gas grill, place bratwurst on grill rack directly over medium heat. Grill 5 to 7 minutes or until browned, turning occasionally.
4. Serve bratwurst in toasted buns. Top with slaw. Makes 6 servings.
EACH SERVING *442 cal, 24 g fat, 61 mg chol, 1,005 mg sodium, 36 g carb, 2 g fiber, 19 g pro.*

FLAVOR SECRET
A little sweetness from the berries and a whole lot of crunch from the cucumber make this bright slaw an unexpected topper for brats. Pile on a big spoonful and serve the rest alongside.

Spicy Chicken Sausage Pasta and Greens

START TO FINISH 30 min.

- 8 oz. medium shell pasta (3 cups)
- 1 bunch Broccolini, cut into 1-inch pieces (3 cups)
- 2 Tbsp. olive oil
- 1 12-oz. package fully cooked spicy chicken sausage links, cut into ½-inch-thick slices
- 1 small onion, coarsely chopped
- 3 cloves garlic, minced
- 1 cup reduced-sodium chicken broth
- ½ tsp. kosher salt
- ¼ tsp. ground black pepper
- 1 to 2 cups arugula
- ¼ cup snipped fresh dill
- ⅓ cup grated Parmesan cheese
  Olive oil (optional)
  Crushed red pepper (optional)

1. In a Dutch oven cook pasta according to package directions, adding the Broccolini the last 4 minutes of cooking time. Drain; rinse with cold water and drain again. Set aside.
2. In a 12-inch skillet heat oil over medium-high heat. Add sausage, onion, and garlic. Cook, about 3 minutes, turning occasionally, until sausage is browned. Add pasta mixture, chicken broth, salt, and pepper. Heat through. Add arugula and dill. Remove from heat; toss to wilt greens.
3. Divide among shallow bowls. Sprinkle each serving with Parmesan cheese. Drizzle with a little olive oil and sprinkle with crushed red pepper, if desired. Makes 4 servings.

EACH SERVING 431 cal, 13 g fat, 69 mg chol, 847 mg sodium, 52 g carb, 4 g fiber, 28 g pro.

FLAVOR SECRET
Fully cooked chicken sausages are convenient and a good-for-you choice. (The lean protein can have 70 percent less fat than traditional pork sausage.) Find a variety of flavors at the grocery store.

Cool Cocktails

Summertime, and the sippin' is easy. Here's to garden-fresh flavor right in the glass!

WATERMELON-BASIL DAIQUIRI

ROSE COLLINS

BLACKBERRY BOURBON LEMONADE

Watermelon-Basil Daiquiri

LOW FAT | FAST

A ripe watermelon is the key to a delicious cocktail. Look for melons with smooth, even color rinds and symmetrical shapes. In precut melon, look for firm, bright color flesh.
START TO FINISH **10 min.**

- 6 to 8 one-inch cubes watermelon
- 4 to 6 basil leaves
- ¼ cup dark aged or white rum (2 oz.)
- 2 Tbsp. lime juice (1 oz.)
- 1½ Tbsp. Simple Syrup (¾ oz.) (see recipe, page 164)
  Ice
  Frozen watermelon spear or wedge

1. In a cocktail shaker combine watermelon and basil; muddle until watermelon is broken up and juiced. Add rum, lime juice, Simple Syrup, and ice; shake until chilled, about 40 seconds. Double-strain into an ice-filled glass. Garnish with a frozen watermelon spear. Makes 1 serving.

Big batch option In a small saucepan combine 1 cup water, 1 cup sugar, and ½ cup packed fresh basil leaves, snipped. Bring just to boiling. Stir until sugar is dissolved. Cool; cover and chill at least 1 hour. Meanwhile, in a blender container add 4 cups watermelon; puree until smooth. Strain watermelon puree and simple syrup into a punch bowl. Add ice, 3 cups aged or light rum, and 1½ cups lime juice. Makes 12 (5-oz.) servings.

EACH SERVING 216 cal, 0 g fat, 0 g chol, 3 mg sodium, 23 g carb, 0 g fiber, 1 g pro.

Rose Collins

LOW FAT | FAST

A dash of bitter Campari tames the perfumed notes of rose in this floral cocktail.
START TO FINISH **10 min.**

- 3 Tbsp. vodka (1½ oz.)
- 6 Tbsp. Homemade Sour Mix (3 oz.)
- 2 Tbsp. rose syrup (1 oz.)
- 1 tsp. Campari
  Ice
  Seltzer water or club soda, chilled

1. In a cocktail shaker combine vodka, sour mix, rose syrup, Campari, and ice; shake until chilled, about 30 seconds. Double-strain into an ice-filled Collins glass. Top with seltzer water. Float a thinly sliced lemon wheel sprinkled with coarse sugar on top. Makes 1 serving.

Homemade Sour Mix In a small jar combine equal parts lemon juice, lime juice, and Simple Syrup (see recipe, page 164). Cover and shake until mixed. Store in refrigerator, covered, up to 1 week.

EACH SERVING 267 cal, 0 g fat, 0 mg chol, 16 mg sodium, 42 g carb, 0 g fiber, 0 g pro.

Blackberry Bourbon Lemonade

LOW FAT | FAST

For a dramatic, swirling presentation, first combine bourbon, lemon juice, and lemonade in a glass, then pour in the Blackberry-Rosemary Syrup.
START TO FINISH **10 min.**

- ¼ cup bourbon (2 oz.)
- 1½ Tbsp. lemon juice (¾ oz.)
- 2 to 3 tsp. Blackberry-Rosemary Syrup
  Ice
- ⅓ cup sparkling lemonade, chilled

1. In a cocktail shaker combine bourbon, lemon juice, Blackberry-Rosemary Syrup, and ice; shake until chilled, about 30 seconds. Strain into an ice-filled glass. Top with sparkling lemonade. Garnish with a few blackberries. Makes 1 serving.

Blackberry-Rosemary Syrup In a small saucepan combine 12 oz. fresh blackberries (about 2 cups), 1½ Tbsp. snipped fresh rosemary, ¼ cup sugar, and ¾ cup water. Bring to boiling; reduce heat and simmer, uncovered, 30 minutes or until blackberries break down and liquid reduces by half. Using a wooden spoon, mash berries to break up. Remove from heat; cool. Strain through a fine-mesh strainer into a jar, pressing fruit against the strainer. Discard fruit. Yields ⅔ cup. Refrigerate cooled syrup up to 1 week.

Big batch option In a punch bowl combine 3 cups bourbon, ⅔ cup lemon juice, and 1 recipe Blackberry-Rosemary Syrup. Add 4 cups chilled sparkling lemonade. Garnish with frozen blackberries, if desired. Makes 12 (5-oz.) servings.

EACH SERVING 211 cal, 0 g fat, 0 mg chol, 16 mg sodium, 17 g carb, 1 g fiber, 0 g pro.

LOW FAT | FAST

Cucumber Gin and Tonic

For a tonic water that doesn't overwhelm the flavor of the gin, choose a brand that is not too sweet.
START TO FINISH **10 min.**

12 ½-inch cubes Persian cucumber
 1 Tbsp. lemon juice (½ oz.)
 3 Tbsp. gin (1½ oz.)
 1 Tbsp. St-Germain or other elderflower liqueur (½ oz.)
    Ice
 ⅓ cup tonic water, chilled
    Cucumber spear

1. In a cocktail shaker combine cucumber and lemon juice; muddle until cucumber is broken up. Add gin, St-Germain, and ice. Shake until chilled, about 20 seconds. To serve, strain into a tall ice-filled glass. Top with tonic water. Garnish with a cucumber spear. Makes 1 serving.
EACH SERVING *185 cal, 0 g fat, 0 mg chol, 12 mg sodium, 12 g carb, 1 g pro.*

LOW FAT | FAST

Cherry Tomato Margarita

This take on the margarita shows off the sweeter side of tomatoes. For a showstopping garnish, grill skewered tomatoes before adding to the drink. Simple Syrup can also be used to sweeten ice tea and lemonade.
START TO FINISH **10 min.**

 3 to 4 sweet yellow cherry tomatoes
    Pinch of coarse or flaked sea salt
 3 Tbsp. silver tequila (1½ oz.)
 1 Tbsp. orange liqueur (½ oz.)
 1 Tbsp. fresh lime juice (½ oz.)
 3 to 4 tsp. Simple Syrup (½ to ¾ oz.)
    Ice
    Cherry tomatoes (optional)

1. Rim a glass with coarse salt; set aside. In a cocktail shaker combine cherry tomatoes and pinch of salt; muddle tomatoes until broken up and juiced. Add tequila, orange liqueur, lime juice, Simple Syrup, and ice; shake until chilled, about 30 seconds. Double-strain into an ice-filled glass. Garnish with a few cherry tomatoes on a bamboo skewer, if desired. Makes 1 serving.
Simple Syrup In a small saucepan combine equal parts sugar and water; bring just to boiling. Stir until sugar is dissolved. Cool; cover and chill at least 1 hour before using. Store in refrigerator, covered, up to 2 weeks.
EACH SERVING *189 cal, 0 g fat, 0 mg chol, 446 mg sodium, 18 g carb, 1 g fiber, 1 g pro.*

LOW FAT | FAST

Spicy Apricot Shandy

A splash of citrus soda and a spoonful of sweet apricot syrup turn a crisp pale ale or lager into a honey-color summertime cocktail.
START TO FINISH **10 min.**

    Ice
 ¼ cup lemon or tangerine Italian soda (2 oz.)
 1 Tbsp. Apricot Syrup
 1 or 2 thin slices serrano chile
 6 oz. pale ale or lager, chilled
    Lemon wedge (optional)

1. In a tall ice-filled glass combine soda, Apricot Syrup, and serrano chile slices. Top with chilled beer. Add a squeeze of lemon, if desired. Makes 1 serving.
Apricot Syrup In a small saucepan combine 1 cup water and ½ cup sugar; bring to boiling. Add 8 dried apricot halves. Cover and simmer 20 minutes or until tender. Cool slightly. Transfer to a blender; puree until smooth. Store in refrigerator, covered, up to 1 week.
EACH SERVING *191 cal, 0 g fat, 0 mg chol, 11 mg sodium, 29 g carb, 0 g fiber, 1 g pro.*

CUCUMBER GIN
AND TONIC

CHERRY TOMATO
MARGARITA

SPICY APRICOT
SHANDY

Dinner on a Dollar

Fire up the grill! These chicken sandwiches burst with the flavor of peppery-sweet ginger and tangy lime.

Ginger-Lime Chicken Sandwiches

Marinating chicken in a mixture of cilantro, lime, and honey for up to 4 hours ensures that meat is tender and moist.

PREP 20 min. MARINATE 1 hr. GRILL 7 min.

- 2 6-oz. skinless, boneless chicken breast halves
- ½ tsp. coarse salt
- ¼ tsp. freshly ground black pepper
- ¼ cup snipped fresh cilantro
- 2 tsp. finely shredded lime peel
- 3 Tbsp. lime juice
- 2 Tbsp. olive oil
- 2 Tbsp. honey
- 1 to 2 Tbsp. grated fresh ginger
- ¼ cup mayonnaise
- 2 cloves garlic, minced
- 4 hamburger buns or kaiser rolls, split
- 4 lettuce leaves

1. Halve chicken breasts horizontally. Sprinkle with salt and pepper; place in a resealable plastic bag set in a shallow dish.

2. For marinade, in a medium bowl whisk together cilantro, lime peel, lime juice, olive oil, honey, and ginger. Pour over chicken in bag. Seal bag; turn to coat. Marinate in refrigerator for 1 to 4 hours, turning occasionally.

3. Meanwhile, for garlic mayonnaise, in a small bowl combine mayonnaise and garlic. Cover and chill.

4. Drain chicken, discarding marinade. For a charcoal or gas grill, grill chicken, covered, over medium heat for 7 to 8 minutes or until no longer pink (170°F), turning once. Brush cut sides of buns lightly with additional olive oil. Grill, cut sides down, for 10 seconds or until lightly toasted.

5. Spread bun tops with garlic mayonnaise. Top bun bottoms with lettuce, chicken breast, red onion slices, if desired, and bun tops. Makes 4 servings.

EACH SERVING *422 cal, 24 g fat, 60 mg chol, 698 mg sodium, 28 g carb, 1 g fiber, 23 g pro.*

Grilling

Turn that old standby grilled chicken into a champion dinner with these flavorful homemade sauces and rubs.

GRILLED CHICKEN WITH JAMAICAN JERK RUB

Grilled Chicken with Jamaican Jerk Rub

PREP 15 minutes   GRILL 10 minutes
MAKES 4 servings

- ½ cup long grain white or brown rice
- ½ tsp. cumin seeds (optional)
- 1 cup canned black beans, rinsed and drained
- ½ cup snipped fresh cilantro
  Salt
  Ground black pepper
- 4 tsp. packed brown sugar
- 2 tsp. ground coffee
- 1½ tsp. garlic powder
- 1½ tsp. dried thyme, crushed
- 1½ tsp. ground allspice
- 1½ tsp. paprika
- ½ tsp. cayenne pepper
- 8 skinless, boneless chicken thighs
- 1 avocado, pitted, peeled, and chopped
- 1 cup canned mandarin oranges, drained
- ¼ cup finely chopped red onion
- 3 Tbsp. lime juice
- 1 tsp. olive oil

1. Cook rice according to package directions, adding cumin seeds to cooking liquid. When rice is cooked, fluff with a fork; stir in beans and cilantro. Season to taste with salt and black pepper; keep warm.
2. In a small bowl combine brown sugar, ground coffee, garlic powder, thyme, allspice, paprika, and cayenne pepper. Pat chicken dry with paper towels. Lay chicken flat; rub with spice mixture. Season with additional salt.
3. For a charcoal or gas grill, place chicken on the rack of a covered grill directly over medium heat. Grill for 10 to 12 minutes or until chicken is no longer pink (180°F), turning once halfway through grilling.
4. For salsa, in a small bowl combine avocado, oranges, onion, lime juice, and oil. Season to taste with additional salt and black pepper.
5. Serve chicken over rice mixture; top with salsa.

PER SERVING *409 cal, 12 g fat, 115 mg chol, 616 mg sodium, 45 g carb, 7 g fiber, 33 g pro.*

Blueberry-Maple BBQ Sauce

1 Tbsp. olive oil
1 cup finely chopped red onion (1 large)
1 jalapeño pepper, seeded and finely chopped (see tip, page 11)
4 cloves garlic, minced
½ cup bourbon
2 cups fresh blueberries
½ cup ketchup
3 Tbsp. pure maple syrup
2 Tbsp. cider vinegar or raspberry vinegar
¼ tsp. freshly grated nutmeg
⅛ tsp. ground allspice

1. In a large skillet heat oil over medium heat. Add onion; cook and stir about 5 minutes or until onion is light brown and tender. Add jalapeño pepper and garlic; cook and stir for 1 minute. Remove skillet from heat. Stir in bourbon. Return skillet to heat and bring mixture to boiling. Cook and stir about 5 minutes or until most of the bourbon has evaporated.
2. In a large bowl, using a potato masher or the back of a fork, slightly mash blueberries. Stir mashed blueberries, ketchup, maple syrup, vinegar, nutmeg, and allspice into skillet. Bring to boiling; reduce heat. Simmer, uncovered, for 15 to 20 minutes or until thickened. If desired, cool mixture slightly; transfer to a blender or food processor. Cover and blend or process until smooth.

Spicy Cajun BBQ Sauce

¼ cup chopped onion
¼ cup chopped red sweet pepper
1 Tbsp. vegetable oil
½ cup beer
½ cup cold water
1 Tbsp. cornstarch
1 Tbsp. Cajun seasoning
¼ tsp. salt

1. In a small saucepan cook onion and sweet pepper in hot oil over medium heat about 4 minutes or until tender.
2. In a small bowl stir together beer, the water, cornstarch, Cajun seasoning, and salt. Add to onion mixture. Cook and stir until thickened and bubbly. Cook and stir for 2 minutes more.

Mango-Lime BBQ Sauce

1⅓ cups chopped mangoes
⅔ cup packed brown sugar
⅔ cup chopped onion
⅓ cup lime juice
¼ cup olive oil
¼ cup guava paste
3 Tbsp. honey
2 Tbsp. tomato paste
2 cloves garlic, minced
¾ tsp. ground cumin

1. In a small saucepan, combine chopped mangoes, brown sugar, chopped onion, lime juice, olive oil, guava paste, honey; tomato paste, garlic, and ground cumin. Bring to boiling; reduce heat. Cover and simmer for 15 minutes. Cool slightly. Transfer to a food processor or blender. Cover and process or blend until slightly chunky.

Mustard-Peppercorn Rub

2 Tbsp. coarse ground brown mustard
1 Tbsp. cracked black pepper
1 Tbsp. snipped fresh tarragon
1 Tbsp. olive oil
1 tsp. coarse salt

1. In a small bowl stir together mustard, pepper, tarragon, oil, and salt.

Chili Rub

2 Tbsp. paprika
1 Tbsp. ground cumin
2 tsp. chili powder
1 tsp. ground coriander
1 tsp. ground black pepper
½ tsp. salt
½ tsp. cayenne pepper

1. In a small bowl stir together paprika, cumin, chili powder, coriander, black pepper, salt, and cayenne pepper.

MUSTARD-PEPPERCORN RUB

CHILI RUB

SAUCES
Brush BBQ sauce on chicken during the last 10 minutes of grilling, allowing 5 minutes per side. Applying sooner will cause sugars in the sauce to burn and the chicken to char.

RUBS
At least 15 minutes before grilling, sprinkle over the chicken. Use your fingers to rub the spice mixture all over until chicken is thoroughly coated.

EASY LIVING It's time to relax and soak up the season's wonderful little pleasures—a tall glass of iced tea, a laid-back picnic where everyone's family, and fruit desserts that make you say "yum!"

175

188

195

Birthday Bash

Throw a party to celebrate America, and pay homage to the grand old flag with a cake that's all about stripes.

Striped Red Velvet Cake

With sides unfrosted, a red velvet cake looks positively patriotic, and food-safe sparklers add extra sizzle. (Expect some ash from the sparklers, which is nontoxic and OK to eat.)

PREP 30 min. BAKE 35 min.
COOL 10 min. OVEN 350°F
MAKES 12 servings

2¼ cups sifted cake flour
2 Tbsp. unsweetened cocoa powder
¼ tsp. kosher salt
½ cup unsalted butter (1 stick)
1½ cups granulated sugar
¼ cup canola or vegetable oil
2 eggs
2 oz. red food coloring
1 cup buttermilk
1 tsp. vanilla
1 tsp. baking soda
1 Tbsp. white vinegar
1 cup whipping cream, cold
2 8-oz. packages cream cheese, softened
1½ cups powdered sugar, sifted
1 tsp. vanilla
Fresh berries (optional)

1. Preheat oven to 350°F. Lightly grease two 8×2-inch round cake pans. Line bottom of pans with parchment paper. Lightly grease the paper. Flour pans, shaking out excess; set aside.
2. In a medium bowl whisk together the flour, cocoa, and salt. Set aside.
3. In a stand mixer fitted with a paddle attachment, combine the butter, sugar, and oil. Beat until light and fluffy. Add the eggs one at a time, beating well after each addition. Beat in the food coloring on low speed (mixture may look curdled).
4. Alternately add flour mixture and buttermilk, beating on low after each addition just until combined. Add vanilla.
5. In a glass measuring cup dissolve the baking soda in the vinegar. Add to the batter; beat on low just until combined.
6. Pour batter into prepared pans. Bake for 35 to 40 minutes or until a wooden pick inserted near centers comes out with a few moist crumbs. Cool cakes on a wire rack for 10 minutes. Remove cakes from pans. Let cool. When cakes are fully cooled, wrap in plastic wrap and refrigerate for at least 2 hours.

7. For the frosting, in a medium bowl beat the cream to nearly stiff peaks with an electric mixer on medium speed; set aside. In a separate large mixing bowl beat the cream cheese, powdered sugar, and vanilla with an electric mixer on medium speed until smooth and fluffy. Add the whipped cream to the cream cheese mixture and beat quickly to combine.
8. Before frosting, with a long serrated knife, cut each cake in half horizontally. Place one half on a serving plate. Frost top with about 1 cup of frosting. Repeat with remaining cake halves and frosting. Arrange fresh berries around cake. Refrigerate to store.
PER SERVING *570 cal, 34 g fat, 121 mg chol, 310 mg sodium, 61 g carb, 1 g fiber, 7 g pro.*

Trisha's Southern Picnic

Travel home with Trisha Yearwood as this darling of country music—and cooking!—celebrates the things that mean the most on the Fourth of July.

No matter what the occasion, family starts showing up at the Yearwood family home in southern Georgia long before the party starts.

"We all just want to be together," Trisha says. And she doesn't worry if nothing's ready. "I never feel like I even need to have the house completely perfect," she said. "We live a completely comfortable life."

Like the true Southerner she is, Trisha always has something out for family and friends to snack on. And she's translated her passion for food into a great second act—from music superstar to celebrity cook.

KID FRIENDLY

Vegetable Pies

"The great thing about this dish is you can vary the ingredients based on what you like or what you have in your garden or refrigerator," Trisha says. For side-size servings, cut the pies into twelfths.
PREP 25 min. COOK 17 min.
BAKE 40 min. STAND 15 min.
OVEN 325°F

- 1 Tbsp. olive oil
- 1 clove garlic, minced
- 1 cup peeled and chopped sweet onion, such as Vidalia
- 1 large zucchini, thinly sliced
- 1 large yellow squash, thinly sliced
- ½ tsp. salt
- ½ tsp. ground black pepper
- 1 cup mayonnaise
- 1 to 1½ cups shredded mozzarella cheese (4 to 6 oz.)
- 1 to 1½ cups shredded cheddar cheese (4 to 6 oz.)
- 2 large tomatoes, peeled and cut into ¼-inch slices
- 2 9-inch deep-dish pie shells, prebaked as directed
- 1 8-oz. can sliced water chestnuts, drained

1. Preheat the oven to 325°F.
2. Heat olive oil in a large skillet over medium heat. When hot add garlic and sauté for 2 minutes; don't let it brown. Add onion, zucchini, yellow squash, and ¼ tsp. each of the salt and pepper.

Cook until squash is tender, about 15 minutes. Divide the mixture in half.
3. Mix the mayonnaise and cheeses and set aside. Layer the sliced tomatoes in the bottom of the baked piecrusts. Sprinkle the tomatoes with the remaining salt and pepper. Layer the squash mixture on the tomatoes, then layer the water chestnuts. Top each pie with half of the mayonnaise and cheese mixture. Bake, uncovered, for 40 minutes. Allow the dish to stand for 15 minutes before cutting into wedges. Makes 12 servings.
EACH SERVING *393 cal, 31 g fat, 23 mg chol, 472 mg sodium, 22 g carb, 2 g fiber, 8 g pro.*

Daddy's Biscuits

"Biscuits are synonymous with Southern cooking," Trisha says. "If I had the time, I would have homemade biscuits at every single meal." For smaller appetizer-friendly biscuits use a 2-inch biscuit cutter.

PREP 20 min. BAKE 8 min.
OVEN 450°F

    4 Tbsp. vegetable shortening
    2 cups self-rising flour*
    ¾ cup buttermilk, well shaken

1. Preheat oven to 450°F. Lightly grease a baking sheet with nonstick cooking spray. Set aside. Using a pastry blender or two table knives, cut the shortening into the flour until it resembles coarse meal. Use a fork to stir in the buttermilk to make a soft dough, or until the dough comes together and leaves the sides of the bowl. Continue stirring with the fork until all the flour is worked into the dough. Turn dough out onto a lightly floured board. Knead three or four times until smooth and manageable.
2. With your hands or a floured rolling pin, flatten dough to a thickness of ½ inch. Cut with a 2½-inch floured biscuit cutter. Reroll the dough for more biscuits if necessary. Place the rounds on the baking sheet 1 inch apart for crisp biscuits or almost touching for softer biscuits. Bake for 8 to 10 minutes, or until lightly browned. Makes 12 servings.
*If you can't find self-rising flour, substitute 2 cups all-purpose flour, 1 Tbsp. baking powder, and ¼ tsp. salt.
EACH SERVING 118 cal, 5 g fat, 1 mg chol, 265 mg sodium, 16 carb, 1 g fiber, 3 g pro.

Pimiento Cheese Spread

"A pimiento cheese sandwich made on fresh white bread is a true Southern staple," Trisha says. Or slather this spread on Daddy's Biscuits with a slice of tomato for a quick appetizer.
START TO FINISH 35 min.

    2 7-oz. jars sliced pimientos, drained
    3 10-oz. bricks sharp cheddar cheese, finely shredded
    1 cup mayonnaise

1. Place the drained pimientos in a blender or food processor and puree until almost smooth. In an extra-large bowl, using an electric mixer, combine the cheese and pimiento, beating until almost smooth. Beat in mayonnaise. Store the spread, covered, in the refrigerator up to 1 week. Remove the spread from the refrigerator and allow it to reach room temperature before serving. Makes 32 servings.
EACH SERVING 157 cal, 14 g fat, 31 mg chol, 211 mg sodium, 1 g carb, 0 g fiber, 7 g pro.

Gwen's Fried Chicken

For Trisha, the secret to flavorful chicken, inside and out, is in the prep. Her mother, Gwen, taught her to soak the chicken overnight in salt brine, resulting in moist and flavorful meat.
PREP 25 min. MARINATE 4 hr.
COOK 30 min.

    10 chicken drumsticks or other serving-size pieces of chicken, light or dark meat
     2 Tbsp. salt
     2 cups peanut oil
     1 tsp. black pepper
     2 cups all-purpose flour

1. Put the chicken pieces in a large bowl and cover with water. Sprinkle salt in the water, cover the bowl, and refrigerate for 4 hours or overnight, up to 24 hours.
2. Pour oil into an electric frying pan or deep, heavy skillet. Heat to 375°F. Check the temperature by sprinkling flour over the oil. If the flour sizzles, the oil is hot enough.
3. Drain the water from the chicken and pat lightly with paper towels. Sprinkle each piece with pepper and coat with flour (you might not use all of the flour). Carefully place chicken in the hot oil. Cover the pan and open the vent to allow a small amount of steam to escape. Partially cover pan if there is no vent on lid. Cook for 15 minutes. Remove the cover. Using tongs, turn each piece of chicken. Replace the cover and cook for 15 minutes more, or until done. Use a sharp, thin-blade knife to check for doneness by slicing a drumstick to the bone. Neither the meat nor the juices should be pink. Drain chicken on paper towels. Makes 10 servings.
EACH SERVING 217 cal, 13 g fat, 104 mg chol, 443 mg sodium, 3 g carb, 0 g fiber, 20 g pro.

His 'n' Hers Deviled Eggs

Trisha says, "Invert each egg in the carton the night before cooking so the yolks become more centered in the white. It makes for a prettier deviled egg!"
PREP 25 min. STAND 25 min.
CHILL 1 hr.

    12 large eggs
        Paprika

His Filling
    ¼ cup mayonnaise
    2 tsp. yellow mustard
    1 Tbsp. butter, softened

Her Filling
    ¼ cup mayonnaise
    1½ Tbsp. sweet pickle relish
    1 tsp. yellow mustard

1. Place eggs in a single layer in a large saucepan with water to cover. Bring to boiling. Remove from the heat, cover the pan, and let stand for 20 minutes. Pour off the hot water and refill the saucepan with cold water. Crack the eggshells all over and let them sit in the cold water for 5 minutes. Peel the eggs, cover, and chill for at least 1 hour.
2. Halve the eggs lengthwise. Carefully remove the yolks and transfer them to a small bowl. Mash the yolks with a fork; divide in half. Stir in filling ingredients to each half. Season to taste with salt and pepper. Scoop a spoonful of the filling into each egg white half. Sprinkle the tops with paprika. Makes 24 servings.
EACH SERVING 73 cal, 6 g fat, 96 mg chol, 132 mg sodium, 1 g carb, 0 g fiber, 3 g pro.

DADDY'S BISCUITS

GWEN'S FRIED CHICKEN

PIMIENTO CHEESE SPREAD

HIS 'N' HERS DEVILED EGGS

BAKED BEAN CASSEROLE

"There is joy in making something my mom made and making it taste like hers," Trisha says.

BARBECUED PORK RIBS

A perfect Fourth of July table includes generous platters of sweet and savory ribs, pickles, and big bowls of the family's favorite salads—including Trisha's Potato Salad and her famed Fourth of July Coleslaw spiked with sweet Georgia onions.

KID FRIENDLY

Barbecued Pork Ribs

"Since moving to Oklahoma, I have noticed that a lot of the barbecue here is made with beef. I started making these Georgia pork ribs a couple of years ago for the Fourth of July, and they quickly became tradition around here," Trisha says.

PREP 20 min. COOL 1 hr.
MARINATE overnight
BAKE 2 hr. 30 min. BROIL 2 min.
OVEN 375°F/ 350°F

Pork Ribs
  2 cups soy sauce
  ½ cup packed light brown sugar
  1 Tbsp. dark molasses
  1 tsp. salt
  5 lb. meaty pork ribs

Barbecue Sauce
  1 14-oz. bottle ketchup
  1 12-oz. bottle chili sauce
  ½ cup packed light brown sugar
  1 tsp. dry mustard

1. In a medium saucepan combine the soy sauce, 1 cup water, ½ cup brown sugar, molasses, and salt. Bring the marinade to a boil; set aside to cool.

2. Put the ribs in a large turkey-size oven baking bag or sealable plastic bag. Support the bag in a 12×14-inch baking pan. Pour marinade over the ribs and seal the bag. Marinate in the refrigerator overnight, turning the bag occasionally to thoroughly coat the meat. The next day, preheat the oven to 375°F.

3. To drain and discard the marinade, cut four slits in the bag (leaving the ribs in the bag; or remove ribs from the plastic bag, place in baking pan, and cover the pan with foil. Bake ribs for 2 hours.

4. While the ribs are baking, prepare the Barbecue Sauce. In a large saucepan blend ⅓ cup water, the ketchup, chili sauce, ½ cup brown sugar, and dry mustard. Bring this mixture to boiling. Stir well to dissolve the sugar; set aside to cool.

5. When the ribs are cooked and tender, open the bag or remove the foil and discard the drippings. Lower the oven temperature to 350°F.

6. Brush the ribs on both sides with the barbecue sauce and return them to the oven to bake, uncovered, for 30 minutes longer. Just before serving, put the ribs on the grill or blacken them under the broiler to give them a bit of a char, about 2 minutes. Makes 10 servings.

EACH SERVING *401 cal, 22 g fat, 97 mg chol, 1,099 mg sodium, 23 g carb, 0 g fiber, 28 g pro.*

KID FRIENDLY

Baked Bean Casserole

"This dish quickly became the new baked bean side at our house. With the addition of ground beef, it is hearty enough for a meal," Trisha says.

PREP 25 min. BAKE 55 min.
STAND 10 min. OVEN 350°F

1½ lb. lean ground beef
  1 small onion, finely chopped
  1 sweet bell pepper, cored, seeded, and finely chopped
  2 15- to 16-oz. cans pork and beans
  ½ cup barbecue sauce
  ½ cup ketchup
  2 Tbsp. spicy brown mustard
  2 Tbsp. Worcestershire sauce
  1 Tbsp. soy sauce
  4 Tbsp. brown sugar
  6 to 8 slices bacon, cooked and crumbled

1. Preheat the oven to 350°F. Spray a 9×13×2-inch casserole dish with nonstick cooking spray.

2. In a 4- to 5-quart Dutch oven brown the ground beef, onion, and bell pepper. Add the pork and beans, barbecue sauce, ketchup, mustard, Worcestershire sauce, soy sauce, and brown sugar to the ground beef mixture. Simmer for 5 minutes.

3. Transfer mixture to the prepared casserole dish. Crumble bacon over the casserole and cover with aluminum foil. Bake 45 minutes. Remove foil and continue to bake for an additional 10 minutes. Let the casserole stand 10 minutes before serving. Makes 12 servings.

EACH SERVING *232 cal, 7 g fat, 41 mg chol, 695 mg sodium, 26 g carb, 4 g fiber, 17 g pro.*

FOURTH OF JULY COLESLAW

Fourth of July Coleslaw

"A lot of coleslaw recipes have sugar as an ingredient, but this one gets that bit of sweetness from salad or sweet pickles, which don't mask the fresh flavors of the cabbage and carrots," Trisha says.

PREP 30 min. CHILL 1 hr.

  1 firm head green cabbage (2 lbs.)
  1 large carrot, peeled
  ½ small sweet onion, such as Vidalia, peeled and finely chopped
  ¼ to ½ cup diced salad pickles or chopped sweet pickles
  ½ cup mayonnaise
  ½ tsp. salt

1. Remove and discard any bruised or undesirable outer leaves from the head of cabbage. Quarter and core the cabbage and, using a large chef's knife or the shredding blade of a food processor, shred the cabbage. Grate the carrot and add it to the cabbage, tossing to combine. Add the onion, pickles, mayonnaise, salt, and a pinch of pepper. Stir until thoroughly mixed. Chill 1 hour before serving. Makes 10 servings.
EACH SERVING *104 cal, 8 g fat, 5 mg chol, 229 mg sodium, 7 g carb, 2 g fiber, 1 g pro.*

KID FRIENDLY | FAST

Potato Salad

"This recipe is mayonnaise-based, but if you like mustard-based potato salad, just experiment a little," Trisha says. "Add some yellow mustard and leave out a little bit of the mayonnaise."

START TO FINISH 30 min.

  5 lb. red potatoes, peeled if desired
  2 tsp. salt
  4 hard-boiled eggs, peeled and diced
  ¾ to 1 cup mayonnaise
  ½ cup sweet pickle relish
    Salt and black pepper

1. Place potatoes in a Dutch oven. Add 2 tsp. salt and enough water to cover. Boil potatoes for 20 to 30 minutes (time depends on size of potatoes) or until they are tender when pierced with the point of a knife yet hold their shape. Drain potatoes, transfer to a large mixing bowl, and cool completely. Cut into ½-inch cubes. Add the chopped eggs, mayonnaise, and sweet relish. Gently fold to combine. Add salt and pepper to taste. Refrigerate until ready to serve. Makes 12 servings.
EACH SERVING *265 cal, 12 g fat, 68 mg chol, 659 mg sodium, 34 g carb, 3 g fiber, 6 g pro.*

KID FRIENDLY | LOW FAT

Trisha's Sweet Tea

This was the first thing Trisha remembers making at home as a child. "Sweet tea is the staple of every good Southern meal. I like it warm, right after it's made, but most people love it cold and over ice."

PREP 20 min. CHILL 2 hrs.

  4 large family-size tea bags
 16 cups cold water
 1½ cups sugar

1. Fill a teakettle or saucepan with enough of the cold water to completely cover the tea bags, about 2 cups. Bring to boiling and remove from heat. Let the tea stand for 10 minutes. Put the sugar into a gallon pitcher and add 1 cup of cold water. Stir to mix slightly. Pour the hot tea into the sugar mixture and stir until the sugar is dissolved. Stir in the remaining 13 cups of cold water to fill the pitcher. Makes 16 servings.
PER SERVING *76 cal, 0 g fat, 0 mg chol, 7 mg sodium, 20 g carb, 0 g fiber, 0 g pro.*

POTATO SALAD

TRISHA'S SWEET TEA

Sweet and Saltines

"Beware of these crackers," Trisha says. "With their combination of sweet and salty flavors, you will just keep eating them."

PREP 5 min. COOK 5 min. BAKE 2 min.
FREEZE 15 min. OVEN 425°F

40 saltine crackers*
 1 cup butter (2 sticks)
 1 cup light brown sugar
 8 oz. semisweet chocolate chips
    (about 1⅓ cups)

1. Preheat oven to 425°F. Line a 15×10×1-inch baking pan with aluminum foil and saltine crackers.
2. In a medium saucepan melt butter and brown sugar and bring to boiling. Boil 5 minutes. Remove from heat and pour over the crackers, covering them evenly. Bake 2 to 4 minutes, or until just bubbly, watching closely to avoid burning. Remove from oven and pour chocolate chips over the crackers. When the chips melt a bit, spread over the crackers with a knife. Transfer the pan to the freezer for 15 to 20 minutes, or until completely cold. They will form one big sheet. Break up into pieces. Store in an airtight container. Makes 20 servings.
*Substitute 24 graham crackers for the saltines for a sweeter snack and use 1 stick of butter. Boil the brown sugar-butter mixture for 3 minutes.
EACH SERVING 203 cal, 13 g fat, 24 mg chol, 147 mg sodium, 23 g carb, 1 g fiber, 1 g pro.

Lizzie's Strawberry Cupcakes

"I always think homemade has to mean strictly from scratch," Trisha says. "But my grandmother, Lizzie Paulk, used this recipe in the 1930s. When I saw it had cake mix in it, I thought to myself, Well, that makes it OK!"

PREP 40 min. BAKE 18 min.
COOL 35 min. OVEN 350°F

Cupcakes
 1 standard box plain white cake
    mix (2-layer)
 1 3-oz. box strawberry-flavor
    gelatin
⅔ cup vegetable oil
½ cup frozen sliced strawberries in
    syrup, thawed
 4 large eggs

Icing
½ cup butter, room temperature
    (1 stick)
 1 to 1½ cups powdered sugar
 1 cup frozen sliced strawberries in
    syrup, thawed*

1. Preheat oven to 350°F. Line twenty-four 2½-inch muffin cups with paper bake cups; set aside.
2. For cupcakes, beat the cake mix, gelatin, oil, ½ cup strawberries, and ½ cup water with an electric mixer until fully combined. Add eggs, one at a time, beating well after each addition. Spoon batter into prepared cups, filling two-thirds full. Bake 18 to 20 minutes or until a toothpick inserted in centers comes out clean. Remove pan(s) from oven; cool on wire rack 5 minutes. Remove cakes from muffin pan and cool completely on wire rack.
3. For icing, in a blender or food processor puree butter, 1 cup powdered sugar, and strawberries until smooth. The mixture will appear curdled then smooth out as you process. Add additional powdered sugar to desired consistency. Spoon desired amount of icing on cupcakes; let stand several hours (icing will remain a bit soft). Chill any remaining icing. Makes 24 servings.
EACH SERVING 218 cal, 11 g fat, 41 mg chol, 194 mg sodium, 28 g carb, 1 g fiber, 2 g pro.

Whole cake variation Preheat oven to 350°F. Lightly coat a 13×9×2-inch baking pan with nonstick cooking spray. Prepare batter as above. Pour batter into prepared pan; gently smooth top. Bake 40 minutes or until a toothpick inserted in center comes out clean. Cool cake in pan on wire rack. Using a toothpick, poke several holes in the top of the cake. Pour icing over the cake, allowing some of it to seep in. Makes 12 servings.
*The more strawberry syrup you add, the thinner the icing will be.

SWEET AND
SALTINES

"When I cook a holiday meal for my family or I cook for my friends, it's a different kind of applause. I love the feeling."

LIZZIE'S
STRAWBERRY
CUPCAKES

RED VELVET
CUPCAKES

GRANDMA YEARWOOD'S
COCONUT CUPCAKES
WITH COCONUT
LEMON GLAZE

Red Velvet Cupcakes

"This is your classic red velvet cake complete with cream cheese frosting," Trisha says. "Only this time, you stir in some pecans!"

PREP 30 min. BAKE 18 min.
COOL 35 min. OVEN 350°F

Cupcakes

2½ cups all-purpose flour
1 tsp. baking soda
1 tsp. salt
2 tsp. unsweetened cocoa powder
2 cups granulated sugar
2 large eggs
1¾ cups vegetable oil
1 cup buttermilk
1 tsp. vanilla extract
1 2-oz. bottle red food coloring

Cream Cheese Frosting

1 8-oz. package cream cheese, room temperature
½ cup butter, room temperature (1 stick)
1 1-lb. box powdered sugar
1 tsp. vanilla extract
1 cup pecans, finely chopped

1. Preheat oven to 350°F. Line thirty 2½-inch muffin cups with paper bake cups; set aside.
2. For cupcakes, sift together flour, baking soda, salt, and cocoa. In a separate large mixing bowl combine the sugar and eggs. Add the oil to the sugar mixture, slowly beating well as the oil is added. To the sugar mixture, alternately add the flour mixture with the buttermilk, beginning and ending with flour and mixing well after each addition. Stir in the vanilla and food coloring. Spoon batter into prepared cups, filling two-thirds full. Bake 18 to 20 minutes or until a toothpick inserted in centers comes out clean. Remove muffin pan from oven; cool on wire rack, 5 minutes. Remove cakes from pan and cool completely on wire rack.

3. Meanwhile, for the frosting, cream the cream cheese and butter. Beat in the powdered sugar until the mixture is smooth. Add the vanilla and nuts, reserving 2 Tbsp. of nuts for garnish. Spread or pipe frosting on the cupcakes. Makes 30 servings.
EACH SERVING *347 cal, 21 g fat, 29 mg chol, 185 mg sodium, 38 g carb, 1 g fiber, 3 g pro.*

Whole cake variation Preheat oven to 350°F. Grease and flour three 9-inch round cake pans. Prepare batter as above. Divide batter evenly among the prepared pans. Bake 25 minutes or until a toothpick inserted in centers comes out clean. Cool cakes in the pan for 10 minutes before turning out onto a wire rack to finish cooling while you prepare frosting. Spread frosting between the layers, on top of the cake, and on the sides, if desired. Makes 12 servings.

Grandma Yearwood's Coconut Cupcakes with Coconut Lemon Glaze

Secret ingredient: This recipe replaces the flour with crushed vanilla wafers, creating a delicious texture.
PREP 25 min. BAKE 25 min.
COOL 35 min. COOK 15 min.
OVEN 325°F

Cupcakes

1 cup butter, room temperature (2 sticks)
2 cups sugar
6 large eggs, room temperature
1 tsp. vanilla extract
1 11- to 12-oz. box vanilla wafers, finely crushed
1 6-oz. package frozen grated coconut, thawed, or 2 cups sweetened flaked coconut, chopped
½ cup chopped pecans

Coconut Lemon Glaze

1 cup sugar
1 Tbsp. cornstarch
Pinch of salt
1 large lemon, zested and juiced
½ 6-oz. package frozen grated coconut, thawed, or 1 cup sweetened flaked coconut, chopped

1. Preheat oven to 325°F. Line eighteen 2½-inch muffin cups with paper bake cups; set aside.
2. For the cupcakes, cream the butter and sugar until light and smooth. Add eggs and vanilla, beating well. Mix in vanilla wafer crumbs, coconut, and pecans. Spoon batter into prepared cups, filling nearly full. Bake 25 minutes or until tops spring back when lightly touched. Remove muffin pan(s) from oven; cool on wire rack for 5 minutes. Remove cakes from pan(s) and cool completely on a wire rack placed over a shallow baking pan.
3. For the glaze, in a small saucepan mix the sugar, cornstarch, salt, lemon zest and juice, ¾ cup water, and coconut. Cook over medium heat, stirring until thickened, about 15 minutes; cool slightly. Using a toothpick, poke several holes in the top of the cakes and spoon the glaze over the cakes. Makes 18 servings.
EACH SERVING *406 cal, 21 g fat, 89 mg chol, 211 mg sodium, 53 g carb, 2 g fiber, 4 g pro.*

Whole cake variation Preheat oven to 325°F. Grease and flour a 9- to 10-inch tube cake pan. Prepare batter as above. Pour the batter into prepared pan. Bake 1 hour and 15 minutes or until a toothpick inserted in center comes out clean. Cool cake in the pan on a wire rack for 10 minutes. Turn out onto a wire rack to finish cooling while you prepare glaze. Prepare the glaze as above; cool slightly. Using a toothpick, poke several holes in the top of the cake and drizzle the glaze over the cake. Makes 12 servings.

Home Cooking

BERRY BEST The time is ripe for cherries and berries galore. Bake a classic like this all-American pie or give dessert a fun new fruit spin.

Cherry-Blackberry Pie

This sweet-tart pie has a juicy filling. If you use frozen cherries, the filling will be even juicier.

PREP **30 min.** STAND **15 min.**
BAKE **55 min.** OVEN **375°F**

- ¾ cup granulated sugar
- ½ cup packed brown sugar
- 6 Tbsp. cornstarch
- 1 tsp. finely shredded orange peel
- 4 cups fresh or frozen* unsweetened tart red cherries, pitted
- 1½ cups blackberries
- 1 recipe Pastry for Double-Crust Pie

1. In a large bowl combine the sugars, cornstarch, and orange peel. Add cherries and blackberries; toss to coat. Let stand 15 minutes or until syrup forms, stirring occasionally.

2. Preheat oven to 375°F. Prepare Pastry for Double-Crust Pie. On a lightly floured surface flatten one portion of dough. Roll dough from center to edge into a 12-inch circle. Wrap pastry circle around rolling pin. Unroll onto a 9-inch pie plate, easing dough into pie plate without stretching. Trim pastry ½ inch beyond pie plate. Pour fruit filling into pastry-lined pie plate.

3. For lattice top, roll remaining dough into a 12-inch circle. Cut pastry into strips ¾ to 1½ inches wide. Weave strips over fruit filling in a lattice pattern. Press ends of strips into bottom pastry rim. Fold pastry over ends of strips; crimp edges as desired. Brush pastry with milk; sprinkle with additional granulated sugar.

4. Place pie on baking sheet; cover edge with foil. Bake 30 minutes. Remove foil; bake 25 to 35 minutes more or until filling is bubbly and pastry is golden. Cool on a wire rack. Makes 8 servings.

Pastry for Double-Crust Pie In a large bowl stir together 2½ cups all-purpose flour and 1 tsp. salt. Using a pastry blender, cut in ½ cup shortening and ¼ cup butter until pieces are pea size. Sprinkle 1 Tbsp. ice water over part of the flour mixture; toss gently with a fork. Push moistened dough to side of bowl. Repeat with additional ice water, 1 Tbsp. at a time (½ to ⅔ cup total), until all the flour mixture is moistened. Gather mixture into a ball, kneading gently until it holds together. Divide dough in half. Shape each portion into a ball.

*If using frozen cherries, let mixture in Step 1 stand 45 minutes or until cherries are partially thawed. In Step 4, bake 45 minutes before removing foil.

EACH SERVING *512 cal, 19 g fat, 15 mg chol, 351 mg sodium, 81 g carb, 4 g fiber, 5 g pro.*

DECORATIVE TOUCH
It's easy to adorn a pie using pastry scraps and a little imagination. Stamp out circles for cherries using small biscuit cutters, make leaves with a small teardrop pastry cutter, or use a knife to cut shapes freehand.

Juicy ripe berries, white chocolate, and crisp vanilla wafers are a made-for-each-other combination in this creamy, crunchy fresh fruit candy bar.

KID FRIENDLY | FAST

Strawberry-Coconut Cream Soda

Refrigerated coconut milk is quickly becoming a popular dairy-free alternative to milk. Its light consistency and subtle hint of coconut flavor are a delicious addition to this refreshing drink. Look for half-gallon cartons in the refrigerated section of the grocery store. START TO FINISH 10 min.

- 3 cups fresh strawberries, halved
- ⅔ cup sugar
- ¾ cup refrigerated coconut milk
- 3 to 4 cups club soda or carbonated water, chilled

1. In a medium bowl combine strawberries and sugar; stir well to combine. Using a pastry blender, coarsely mash the strawberries.
2. Place ⅓ cup of the mashed strawberries in each of six glasses. To each glass add ice, 2 Tbsp. coconut milk, and ½ to ⅔ cup club soda. Stir drinks just before serving. Makes 6 servings.
EACH SERVING *183 cal, 7 g fat, 0 mg chol, 30 mg sodium, 31 g carb, 2 g fiber, 1 g pro.*

KID FRIENDLY | FAST

Fresh Berry-White Chocolate Bark

When adding food coloring to the white chocolate, make sure you use the paste form. Liquid food coloring can cause the chocolate to seize up. PREP 20 min. COOL 5 min.

- 25 vanilla wafers
- 12 oz. quality white chocolate, chopped
  Pink or red paste food coloring (optional)
- ⅓ to ½ cup fresh blueberries
- ⅓ to ½ cup fresh raspberries

1. Line an 8×8-inch baking pan with foil. Arrange vanilla wafers in a single layer on the bottom of the pan.
2. In a medium saucepan melt 8 oz. of the white chocolate over low heat. Place remaining white chocolate in a bowl. Pour melted chocolate on top; stir until melted. Add a small amount of food coloring to chocolate to tint, if desired.
3. Pour the melted chocolate over cookies in the prepared pan. Using a spatula, spread chocolate into an even layer. Cool 5 minutes. Gently press berries into chocolate. Refrigerate up to 24 hours. Makes 16 servings.
EACH SERVING *162 cal, 9 g fat, 4 mg chol, 45 mg sodium, 20 g carb, 0 g fiber, 2 g pro.*

WHITE HOT
Melting some chocolate over direct heat then stirring it into unmelted pieces ensures a smooth chocolate that will spread easily yet still set when cooled. Be sure the burner is on low heat and watch closely to avoid burning.

Cherry-Berry Shortcake Stars

The dough for these shortcakes will be sticky. To easily cut out the star shapes, dip the cutter in flour between each cut.

PREP 20 min. BAKE 12 min.
COOL 5 min. OVEN 400°F

1½ cups fresh or frozen* tart red cherries, pitted
1½ cups fresh or frozen* blueberries
⅓ cup sugar
2 cups all-purpose flour
1½ tsp. baking powder
¼ tsp. salt
⅓ cup butter
1 egg
½ cup whipping cream
¼ cup honey
¼ cup fresh or frozen* tart red cherries, pitted and chopped
¼ cup fresh or frozen* blueberries, chopped
1 recipe Vanilla Whipped Cream

1. Preheat oven to 400°F. In a medium bowl combine 1½ cups cherries, 1½ cups blueberries, and sugar. Set aside.
2. For shortcakes, in a large bowl combine flour, baking powder, and salt. Using a pastry blender cut in butter until mixture resembles coarse crumbs. In a small bowl combine egg, cream, honey, ¼ cup cherries, and ¼ cup blueberries; add to flour mixture. Using a fork, gently stir mixture until moistened and dough comes together.
3. On a floured surface knead dough by gently folding and pressing just until it holds together. Pat dough out to ¾-inch thickness. Using a floured 2½-inch star cutter, cut out shortcakes; reform scraps as necessary.
4. Place shortcakes 1 inch apart on an ungreased baking sheet. Bake for 12 to 15 minutes or until golden. Cool on baking sheet for 5 minutes. Serve with cherry-berry mixture and Vanilla Whipped Cream. Makes 6 servings (about 12 shortcakes).

Vanilla Whipped Cream Combine ½ cup whipping cream and 1 tsp. vanilla; beat to soft peaks.
*If using frozen cherries and/or berries, thaw and drain well before using.
EACH SERVING *527 cal, 27 g fat, 113 mg chol, 339 mg sodium, 68 g carb, 3 g fiber, 7 g pro.*

JUICY FRUIT
Tossing the cherries and blueberries with a little sugar draws out the fruit juices. The sweet syrup is a perfect complement to the flaky sconelike shortcakes.

Delicious Every Day

Fresh and easy ideas for dinner.

LIME COUSCOUS WITH SUMMER VEGGIES

Lime Couscous with Summer Veggies

When you're really crunched for time, reach for couscous—most varieties cook in just 5 minutes. Plus, you can adapt this meal to whatever's on hand or make it your own by exploring a new vegetable when it's in season.

PREP 15 min. COOK 8 min.

- 1 10-oz. package couscous
- 4 medium carrots, coarsely chopped (2 cups)
- 1 Tbsp. olive oil
- 2 medium zucchini and/or yellow summer squash, quartered lengthwise and sliced into ½-inch pieces
- 6 green onions, sliced into 1-inch pieces
- ½ cup lime or lemon juice
- ¼ cup olive oil
- 1 Tbsp. honey
- 1 tsp. salt
- ½ tsp. freshly ground black pepper
- ½ cup chopped walnuts, toasted (see tip, page 35)
- 2 oz. Parmigiano-Reggiano cheese, shaved

1. Prepare couscous according to package directions.
2. Meanwhile, in a large skillet cook and stir carrots in hot oil for 2 minutes. Add zucchini and green onions; cook and stir 6 minutes or just until vegetables are tender. Transfer couscous to large bowl and fluff with a fork. Add vegetables.
3. In a screw-top jar combine lime juice, oil, honey, salt, and black pepper. Cover and shake well. Pour over couscous and vegetables; toss to combine. Top with walnuts and cheese. Makes 4 servings.

EACH SERVING 643 cal, 31 g fat, 10 mg chol, 884 mg sodium, 75 g carb, 8 g fiber, 19 g pro.

CHICKEN, BRIE, AND NECTARINE FLATBREAD

Chicken, Brie, and Nectarine Flatbread

A swipe of peach preserves works as a spread for these quick flatbreads, adding a pleasant sweet note to balance rich Brie. Topped with peppery arugula and Italian salad dressing for a final punch of flavor, every bite is an unexpected treat for your taste buds.

PREP 15 min. BAKE 10 min.
OVEN 425°F

- 4 7-inch flatbreads
- ¼ cup peach preserves
- 2 cups shredded purchased roasted chicken
- 4 oz. Brie, sliced
- 2 nectarines, pitted and sliced
- 4 thin red onion slices
- 3 cups arugula, baby lettuce, and/or spinach
- ¼ cup bottled Italian salad dressing

1. Preheat oven to 425°F. Place flatbreads on a baking sheet. Brush preserves over each flatbread to within ½ inch of edge. Layer on chicken, Brie, nectarines, and red onion slices.
2. Bake flatbreads 10 to 12 minutes or until edges are golden and cheese just begins to melt. Top with greens and drizzle with dressing. Makes 4 servings.

EACH SERVING 603 cal, 24 g fat, 108 mg chol, 998 mg sodium, 62 g carb, 5 g fiber, 35 g pro.

GRILLED CHERRY
TOMATO TURKEY
BURGERS

Grilled Cherry Tomato Turkey Burgers

Turkey burgers get a bad rap for being dry, but a healthy dose of Dijon-style mustard makes them both flavorful and moist. Grilled cherry tomatoes lend a juicy burst of sweetness. Serve burgers as open-face sandwiches with a big salad for a light yet filling meal.
PREP 30 min.   GRILL 11 min.

- 2 Tbsp. Dijon-style mustard
- 2 Tbsp. whole wheat or plain panko (Japanese-style bread crumbs)
- 2 Tbsp. fat-free milk
- 2 cloves garlic, minced
- 1 shallot, finely chopped (2 Tbsp.)
- 1 Tbsp. snipped fresh basil
- ½ tsp. salt
- ½ tsp. freshly ground black pepper
- 1 lb. uncooked ground turkey breast
- 1 pint assorted cherry tomatoes or baby heirloom tomatoes
- 2 4-inch squares split focaccia bread or ciabatta rolls, toasted
- 1 tsp. lemon juice
  Snipped fresh basil

1. In a medium bowl combine 1 Tbsp. of the mustard, the panko, milk, garlic, shallot, basil, and ¼ tsp. each of the salt and pepper. Add ground turkey; mix well. Form into four ½-inch-thick patties.
2. Thread cherry tomatoes on skewers (see tip, page 111). Brush lightly with olive oil.
3. For a charcoal or gas grill, grill patties on the rack of a covered grill directly over medium heat for 11 to 13 minutes or until done (165°F), turning once. Add the tomato kabobs the last 6 minutes of grilling, turning to cook evenly.
4. Spread the cut sides of the toasted bread with the remaining Dijon mustard. Place patties on top. Remove tomatoes from skewers and pile on burgers. Drizzle with lemon juice, then sprinkle remaining salt and pepper and additional fresh snipped basil. Makes 4 servings.
EACH SERVING *297 cal, 7 g fat, 55 mg chol, 821 mg sodium, 24 g carb, 2 g fiber, 33 g pro.*

Dinner on a Dollar

The slight char of grilled sweet corn lends a hint of smoky flavor to this summery chowder.

Grilled Corn Chowder

PREP 25 min. GRILL 12 min.
COOK 18 min. COST $1.45 per serving

- 4 ears fresh sweet corn, husked and silks removed (to yield 2 cups corn kernels)
- 1 poblano pepper, halved and seeded with membranes removed
- 1 Tbsp. olive oil
- 1 medium onion, chopped
- 2 cloves garlic, minced
- 1 tsp. cumin
- 1 14-oz. can reduced-sodium chicken broth
- 1 medium potato, peeled and cubed (1 cup)
- 2 Tbsp. all-purpose flour
- ½ tsp. salt
- ¼ tsp. pepper
- 1½ cups half-and-half or milk

1. Heat a charcoal or gas grill to medium-high heat. Grill corn and pepper halves, cut sides down, 12 to 16 minutes, or until the pepper is charred and the corn is tender. Remove from grill; wrap pepper in foil. When corn is cool enough to handle, cut kernels from cobs. Remove pepper from foil. Remove charred skin and coarsely chop.
2. In a large saucepan heat oil over medium heat. Add onion and garlic. Cook until tender, about 5 minutes. Add cumin; cook until fragrant, about 30 seconds. Stir in 1½ cups of the grilled corn kernels, the chicken broth, and potato. Bring to boiling; reduce heat. Simmer, covered, 10 to 15 minutes, stirring occasionally.
3. In a small bowl combine flour, salt, and pepper. Stir half-and-half into flour mixture until smooth. Gradually stir into chicken broth mixture. Cook and stir until slightly thickened and bubbly; cook and stir 1 minute more. Using an immersion blender, puree mixture until smooth. Top with remaining grilled corn kernels and chopped pepper before serving. Makes 4 servings.

EACH SERVING *294 cal, 15 g fat, 34 mg chol, 584 mg sodium, 35 g carb, 3 g fiber, 9 g pro.*

GRILLED CORN
CHOWDER

BLT CORN CAKES WITH BUTTERMILK DRESSING

august

GROWING SEASON Ripe summer tomatoes mean BLTs. Try a sandwich, pie, casserole, and even a drink! For dishes to share, check out the chilled pasta salads.

215

217

221

Cool Twist

Layer after layer of strawberries, sugar cookies, and cream make this an irresistible icebox treat.

Strawberry Shortcake Icebox Bars

Bake, assemble, and chill this playful summer dessert in the same pan. With an overnight chill time, it's an easy make-ahead treat.

PREP 45 min. CHILL 1 hr. 30 min. + overnight BAKE 40 min. OVEN 375°F

Strawberry Sauce
- 4 cups strawberries, cut up
- ¾ cup sugar
- 1 Tbsp. cornstarch
- 1 tsp. finely shredded lemon peel
- 1 Tbsp. lemon juice
- 2 Tbsp. butter, cut up

Cookies
- ⅔ cup butter, softened
- ⅔ cup shortening
- 1½ cups sugar
- 2 tsp. baking powder
- 2 tsp. finely shredded lemon peel
- ⅛ tsp. salt
- 2 eggs
- 2 tsp. vanilla
- 4 cups all-purpose flour
- 2 cups strawberries, sliced
- 1 recipe Sweetened Whipped Cream

For Serving
- 1 recipe Sweetened Whipped Cream
- 1 cup strawberries, sliced

1. For Strawberry Sauce, in a blender puree strawberries until smooth.
2. In a medium saucepan combine sugar and cornstarch; stir in pureed strawberries. Cook and stir over medium heat until thickened. Cook and stir 2 minutes more. Stir in lemon peel, lemon juice, and butter. Remove from heat. Transfer to a bowl; cover surface with plastic wrap. Chill at least 1½ hours.
3. Preheat oven to 375°F. For cookies, in a large mixing bowl beat butter and shortening with an electric mixer on medium speed for 30 seconds. Add the sugar, baking powder, lemon peel, and salt. Beat until combined, scraping sides of bowl as needed. Beat in eggs and vanilla until combined. Beat in as much of the flour as you can with the mixer. Stir in any remaining flour. Divide dough into fourths.
4. Grease a 9×9×2-inch baking pan. Line with parchment paper; evenly pat in a quarter of the dough. Bake 10 to 12 minutes or until edges start to brown. Cool in pan on wire rack for 1 minute. Turn out onto a wire rack; remove parchment and cool completely. As soon as pan is cool, repeat using remaining cookie dough to make two more layers. For the fourth layer, line pan with enough parchment to extend up two opposite sides of the pan. Bake 10 to 12 minutes. Cool final layer of cookie in pan on a wire rack.

5. To assemble, spoon half the strawberry sauce over the baked cookie in the pan. Add another cookie layer, the Whipped Cream, and sliced strawberries. Add another cookie layer. Top with remaining strawberry sauce and remaining cookie layer. Gently press cookie layers down. Cover and chill overnight.
6. Using the parchment paper, lift uncut bars from the pan. Cut into pieces. Top with Whipped Cream and sliced strawberries before serving. Makes 16 servings.

Sweetened Whipped Cream In a large chilled mixing bowl beat ¾ cup whipping cream and 1 Tbsp. sugar until soft peaks form.

Note To freeze, transfer the uncut bars to a freezer-safe container and cover. Store up to 1 month. Transfer to the refrigerator to thaw. If still icy, allow to stand at room temperature until thawed.

EACH SERVING 497 cal, 27 g fat, 78 mg chol, 179 mg sodium, 60 g carb, 2 g fiber, 5 g pro.

BLT!

Crispy bacon + cool lettuce + juicy tomatoes = summer's best combo. The sandwich is just the beginning. Turn the pages for seven new ways to stack, toss, or stir up BLTs.

KID FRIENDLY

Ultimate Bacon Sandwich

"Toward the end of summer, everyone's looking for a way to use all those extra cherry tomatoes," Chadwick says. "I make chutney and spread it on anything from burgers to grilled cheese. It's amazing in this sandwich because it's a fun way to sneak in some sweetness."

PREP 45 min. COOK 16 min.

- 8 slices Texas toast
- 4 to 5 Tbsp. butter, melted
- 1 recipe Tomato-Peach Chutney
- 4 slices thick-cut pepper bacon, cooked and halved
- 6 to 8 oz. fresh mozzarella, sliced ¼ inch thick
- 4 crisp leaves of butter lettuce, center veins removed

1. Lightly brush one side of each slice of toast with melted butter. Place four slices, buttered sides down, on a cutting board. Spread each with ¼ cup Tomato Peach Chutney. Layer on bacon, mozzarella, and lettuce. Top with remaining bread slices, buttered sides up.

2. Heat a grill pan over medium heat. Place sandwiches on heated pan. Cook 2 to 3 minutes on each side or until golden, turning once. Makes 4 servings.

Tomato-Peach Chutney In a large skillet over medium-high heat cook 1½ cups chopped sweet onion and 2 Tbsp. minced garlic in ⅓ cup water until tender. Add 3 cups cherry tomatoes. Cook 5 to 7 minutes more until tomatoes begin to pop. Using a potato masher or the back of a wooden spoon, gently mash tomatoes. Add 1½ cups coarsely chopped peaches, ⅓ cup water, 2 Tbsp. cider vinegar, 2 Tbsp. packed brown sugar, 1 tsp. sea salt, and ¼ tsp. crushed red pepper. Bring just to boiling. Stir to dissolve sugar; reduce heat. Simmer, uncovered, 10 to 15 minutes or until chutney thickens. Store chutney in an airtight container in the refrigerator up to 5 days.

EACH SERVING *527 cal, 28 g fat, 71 mg chol, 1,160 mg sodium, 49 g carb, 3 g fiber, 19 g pro.*

TOP TOMATO PICKS

"The secret to choosing the best tomatoes is to pick one up," Chadwick says. "Looking at it isn't enough. You have to touch it and smell it to be sure of what you're getting!" Keep his tips in mind next time you buy tomatoes:

- Look for fruit with firm, even-color skin and a weighty feel. The tomato should feel a little heavy for its size.

- Check stems and leaves. If they're healthy, that's an indication the tomatoes ripened on the vine.

- Smell it! Ripe tomatoes emit a rich and earthy fragrance.

- Avoid tomatoes that are blemished or bruised, or give too much when lightly squeezed.

- Never store tomatoes in the fridge. They'll quickly grow bland and mushy.

MEET CHADWICK

Chadwick Boyd is a food and lifestyle expert. From his grandparents' vegetable garden to the simple and delicious summer food prepared by his stepmother, memories of food and family have long been an inspiration for Chadwick. Growing up, BLTs always began with a trip to the farmer's market for fresh tomatoes. His stepmother's classic recipe of toasted bread, mayonnaise, tomatoes, bacon, and iceberg lettuce is still how Chadwick enjoys BLTs, although now you'll likely find him adding a few slices of avocado.

KID FRIENDLY

Orecchiette with Bacon Meatballs

"Bacon meatballs are the key flavor moment in this pasta," Chadwick says. "When shaping the meatballs, make sure you can see bits of the bacon sticking out. They crisp up in the skillet, and their drippings form the base for the simple pan sauce."

PREP 30 min. COOK 21 min.

12 oz. ground pork
4 slices bacon or uncured smoked bacon, cut into ½-inch pieces
2 cloves garlic, finely chopped
½ tsp. black pepper, divided
2 to 3 Tbsp. olive oil
8 oz. dried orecchiette pasta
2 small shallots, thinly sliced
3 red tomatoes, coarsely chopped
4 cups kale, coarsely chopped, or spinach
¼ tsp. salt
¼ cup shaved Parmesan cheese

1. In a medium bowl combine pork, bacon, garlic, and ¼ tsp. of the pepper until well mixed. Using a teaspoon, scoop the mixture into the palm of your hand and shape into 1-inch meatballs. Pieces of the bacon should be visible.
2. In a large skillet heat olive oil over medium-high heat. Add half the meatballs. Cook and stir until meatballs are browned on all sides and the bacon is crisp, 8 to 10 minutes. Using a slotted spoon, transfer meatballs to paper towels; drain. Repeat with remaining meatballs. Reserve 1 Tbsp. bacon drippings in the skillet; set aside.
3. Cook pasta according to package directions in lightly salted water; drain. Reserve about ¼ cup pasta liquid.
4. Cook shallots in reserved bacon drippings, over medium-high heat, for 3 to 4 minutes, scraping the bottom of the pan with a wooden spoon to release the brown bits. Return meatballs to skillet. Add tomatoes; cook 2 to 3 minutes. Add pasta and kale; toss to combine, adding pasta liquid as needed to moisten the pasta. Season with salt and the remaining ¼ tsp. pepper. Top with Parmesan before serving. Makes 4 servings.

EACH SERVING *673 cal, 37 g fat, 83 mg chol, 490 mg sodium, 55 g carb, 5 g fiber, 32 g pro.*

ORECCHIETTE WITH BACON MEATBALLS

**BLT CORN CAKES
WITH
BUTTERMILK
DRESSING**

KID FRIENDLY

BLT Corn Cakes with Buttermilk Dressing

"This dish has such an elegant look about it, but it's a breeze to make," Chadwick says.

PREP **30 min.** COOK **12 min.**
BAKE **14 min.** OVEN **400°F**

- ½ cup yellow cornmeal
- ½ cup all-purpose flour
- 1 Tbsp. baking powder
- ¾ tsp. salt
- ⅛ tsp. ground black pepper
- 2 eggs
- 1 cup whole milk
- 1 cup fresh sweet corn kernels or frozen whole corn kernels, thawed and drained
- 8 thick-cut slices applewood-smoked bacon
- 3 Tbsp. packed brown sugar
- ¼ tsp. cayenne pepper

- 2 large green or red tomatoes, sliced
- 3 cups fresh mesclun
- 1 recipe Buttermilk Dressing
- 1 cup cherry tomatoes, halved or quartered

1. Preheat oven to 400°F. For corn cakes, in a small bowl combine cornmeal, flour, baking powder, salt, and pepper. In a medium bowl lightly whisk together eggs and milk. Add cornmeal mixture to egg mixture; mix well. Stir in corn.
2. Evenly coat a griddle or skillet with nonstick cooking spray; heat on medium-high until hot. Pour about ⅓ cup batter for each cake onto the griddle, spread to about 4 inches in diameter. Cook 2 to 3 minutes on each side until golden brown. Transfer to platter; cover and keep warm. Repeat with remaining batter. (Yields about 8 corn cakes.)
3. Meanwhile, for candied bacon, line a 15×10×1-inch baking pan with foil.

Arrange bacon strips about 1½ inches apart. In a small bowl stir together brown sugar and cayenne pepper. Spoon mixture evenly over bacon. Bake 14 to 16 minutes until bacon is browned and crisp. Transfer to paper towels; cool. Halve slices.
4. To assemble, place one corn cake on each of four plates. Layer half the bacon pieces, the tomato slices, some mesclun, and remaining corn cakes. Drizzle with Buttermilk Dressing, and top with remaining bacon, mesclun, and cherry tomatoes. Makes 4 servings.
Buttermilk Dressing In a screw-top jar combine ⅓ cup buttermilk, ¼ cup fat-free plain Greek yogurt, 2 tsp. snipped fresh dillweed, 1 tsp. fresh lemon juice, and ¼ tsp. ground black pepper. Shake to combine. Makes ⅔ cup.
EACH SERVING *442 cal, 16 g fat, 120 mg chol, 1,429 mg sodium, 56 g carb, 4 g fiber, 22 g pro.*

Grilled Pork Chops with Bacon and Tomato

"Sometimes the best way to use bacon is as a condiment. I mix salty bacon with onions and garlic, then add sweet and sour flavors for a quick bacon jam," Chadwick says.

PREP 45 min. GRILL 14 min.
COOK 3 min.

- 4 bone-in pork loin chops, about 1 inch thick
- 1 recipe Quick Bacon Jam
- 1 large tomato or 2 medium tomatoes, cut into ¾-inch-thick slices
- 2 Tbsp. olive oil
- 1 medium shallot, thinly sliced
- 4 cups baby kale or chopped kale

1. Season chops with salt and pepper. Spread both sides lightly with 2 to 3 Tbsp. Quick Bacon Jam.
2. For a charcoal or gas grill, grill chops, covered, over medium heat for 7 minutes. Turn and grill 7 to 9 minutes more or until done (145°F), adding tomato slices the last 3 minutes of grilling, turning once.
3. In a large skillet heat olive oil over medium-high heat. Add shallot; cook 1 to 2 minutes until tender. Add kale and ¼ cup water; cook and stir 2 minutes until tender. Using a slotted spoon, transfer to a plate. Season to taste with salt and pepper.
4. Spoon Quick Bacon Jam over chops and serve with kale and tomatoes. Makes 4 servings.

Quick Bacon Jam In a large skillet cook 6 slices of bacon until browned and crispy. Transfer to paper towels; drain and cool. Reserve bacon drippings in skillet. Chop bacon into small pieces; set aside. Heat bacon drippings over medium heat. Add 1 small sweet onion, chopped, and 2 cloves of minced garlic to the skillet. Cook until tender. Stir in ⅓ cup brown sugar, ¼ cup cider vinegar, ¼ cup orange juice, and 1 tsp. grated fresh ginger. Bring mixture to boiling; reduce heat. Simmer, uncovered, 15 minutes or until thickened. Remove from heat. Fold in chopped bacon and ½ tsp. crushed red pepper. Serve with Grilled Pork Chops.

EACH SERVING *601 cal, 34 g fat, 116 mg chol, 540 mg sodium, 29 g carb, 2 g fiber, 41 g pro.*

BRING ON THE BACON
With bacon's popularity at an all-time high, many options are available at grocery stores. Use these must-know terms to demystify the bacon aisle.

Slab Cut This unsliced, smoked, and cured pork belly (also called slab bacon) is the best option when you want a range thicknesses for slices.

Center Cut Considered a premium cut, this is bacon with the ends trimmed off for uniform strips. It's a good choice when strips are the star of a dish, like in a sandwich.

Curing This preservation process uses salts and sometimes sugars to draw out moisture. The harder the cure, the crispier the bacon. Uncured bacon uses natural salts, unlike standard cured bacon, and is regularly labeled nitrate-free.

Smoking Another preservation process, smoking gives bacon the flavor of the wood used. Explore the varieties—basic applewood for classic taste, or maple or pecan for richer flavor.

"Double-lining your pie dish forms an extra-sturdy shell, and it's especially delicious if you love the crust as much as the filling."

Cherry Tomato Pie

"When you have a really juicy filling like the one in this pie, try a double-crust base," Chadwick says.

PREP 30 min. BAKE 50 min.
STAND 1 hr. 20 min. OVEN 400°F/375°F

6   strips bacon
1   15-oz. package rolled refrigerated unbaked piecrust (2 crusts)
⅔   cup finely shredded Parmesan cheese
¾   cup finely chopped sweet onion
4   cups cherry tomatoes
1   Tbsp. olive oil
¼   cup fresh basil, finely chopped
½   tsp. kosher salt
½   tsp. black pepper
½   8-oz. package cream cheese, softened
¼   cup mayonnaise
1   egg yolk, lightly beaten
1   tsp. finely shredded lemon peel
    Chopped leaf lettuce

1. Preheat oven to 400°F. In a large skillet cook bacon just until done but not crisp. Transfer to paper towels; drain. Reserve 1 Tbsp. bacon drippings in skillet; set aside.
2. Let piecrust stand at room temperature for 20 minutes. On a lightly floured surface stack the two piecrusts. Roll from center to edges to form a 12-inch circle. Wrap pastry around rolling pin; unroll into a 9-inch deep-dish pie plate. (Sides should be 2 to 2½ inches deep.) Ease pastry into pie plate, allowing edges to form a loose ruffled or scalloped effect. Gently press pastry into bottom of pie plate. Sides will not lay flat against pie plate. Prick bottom of pastry.
3. Line pastry with a double thickness of foil; bake 10 minutes. Remove foil; bake 5 minutes more. Remove, and reduce oven temperature to 375°F. Sprinkle ½ cup of the cheese over the piecrust. Place half the bacon around the edge of crust. Set aside.
4. Cook onion in reserved bacon drippings over medium heat until tender. Drain drippings; set aside.

5. Halve 2 cups of the cherry tomatoes, leaving the remaining 2 cups whole. Place halved and whole tomatoes in a large mixing bowl. Add olive oil, 2 Tbsp. of the basil, the salt, and ¼ tsp. of the pepper; stir to combine.
6. In a separate mixing bowl beat together cream cheese, mayonnaise, egg yolk, cooked onion, lemon peel, and remaining Parmesan, basil, and pepper.
7. Spoon cream cheese mixture into piecrust. Top with tomato mixture. Nestle the remaining bacon slices among the tomatoes, weaving bacon between tomatoes. Gently press tomatoes and bacon into cream cheese mixture.
8. Bake pie until tomatoes just begin to brown, about 35 minutes. (Loosely cover pie with foil if edges begin to brown too quickly.) Let stand 60 minutes.
9. Top with chopped leaf lettuce. Makes 8 servings.
EACH SERVING *432 cal, 30 g fat, 59 mg chol, 714 mg sodium, 30 g carb, 1 g fiber, 8 g pro.*

**BLT AND CHIPS
CASSEROLE**

BLT and Chips Casserole

"Kettle chips are the secret ingredient in this casserole. They soften during baking, but the bits that peek out of the mixture get crisp and crunchy," Chadwick says. "Kids, especially, will love this dish."

PREP **20 min.** BAKE **50 min.**
STAND **10 min.** OVEN **350°F**

10	eggs
¾	cup whole milk
1	tsp. kosher salt
¼	tsp. cayenne pepper
3	cups kettle-cooked potato chips (3 oz.)
3	cups fresh arugula, shredded
1½	cups shredded sharp cheddar cheese
1½	cups cherry tomatoes, halved
10	strips bacon, coarsely chopped and crisp-cooked
¼	cup fresh basil, chopped
	Arugula
	Cherry tomatoes

1. Preheat oven to 350°F. Lightly grease a 2-quart baking dish; set aside. In a large mixing bowl whisk together eggs and milk. Add salt and cayenne. Gently fold in the potato chips until completely covered by egg mixture. Stir in shredded arugula, cheddar cheese, cherry tomatoes, bacon, and basil. Transfer to prepared baking dish.
2. Bake 50 minutes or until golden brown and a knife inserted near the center comes out clean. Let stand 10 to 15 minutes.
3. Top with arugula and cherry tomatoes before serving. Makes 6 servings.

EACH SERVING *410 cal, 29 g fat, 357 mg chol, 1,001 mg sodium, 13 g carb, 1 g fiber, 25 g pro.*

TOMATO BACON SIPPER

Tomato Bacon Sipper

"Tomato-based drinks are refreshing and a nice alternative to the sweet drinks that are popular when the weather warms up," Chadwick says. "I enjoy this as a cocktail with vodka or gin, but lemon seltzer works well too."
START TO FINISH **15 min.**

1	clove garlic
5	fresh basil leaves
2	tsp. lime juice
¼	tsp. celery salt
2	medium ripe red heirloom tomatoes, halved
1½	oz. vodka
1	Tbsp. pepper bacon, chopped and crisp-cooked
½	tsp. Asian chili sauce (Sriracha)
1	to 2 tomato slices
1	center leaf romaine
1	slice pepper bacon, crisp-cooked

1. In a cocktail shaker combine garlic, basil, lime juice, and celery salt. Using a muddler or wooden spoon, mash mixture to combine. Add tomatoes; mash until smooth and well incorporated. Add vodka, bacon, chili sauce, and ice to fill. Cover; shake well for 20 to 30 seconds.
2. Strain mixture through a wire mesh strainer over a liquid measuring cup. Using the back of a spoon, press out all the juice. Discard solids.
3. Pour mixture into an ice-filled glass. Add tomato slices. Garnish with romaine lettuce and bacon. Makes 1 serving.
Tip To rim glass run a lime wedge along the lip of the glass, then dip into a mixture of celery salt and paprika.

EACH SERVING *231 cal, 6 g fat, 15 mg chol, 712 mg sodium, 13 g carb, 4 g fiber, 8 g pro.*

Home Cooking

CALL IT MACARONI Just don't call it the same old thing! These pasta salads put a whole new flavor spin on humble potluck food.

FAST

Deviled Egg Macaroni Pasta Salad

For perfect hard-cooked eggs, place eggs in a single layer in a saucepan. Add cold water to cover by 1 inch and bring to a rapid boil over high heat. Remove from heat, cover, and let stand for 15 minutes. Drain and transfer to a bowl of ice water until cool enough to handle. To peel, gently tap each egg on the countertop and roll between the palms of your hands. Peel eggs, starting at the large end, under cool running water.

START TO FINISH **30 min.**

- ½ cup thinly sliced red onion
- ¼ cup cider vinegar
- 1 tsp. sugar
- 8 oz. large elbow macaroni
- 12 hard-cooked eggs
- ½ cup mayonnaise
- 3 Tbsp. country Dijon-style mustard
- ½ tsp. salt
- ½ tsp. smoked paprika
- ¼ tsp. cracked black pepper
- ½ cup chopped sweet pickles
- 1½ cups very thinly sliced celery

1. In a small saucepan combine onion, vinegar, and sugar. Bring to a simmer, stirring occasionally. Remove from heat; set aside.

2. Meanwhile, cook macaroni according to package directions. Drain and rinse well with cold water; set aside.

3. Slice 1 egg; set aside. Halve remaining eggs; separate yolks from whites. Coarsely chop egg whites; set aside.

4. For dressing, place yolks in a medium bowl; mash with a fork. Add mayonnaise, mustard, and vinegar mixture; mix well. Gradually stir in 2 Tbsp. water, the salt, paprika, and pepper. Set aside.

5. In a large bowl combine the egg whites, pickles, celery, macaroni, and dressing; toss to combine. Top with reserved egg; sprinkle with additional smoked paprika and pepper. Serve at once or cover and chill up to 6 hours. Makes 10 servings.

EACH SERVING *273 cal, 15 g fat, 228 mg chol, 422 mg sodium, 21 g carb, 1 g fiber, 11 g pro.*

PASTA PREP
Want to get ahead and cook the pasta the night before? Toss the cooked, drained pasta with 2 Tbsp. olive oil and 1 Tbsp. lemon juice before chilling it overnight to keep the pasta from absorbing too much of the dressing, making for a dry pasta salad.

Double pickle goodness—from chopped sweet pickles and quick-pickled red onions—makes for a sweet-and-sour punch of flavor.

Southwestern Chicken and Macaroni Salad

Salsa taquera is a traditional Mexican salsa with a thin consistency and slightly smoky flavor. Find it at Mexican markets or in the Mexican section of the grocery store. If you prefer, you can substitute your favorite salsa.

PREP **18 min.** ROAST **20 min.** STAND **15 min.** OVEN **450°F**

- 2 poblano peppers, halved lengthwise
- 1 25-oz. package frozen fully cooked crispy chicken strips
- 8 oz. large elbow macaroni
- ½ 8-oz. package cream cheese, softened
- 1 7-oz. can salsa taquera
- 1 avocado, halved, pitted, peeled, thinly sliced, and coarsely chopped

1. Preheat oven to 450°F. Line a baking sheet with heavy-duty foil. Place peppers on baking sheet, cut sides down. Roast 20 to 25 minutes or until skin is blistered and charred. Bring the foil up around peppers and fold edges together to enclose. Let stand 15 minutes or until cool enough to handle. Using a sharp knife, loosen the edges of the skins. Gently pull off skins and discard. Chop peppers.
2. Meanwhile, cook chicken and macaroni according to package directions. Drain pasta and rinse well under cold water; set aside. Cut chicken into ½-inch chunks.
3. In a large mixing bowl combine cream cheese and half the salsa. Beat with an electric mixer on low speed until smooth; gradually beat in remaining salsa. Add chopped peppers and macaroni; toss to combine. Gently fold in avocado and chicken. Serve at once or cover and chill up to 2 hours. Makes 10 servings.
EACH SERVING *312 cal, 14 g fat, 37 mg chol, 600 mg sodium, 30 g carb, 3 g fiber, 17 g pro.*

Italian Pesto Pasta Salad

The key to this easy dish is quality pesto. If you have a few extra minutes, make your own. In a food processor combine 2 cups packed fresh basil leaves, ¼ cup toasted pine nuts, ¼ cup grated Parmigiano-Reggiano cheese, 3 Tbsp. extra-virgin olive oil, 2 Tbsp. water, 1 clove garlic, and ½ tsp. each salt and freshly ground pepper. Process until desired consistency.

START TO FINISH **30 min.**

8	oz. elbow macaroni
1	7- to 8-oz. jar basil pesto or homemade pesto
¼	cup red wine vinegar
½	tsp. kosher salt
2	15-oz. cans cannellini beans, rinsed and drained
½	5-oz. package baby arugula (3 cups)
2	oz. Parmigiano-Reggiano cheese, shaved
¼	cup pine nuts, toasted

1. Cook macaroni according to package directions. Drain and rinse well under cold water; set aside.

2. In a large bowl stir together pesto, vinegar, and salt. Add beans, cooked macaroni, arugula, half the cheese, and half the pine nuts. Toss well. Serve at once or cover and chill up to 6 hours. Top with remaining cheese and pine nuts before serving. Makes 10 servings.

EACH SERVING *244 cal, 12 g fat, 5 mg chol, 474 mg sodium, 25 g carb, 3 g fiber, 9 g pro.*

SALTWATER

To get the most flavor from macaroni, use a heavy hand when salting the boiling pasta water. For a 6-qt. pot, 2 Tbsp. of salt seasons the pasta as it cooks, which means you'll need less salt overall.

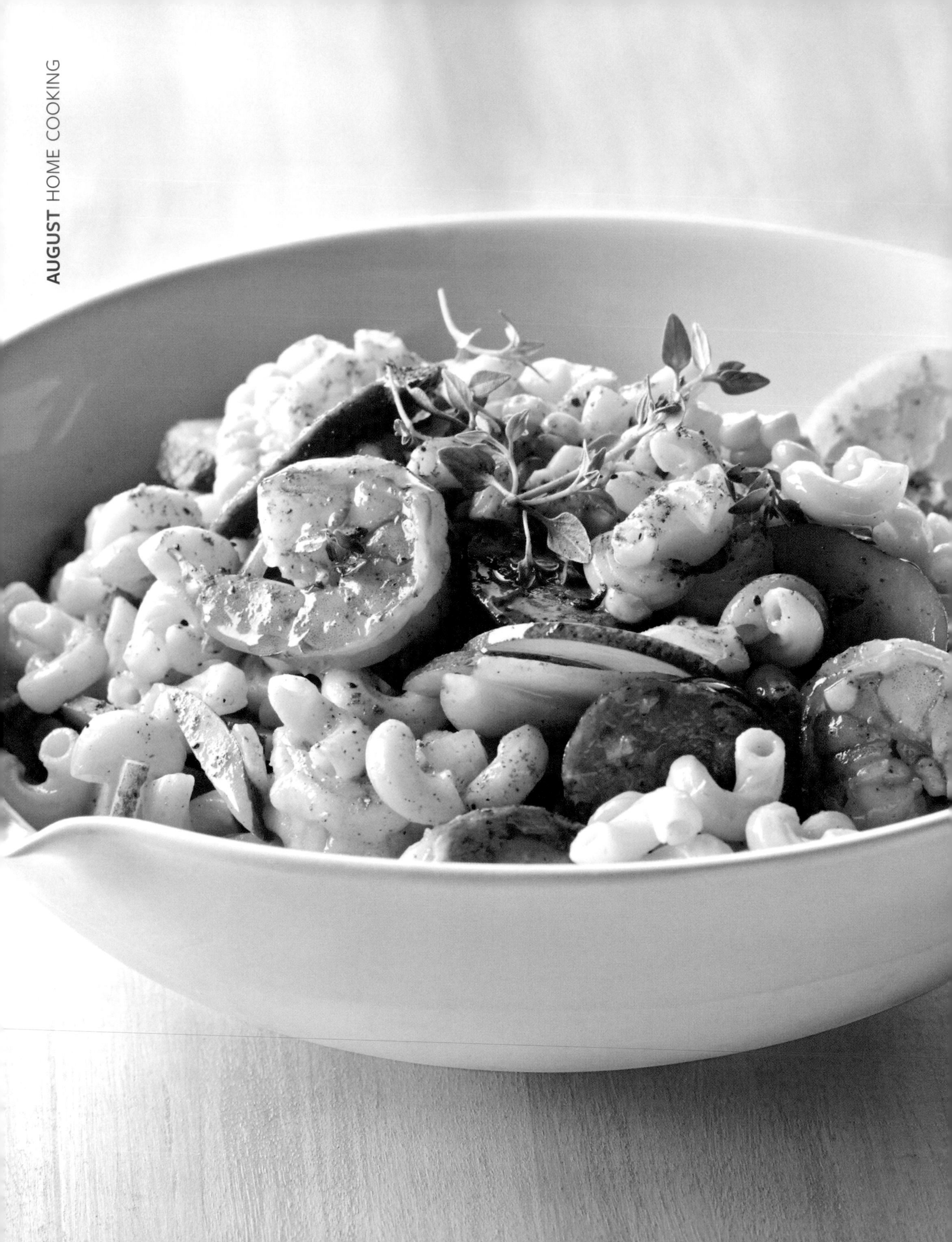

LOW FAT

Shrimp Boil Macaroni Salad

Simmering the shrimp shells in the cooking liquid adds an extra layer of flavor.

PREP 45 min. COOK 27 min.

- 8 oz. elbow macaroni
- 1 lb. medium shrimp
- 1 bay leaf
- 2 sprigs fresh thyme
- 1 qt. reduced-sodium chicken broth
- ½ cup chopped onion
- 2 Tbsp. lemon juice
- 2 tsp. Old Bay seasoning
- 4 ears of corn, halved crosswise
- 8 oz. small red potatoes, halved lengthwise and sliced ⅛ inch thick
- 8 oz. cooked andouille sausage, sliced
- 1 tsp. Old Bay seasoning
- 1 tsp. lemon peel
- ¼ cup lemon juice
- ¼ cup extra-virgin olive oil
- 1 Tbsp. snipped fresh thyme

1. Cook macaroni according to package directions. Drain and rinse well under cold water; set aside.

2. Peel and devein shrimp, reserving the shells. For a seasoning bag, in the center of a 15-inch square of double-thickness cheesecloth, combine shrimp shells, bay leaf, and 2 sprigs fresh thyme. Bring up cheesecloth sides; tie with clean kitchen string. In a 5-quart Dutch oven combine broth, onion, 2 Tbsp. lemon juice, 2 tsp. Old Bay seasoning, and seasoning bag. Bring to a simmer.

3. Add shrimp to Dutch oven. Simmer 1 minute or until shrimp is opaque; remove with slotted spoon. Add corn to Dutch oven. Simmer, covered, for 10 minutes, rearranging corn once. Remove corn and set aside to cool. Add potatoes and sausage to Dutch oven. Simmer, covered, about 8 minutes or until potatoes are tender. Drain, reserving ½ cup cooking liquid. Discard seasoning bag. When corn is cool enough to handle, cut kernels from cobs.

4. For dressing, in a blender combine reserved ½ cup cooking liquid, 1 tsp. Old Bay seasoning, lemon peel, and ¼ cup lemon juice. With blender running, slowly add oil.

5. In a large bowl combine macaroni, corn kernels, shrimp, potatoes, and sausage. Add dressing and 1 Tbsp. thyme; toss gently to combine. Serve at once or cover and chill up to 24 hours. Sprinkle with additional fresh thyme and Old Bay seasoning, and serve with lemon wedges. Makes 12 servings.

EACH SERVING *247 cal, 11 g fat, 56 mg chol, 329 mg sodium, 25 g carb, 2 g fiber, 12 g pro.*

NO-STICK TRICK
Stir the pasta during the first couple minutes of cooking, the time when the pasta releases some of its gluey starch, which can make it stick together as it cooks.

Delicious Every Day

Fresh and easy ideas for dinner.

CHICKEN MEATBALL NOODLE BOWL

Chicken Meatball Noodle Bowl

Set out dishes of fresh cilantro, sliced Fresno peppers, and sliced green onions and let everyone top their own bowls. Squeeze a little fresh lime juice right before digging in—it gives a bright spark to this Vietnamese-inspired dish.

START TO FINISH **25 min.**

- 4 oz. thin rice noodles
- 12 oz. ground chicken
- 1 Tbsp. grated fresh ginger
- 2 Tbsp. snipped fresh cilantro
- ½ tsp. salt
- 3 Tbsp. coconut oil
- 1 red Fresno chili pepper, seeded and finely chopped
- ⅓ cup rice vinegar
- 2 Tbsp. honey
- 1 Tbsp. lime juice
- 3 cups shredded leaf lettuce
- ½ cup finely shredded carrot

1. Prepare noodles according to package directions; drain and set aside.
2. Meanwhile, in a large bowl combine ground chicken, ginger, cilantro, and salt. Shape into 16 meatballs.
3. In a large skillet heat 1 Tbsp. of the coconut oil over medium heat. Add meatballs. Cook, turning occasionally, until browned and cooked through, about 10 minutes. Transfer meatballs to a plate. Turn off heat.
4. Add the remaining 2 Tbsp. coconut oil and chili pepper to the still-warm pan. Stir in vinegar, honey, and lime juice.
5. Divide lettuce, noodles, and carrots among bowls. Top with meatballs and drizzle with pan sauce. Makes 4 servings.

EACH SERVING *358 cal, 17 g fat, 73 mg chol, 412 mg sodium, 35 g carb, 1 g fiber, 16 g pro.*

GRILLED FISH SANDWICHES WITH AVOCADO SPREAD

Grilled Fish Sandwiches with Avocado Spread

These quick fish sandwiches get extra zing from thin slices of fennel and orange—a zippy pair teamed with an easy avocado spread. Save the fronds from the fennel and sprinkle on a few of those to add lovely, subtle anise flavor.

START TO FINISH **30 min.**

- 1 avocado, halved, seeded, and peeled
- ⅓ cup olive oil
- 2 Tbsp. lemon juice
- 1 Tbsp. Dijon-style mustard
- 2 tsp. sugar
- 4 4-oz. skinless, boneless salmon fillets
- 2 Tbsp. butter, melted
- ½ tsp. sea salt or kosher salt
- ½ tsp. salt-free lemon pepper seasoning
- 4 onion buns, split
- 1 small fennel bulb, cored and thinly sliced, about ¾ cup
- 1 orange, peeled, halved, and thinly sliced

1. For Avocado Spread, in a blender combine avocado, olive oil, lemon juice, 2 Tbsp. water, mustard, and sugar. Cover and blend until smooth; set aside.
2. Rinse fish; pat dry. Brush both sides with melted butter and sprinkle with sea salt and lemon pepper.
3. For a charcoal or gas grill, grill salmon on the greased rack of a covered grill directly over medium heat for 3 to 4 minutes per side or until fish flakes easily with a fork. Grill buns, cut sides down, until toasted, about 1 minute.
4. Serve salmon on buns with Avocado Spread and fennel and orange slices. Makes 4 servings.

EACH SERVING *667 cal, 39 g fat, 77 mg chol, 789 mg sodium, 48 g carb, 6 g fiber, 31 g pro.*

Roasted Red Pepper Gazpacho with Pepperoni Cheese Toasts

Make a big batch of this cold soup to enjoy throughout the week on sweltering nights when you just don't want to cook. Before serving, drizzle the gazpacho with olive oil and sprinkle crushed red pepper for a little heat.
START TO FINISH **30 min.**

1	12-oz. jar roasted red sweet peppers, drained
2	14½-oz. cans no-salt-added diced tomatoes
1½	cups reduced-sodium chicken broth
2	Tbsp. olive oil
1	Tbsp. snipped fresh tarragon
1	tsp. celery seeds
1	tsp. bottled minced garlic
½	tsp. sugar
8	slices bread
¼	cup light mayonnaise
24	thin slices pepperoni
4	1-oz. slices Monterey Jack cheese
½	cup coarsely chopped cucumber

ROASTED RED PEPPER GAZPACHO WITH PEPPERONI CHEESE TOASTS

1. In food processor combine peppers, tomatoes, broth, olive oil, tarragon, celery seeds, garlic, and sugar. Cover and process, half at a time if necessary, to desired consistency. Season to taste with salt and pepper; set aside.
2. For Pepperoni Cheese Toasts, brush one side of each bread slice with mayonnaise. Layer pepperoni and cheese on the unbrushed sides of 4 slices. Top with remaining bread slices, mayonnaise sides up. On a large griddle or skillet toast sandwiches over medium heat until cheese is melted and bread is golden, turning once, about 3 to 5 minutes.
3. Divide soup among bowls; top with cucumber. Serve with Pepperoni Cheese Toasts. Makes 4 servings.
EACH SERVING *478 cal, 26 g fat, 39 mg chol, 1,022 mg sodium, 44 g carb, 6 g fiber, 18 g pro.*

Dinner on a Dollar

Creamy ricotta filling gets bright flavor from a double dose of lemon in this savory summer pie.

Lemony Ricotta Summer Squash Galette

Using refrigerated piecrust takes all the hard work out of this rustic weeknight-friendly dish. The key to a successful galette is a filling that doesn't become runny while baking. Salting the squash helps remove excess water to prevent a soggy crust.

PREP **40 min.** BAKE **35 min.**
OVEN **400°F** COST **$1.40 per serving**

- 2 medium zucchini and/or yellow summer squash, thinly sliced (2½ cups)
- ½ 15-oz. package rolled refrigerated unbaked piecrust (1 piecrust)
- ¾ cup ricotta cheese
- ½ cup grated Parmesan cheese
- ¼ cup shredded mozzarella cheese
- 1 clove garlic, minced
- 1 Tbsp. olive oil
- 2 tsp. finely shredded lemon peel
- 1 Tbsp. lemon juice
- ¼ tsp. salt
- ¼ tsp. freshly ground black pepper
- 1 egg yolk
  Fresh dillweed (optional)

1. Sprinkle zucchini lightly with salt. Transfer to a colander; drain for 15 minutes. Pat dry with paper towels. Preheat oven to 400°F.
2. Meanwhile, on a large piece of lightly floured parchment, roll dough to a 12-inch circle. Transfer parchment and dough to a large baking sheet; set aside.
3. For ricotta filling, in a medium bowl whisk together ricotta, Parmesan, mozzarella, garlic, 1 tsp. of the olive oil, lemon peel, lemon juice, salt, and pepper. Using a spatula, spread ricotta filling over dough, leaving a 1½-inch border. Top with squash rounds. Drizzle with remaining olive oil. Gently fold over pastry edges, pleating as necessary.
4. In a small bowl whisk together egg yolk and 1 tsp. water. Lightly brush pastry edges with egg mixture. Transfer galette to oven. Bake 35 to 40 minutes or until edges are golden brown. Sprinkle with fresh dillweed, if desired. Serve warm or at room temperature. Makes 6 servings.

EACH SERVING *283 cal, 18 g fat, 59 mg chol, 444 mg sodium, 20 g carb, 1 g fiber, 9 g pro.*

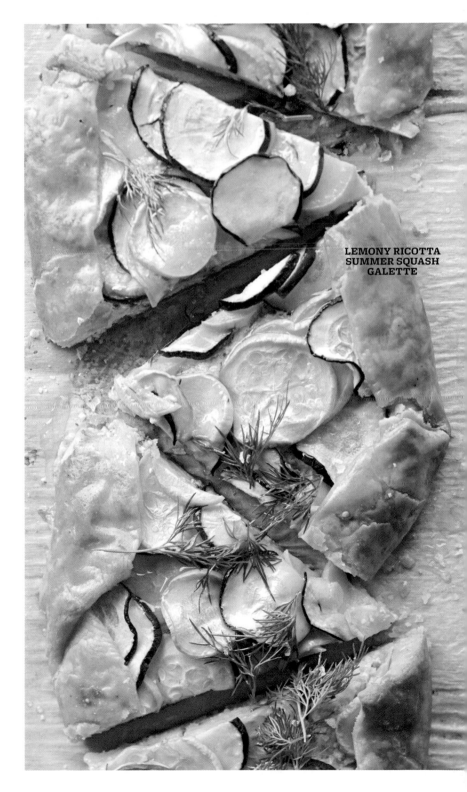

LEMONY RICOTTA SUMMER SQUASH GALETTE

ROSÉ RASPBERRY
TEA THYME POP

MANGO-OVERBOARD
POP

MOSCATO MELON
AND KIWI POP

Chill Out

Put the "ah" in August with a cool-off party starring juiced-up pops. Serve the frozen fruity cocktails in glasses so you don't miss a drop.

LOW FAT

Rosé Raspberry Tea Thyme Pop

No special molds are required! Paper cups are an easy way to prepare ice pops. Peel them off and enjoy.
PREP **15 min.** STAND **10 min.** FREEZE **8 hr.**

- 6 raspberry herb tea bags
- 3 Tbsp. sugar
- 6 sprigs fresh thyme
- 3 cups fresh raspberries
- ¾ cup rosé wine
  Wooden craft sticks or heavy-duty straws

1. Place eight 5-oz. paper cups in a shallow baking pan. In a medium bowl combine tea bags, sugar, and thyme sprigs. Add 2 cups boiling water. Let stand 5 minutes. Remove and discard tea bags and thyme.
2. In a blender combine tea mixture and raspberries. Cover; blend to combine. Strain mixture through a fine-mesh sieve; discard seeds. Let stand 5 minutes. Using a spoon, remove any foam from top of the tea mixture. Stir the wine into the mixture; pour into prepared paper cups. Cover each cup with a square of foil. Using a knife, make a small hole in center of each foil square. Slide a wooden craft stick or straw through each hole and into the mixture. Freeze 8 to 12 hours.
3. To serve, peel paper cup off pop. Serve at once or place in a larger glass set in ice. Makes 8 servings.
EACH SERVING *62 cal, 0 g fat, 0 mg chol, 2 mg sodium, 12 g carb, 3 g fiber, 1 g pro.*

LOW FAT

Mango-Overboard Pop

Not only are mango juice smoothies packed with concentrated flavor, they're also thick—perfect for making pops!
PREP **15 min.** FREEZE **8 hr.**

- 1¾ cups refrigerated mango juice smoothie
- 3 oranges, peeled, seeded, and sectioned
- 3 Tbsp. tequila
- 1 Tbsp. triple sec or other orange liqueur
  Wooden craft sticks or heavy-duty straws

1. Place eight 5-oz. paper cups in a shallow baking pan. In a blender combine mango juice smoothie, oranges, tequila, and triple sec. Cover; blend just until smooth. Pour into prepared paper cups. Cover each cup with a square of foil. Using a knife, make a small hole in center of each foil square. Slide a wooden craft stick or straw through each hole and into the mixture. Freeze 8 to 12 hours.
2. To serve, peel paper cup off pop. Serve at once or place in a larger glass set in ice. Makes 8 servings.
EACH SERVING *73 cal, 0 g fat, 0 mg chol, 2 mg sodium, 14 g carb, 1 g fiber, 1 g pro.*

LOW FAT

Moscato Melon and Kiwi Pop

Moscato wine has a sweet and fruity flavor, it a favorite to enjoy during the summer. This recipe is one way to use any extra you have.
PREP **15 min.** FREEZE **8 hr.**

- 3 cups cubed honeydew melon
- ½ cup Moscato wine
- 4 fresh kiwi, peeled
  Wooden craft sticks or heavy-duty straws

1. Place ten 5-oz. paper cups in a shallow baking pan. In a blender combine honeydew melon, Moscato, and two of the kiwi; blend until smooth. Add remaining kiwi; process with on/off turns until almost smooth. Pour into prepared paper cups. Cover each cup with a square of foil. Using a knife, make a small hole in center of each foil square. Slide a wooden craft stick or straw through each hole and into the mixture. Freeze 8 to 12 hours.
2. To serve, peel paper cup off pop. Serve at once or place in a larger glass set in ice. Makes 10 servings.
EACH SERVING *48 cal, 0 g fat, 0 mg chol, 10 mg sodium, 10 g carb, 1 g fiber, 1 g pro.*

When life gives you summer scorchers, make lemonade! Stir up a pitcher, and give it a fresh flavor twist with herbs, other fruits, even flowers. Then listen to the ice clink and savor every cool sip.

KID FRIENDLY | LOW FAT | FAST
Melon and Mint Lemonade

Ripe honeydew delivers the best flavor. To sniff a ripe melon, find one with an intense floral perfume.
START TO FINISH **20 min.**

     6 cups cubed ripe honeydew melon
     2 cups lemon juice
     1 cup water
     1 cup Plain or Mint Simple Syrup
        Ice
        Fresh mint leaves (optional)
        Honeydew melon balls (optional)

1. In a blender place honeydew cubes. Cover and blend until smooth; add lemon juice, the water, and Simple Syrup. Cover; blend just until combined. Transfer mixture to a serving pitcher. Pour into ice-filled glasses. Add mint leaves and melon balls, if desired, to garnish. Makes 2 quarts.
Plain Simple Syrup In a small saucepan combine 2 cups sugar and 2 cups water. Bring just to boiling. Stir until sugar is dissolved. Cool; cover and chill at least 2 hours before using. Refrigerate, covered, up to 2 weeks.
Mint Simple Syrup Stir in ½ cup fresh mint with the sugar and water. Strain after cooling. (Let stand up to 2 hours before straining; mint flavor grows stronger the longer it steeps.) Makes 3 cups.
EACH 8-OZ. SERVING *124 cal, 0 g fat, 0 mg chol, 30 mg sodium, 32 g carb, 2 g fiber, 1 g pro.*

KID FRIENDLY | LOW FAT | FAST
Mango Limeade

Avoid adding sweetened or flavored sparkling water to lemonade; they overpower the fresh taste of fruit.
START TO FINISH **20 min.**

     4 cups fresh mangoes or 4 cups frozen mango cubes, thawed
     1 cup mango nectar
     1 cup fresh lime juice
     ¼ cup Plain or Ginger Simple Syrup
     1 750-ml. bottle sparkling water, chilled (about 3 cups)
        Ice
        Lime slices (optional)

1. Seed, peel, and cut up fresh mangoes, if using. In a blender combine mangoes and mango nectar. Cover; blend until smooth. In a serving pitcher stir together the mango mixture, lime juice, and Simple Syrup. Stir in sparkling water before serving. Pour into ice-filled glasses. Garnish with lime slices, if desired. Makes 2 quarts.
Ginger Simple Syrup Stir in ½ cup sliced fresh ginger with the sugar and water. Strain after cooling. Makes 3 cups.
EACH 8-OZ. SERVING *101 cal, 0 g fat, 0 mg chol, 5 mg sodium, 26 g carb, 2 g fiber, 1 g pro.*

LOW FAT | FAST
Lavender-Peach Lemonade

It takes about 4 to 6 lemons to get 1 cup of lemon juice. Lemons with soft rinds that are heavy for their size are best for juicing.
START TO FINISH **20 min.**

     2 cups lemon juice
    1⅓ cups peach nectar, chilled
    1⅓ cups Chamomile-Lavender Simple Syrup
     1 cup white grape juice, chilled
        Ice
        Cantaloupe and/or honeydew melon balls (optional)
        Lemon slices (optional)

1. In a serving pitcher combine lemon juice, peach nectar, Simple Syrup, and white grape juice. Pour into ice-filled glasses. Garnish with melon balls and lemon slices, if desired. Makes 2 quarts.
Chamomile-Lavender Simple Syrup Stir in ¼ cup chamomile-lavender herbal tea with the sugar and water. Strain after cooling. Makes 3 cups. (Chamomile and lavender is available as a loose tea blend, but a combination of chamomile tea and dried lavender flowers works as well.)
EACH 8-OZ. SERVING *234 cal, 0 g fat, 0 mg chol, 13 mg sodium, 63 g carb, 1 g fiber, 1 g pro.*

MELON AND MINT LEMONADE

MANGO LIMEADE

LAVENDER-PEACH LEMONADE

ROAST BEEF WITH
ROSEMARY

SIMPLY IMPRESSIVE Follow stylemakers Anna Last and Stephanie Izard for effortless entertaining and recipes that make you say "wow! " These dishes make the best of seasonal ingredients.

233

235

241

Anna in the City

Not even a move to San Francisco and a demanding job as the creative director of Williams-Sonoma keep Anna Last from having friends over. Her secret: go-to recipes and a table set with signature pieces.

"We live in a very busy virtual world, and preparing food for others is personal, authentic, and real. It takes us away from our computer screens and puts us in touch with one another. For me, the purpose of dinner is quality time." And so the woman who spearheads the look of a brand that's found its way into kitchens across the country invites friends into her own.

Anna believes spontaneous dinners are the best kind because there's no time to overplan. "The real key to spontaneity is relying on a handful of go-to dishes that I can easily tweak to incorporate seasonal ingredients," Anna says. "I love that people know me for certain dishes, like my roasted tomatoes."

She often hits the market on her way home from the office, inspired by what is fresh, local, and easy to prepare. "If I have an entrée that needs more work or special attention," she says, "I'll make sides that require next to none."

KID FRIENDLY

Zucchini and Prosciutto Focaccia

Any shape of focaccia will work, but Anna likes to serve rectangular loaves, about 13×9 inches wide and 1 inch thick. They're large enough to hold a generous amount of toppings. For a smaller focaccia, use about 1 cup of arugula.

PREP 10 min. STAND 30 min.
BAKE 30 min. COOK 15 min.
OVEN 400°F

3 small zucchini
1 16-oz. purchased baked focaccia
3 Tbsp. olive oil
   Crushed red pepper (optional)
1 Tbsp. balsamic vinegar
2 oz. sliced prosciutto, cut in thin strips
1 to 2 cups chopped arugula

1. Using a mandoline or very sharp knife, thinly slice zucchini lengthwise. Place in a colander; sprinkle with 1 tsp. salt. Let stand 30 minutes. Rinse and drain; pat dry with paper towels.
2. Preheat oven to 400°F. Place focaccia on a baking sheet. Prick generously with a fork. Bake 5 to 10 minutes until lightly toasted and heated through. Remove from oven; set aside.
3. Meanwhile, in a 12-inch skillet heat 2 Tbsp. of the olive oil over medium-high heat. Working in three batches, slightly brown zucchini slices on both sides, about 5 minutes per batch. Transfer zucchini to a bowl. Sprinkle with crushed red pepper, if using. Set aside. Remove skillet from heat. Add remaining 1 Tbsp. of olive oil and balsamic vinegar to the same skillet. Warm mixture for 1 minute. Spoon balsamic mixture over the focaccia.
4. Place focaccia on a serving tray. Top with zucchini, prosciutto, and arugula (arranging each in lengthwise rows, if desired). To serve, cut crosswise into slices. Makes 12 servings.
EACH SLICE *133 cal, 6 g fat, 5 mg chol, 490 mg sodium, 15 g carb, 1 g fiber, 5 g pro.*

**ROAST BEEF WITH
ROSEMARY**

KID FRIENDLY

Roast Beef with Rosemary

"Even anchovy haters will love this—I promise," Anna says. "The anchovies form the base of the paste that gets rubbed over the meat and provide all the savory, salty flavor you need in this dish." If you want to skip the anchovies, purchased black olive tapenade provides a similar flavor to Anna's paste.

PREP 20 min. CHILL 1 hr. ROAST 1 hr. STAND 15 min. OVEN 500°F/350°F

- 1 sprig rosemary
- 1 2-oz. can anchovies, drained
- 1 clove garlic, peeled and smashed
- 1 tsp. freshly ground black pepper
- 1 Tbsp. red wine vinegar
  Olive oil
- 2½ to 3 lb. strip loin roast or top sirloin roast

1. Remove leaves from the rosemary sprig. Place rosemary leaves, anchovies, garlic, and black pepper on a cutting board. Roughly chop mixture. Drag the flat, broad side of the knife across the mixture in one direction and then the other until it forms a smooth paste. Transfer to a small bowl. Stir in vinegar and enough olive oil to make a spreadable paste. Set aside.
2. Trim most of the fat from the roast; score any fat that remains. Rub anchovy paste over beef. Tuck under edges of the roast and tie with kitchen string. Cover and chill at least 1 hour.
3. Preheat oven to 500°F. Place the roast on a rack in a shallow roasting pan. Insert an oven-going meat thermometer in the center of the roast. Roast, uncovered, for 15 minutes. Reduce temperature to 350°F; roast for 45 to 60 minutes more or until the thermometer registers 135°F for medium-rare. Remove roast from oven. Cover with foil; let stand 15 minutes. (The temperature of meat will rise to 145°F after standing.) Top with fresh rosemary leaves. Makes 6 servings.
EACH SERVING 239 cal, 11 g fat, 75 mg chol, 361 mg sodium, 0 g carb, 0 g fiber, 33 g pro.

GREEN BEANS WITH GREEN OLIVE DRESSING

KID FRIENDLY

Green Beans with Green Olive Dressing

"This dressing is so delicious and versatile," Anna says. "Spoon some onto halved hard-cooked eggs, serve with steamed fish, or spread over a really good crusty sourdough bread. It keeps well in the fridge, so it's always nice to have extra."

PREP 15 min. STAND 30 min. COOK 10 min.

- 2 cups pitted green olives
- ¼ cup extra-virgin olive oil
- ¼ cup fresh flat-leaf Italian parsley
- 2 tsp. finely shredded lemon peel
- 2 Tbsp. lemon juice
- 1½ lb. green beans, trimmed

1. For dressing, in a food processor combine olives, olive oil, parsley, lemon peel, and lemon juice. Cover and pulse with on/off turns until dressing is almost a paste. Season to taste with salt and freshly ground black pepper. Set aside for at least 30 minutes.
2. Meanwhile, place green beans in a steamer basket; set over boiling water. Cover and steam for 10 to 12 minutes or just until tender. Transfer to a large bowl filled with ice water; drain well.
3. Toss green beans with about half the dressing before serving. Refrigerate any remaining dressing up to 3 days. Makes 6 servings.
EACH SERVING 135 cal, 11 g fat, 0 mg chol, 279 mg sodium, 10 g carb, 3 g fiber, 2 g pro.

"There's something so exciting about not knowing what you're going to cook until the last minute—allowing the ingredients to decide the menu for you."

FENNEL AND PARSLEY SALAD

KID FRIENDLY | **LOW FAT**

Smashed Potatoes

Anna preps this recipe while the roast is chilling. Store the cooled, smashed potatoes in the fridge, then pop them in the oven to cook as guests arrive.

PREP 10 min. COOK 15 min.
COOL 15 min. BAKE 20 min.
OVEN 400°F

1½ lb. small new potatoes
2 Tbsp. olive oil
1 Tbsp. fresh thyme leaves

1. In a large saucepan cook potatoes in lightly salted boiling water, covered, for 15 minutes or until tender; drain. Cool at least 15 minutes.
2. Preheat oven to 400°F. Gently flatten or smash potatoes with the bottom of a skillet or the heel of your hand. Place on a greased baking sheet. Drizzle with olive oil. Sprinkle with thyme leaves, salt, and pepper. Bake 20 minutes or until crisp. Makes 6 servings.
EACH SERVING *127 cal, 5 g fat, 0 mg chol, 200 mg sodium, 20 g carb, 2 g fiber, 2 g pro.*

Oven-Melted Tomatoes with Goat Cheese and Mint

"One hour of low and slow baking concentrates the tomato flavor in this appetizer," Anna says. "You can pop them in the oven and get started on another dish while they cook."

PREP 15 min. BAKE 1 hr. OVEN 300°F

12 small roma tomatoes, halved
2 tsp. sugar
½ tsp. kosher salt
½ tsp. freshly ground black pepper
1 Tbsp. olive oil
2 oz. goat cheese, crumbled
⅓ cup fresh mint leaves

1. Preheat oven to 300°F. Place tomatoes, cut sides up, on a 15×10×1-inch baking pan. Sprinkle with sugar, salt, and pepper. Bake for 1 hour or until sides of tomatoes just begin to crinkle. Let cool. Drizzle with olive oil. Top with goat cheese and mint. Serve at room temperature. Makes 6 servings.
EACH SERVING *85 cal, 5 g fat, 7 mg chol, 220 mg sodium, 7 g carb, 2 g fiber, 3 g pro.*

LOW FAT | **FAST**

Fennel and Parsley Salad

"This salad is incredibly refreshing," Anna says. "I like to dress it with the olive oil right before serving so the fennel remains crisp."

START TO FINISH 20 min.

3 fennel bulbs
2 lemons, juiced
2 Tbsp. extra-virgin olive oil
¼ cup fresh flat-leaf Italian parsley
   Shaved Parmesan cheese
   (optional)

1. Cut off and discard fennel stalks. Trim base and remove any wilted outer layers. Cut into quarters lengthwise and remove core. Using a mandoline or very sharp knife, finely slice fennel. In a mixing bowl combine fennel and lemon juice; toss to combine. Just before serving drizzle with olive oil and season to taste with salt and freshly ground black pepper. Add parsley; toss to combine. Top with Parmesan, if desired. Makes 6 servings.
EACH SERVING *81 cal, 5 g fat, 0 mg chol, 128 mg sodium, 10 g carb, 4 g fiber, 2 g pro.*

**OVEN-MELTED
TOMATOES
WITH GOAT
CHEESE AND MINT**

**POACHED
NECTARINES
WITH HONEY
ICE CREAM**

APEROL COCKTAIL

Poached Nectarines with Honey Ice Cream

"Last-minute desserts shouldn't be fussy," Anna says. "Poaching takes advantage of the freshness of seasonal fruit while adding a little extra sweetness."

PREP 25 min. COOK 12 min.
COOL 10 min.

    2 cups Moscato wine
    ½ cup water
    2 Tbsp. sugar
    1 vanilla bean, halved lengthwise
    6 small nectarines, halved and
       pitted
    1 quart purchased honey ice cream
       Fresh mint leaves (optional)

1. In a large saucepan combine wine, the water, sugar, and vanilla bean. Bring just to a simmer. Add nectarines. Return to a simmer. Cook, uncovered, over medium-low heat for 7 minutes or just until tender, turning nectarines once or twice for even poaching. Transfer to a serving bowl. Let cool 10 minutes. Return the cooking liquid to a simmer. Cook, uncovered, until the liquid has reduced by half, about 5 minutes.
2. To serve, remove and discard vanilla bean. Scoop ice cream and drizzle with additional honey. Top with poached nectarines and the reduced syrup. Add mint leaves, if desired. Makes 6 servings.
EACH SERVING 352 cal, 12 g fat, 66 mg chol, 48 mg sodium, 45 g carb, 2 g fiber, 4 g pro.

LOW FAT FAST
Aperol Cocktail

Choosing just one cocktail takes all the fuss out of drink preparation. Anna always serves an aperitif or predinner cocktail of Aperol spritzes. Aperol is an Italian alcohol made from sweet and bitter orange peels and a blend of herbs and spices. It has relatively low alcohol content and a slightly bitter flavor, ideal for stimulating appetites. Spritzes, the most popular Aperol cocktail, are a breeze to make.

PREP 5 minutes MAKES 1 serving

       Ice
    3 to 4 tsp. aperol liqueur
       (1½ to 2 ounces)
    ½ cup chilled Prosecco
       Splash chilled club soda

1. In an ice-filled glass combine aperol, Prosecco, and a splash of club soda.
PER SERVING 204 cal, 0 g fat, 0 mg chol, 12 mg sodium, 21 g carb, 0 g fiber, 0 g pro.

MEET ANNA

Anna grew up on a sheep and cattle ranch in Australia, where her parents lived off the land and loved to entertain. Anna was a willing helper.

Anna's culinary interests led her to New York, where she styled, produced, and edited food and entertaining stories for national and international magazines. Her current role at Williams-Sonoma brought her to San Francisco. "This city reminds me so much of home," Anna says. It's all about fresh, quality ingredients."

Home Cooking

FRUIT TWIST Top Chef Stephanie Izard shows how to dress up even the simplest of savory main dishes with sweet harvest surprises.

Pear and Potato Salad with Pickled Mustard Seeds and Sausage

Pickled mustard seeds are a breeze to make, and they give this simple dish a major wow factor. "I love the pop you get, a little burst of flavor and texture," Stephanie says.

PREP 30 min. COOK 15 min.
ROAST 12 min. OVEN 375°F

- 1 Tbsp. olive oil
- 8 oz. cooked chicken-and-apple sausage, or your favorite brown-and-serve sausage, sliced ¼ inch thick
- 1 lb. Yukon Gold potatoes, coarsely chopped
- 3 firm Anjou pears, cored and cut into thin wedges
- 1 recipe Pickled Mustard Seeds
- ¼ cup lemon juice
- ¼ cup cider vinegar
- ¼ cup extra-virgin olive oil
- 1 Tbsp. Dijon-style mustard
- 1 Tbsp. soy sauce
- 1 Tbsp. pure maple syrup
- ¼ cup thinly sliced fresh mint leaves
- 1 small onion, chopped
- 4 cups torn kale or baby kale
  Kosher salt and freshly ground black pepper

1. Preheat oven to 375°F. In a 12-inch oven-going skillet heat 1 Tbsp. oil over medium-high heat. Add sausage; cook and stir until browned. Add potatoes and pears; cook until browned on edges. Transfer to oven. Roast, uncovered, for 12 minutes or just until tender.
2. Meanwhile, for vinaigrette, in a medium bowl whisk together the Pickled Mustard Seeds, lemon juice, cider vinegar, the ¼ cup oil, mustard, soy sauce, and maple syrup. Stir in mint.
3. In a very large bowl combine potato mixture, onion, and kale. Add vinaigrette; toss to coat. Season to taste with salt and pepper. Serve at once. Makes 6 servings.

Pickled Mustard Seeds In a small saucepan combine ⅓ cup champagne vinegar, 1 Tbsp. salt, and 1 Tbsp. sugar; bring to boiling. Place ¼ cup mustard seeds in a small glass bowl; pour boiling vinegar mixture over seeds. Cover and cool to room temperature. Pickled mustard seeds can be made up to 48 hours ahead and stored in the refrigerator.
EACH SERVING *339 cal, 17 g fat, 27 mg chol, 1,047 mg sodium, 37 g carb, 6 g fiber, 12 g pro.*

MEET STEPHANIE
Stephanie Izard is the chef at Girl & The Goat restaurant and Little Goat Diner in Chicago. Her go-to ingredient is vinegar, and she believes the most underrated spice is mustard seeds. Her signature cocktail is Strawberry Rhubarb Gin Fizz and the most requested dish at her restaurant is Roasted Cauliflower with Pickled Peppers, Pine Nuts, and Mint. Her favorite comfort food? Pasta with lots of Parmesan.

"Figs are everywhere this time of year. Their mellow sweetness goes perfectly with the briny saltiness of the olives—a nice counterpoint for a juicy, rich steak."

FAST

Steak with Fig Tapenade

"This tapenade would also be great as an easy appetizer," Stephanie says. "Spoon it over pieces of grilled crusty bread topped with ricotta or fresh mozzarella."

START TO FINISH **30 min.**

- 2 Tbsp. olive oil
- 2 Tbsp. malt vinegar
  Juice of 1 lemon
- 2 tsp. soy sauce
  Pinch cayenne pepper
- 4 ribeye steaks, 1 inch thick
- 6 firm figs, quartered and coarsely chopped
- 2 Tbsp. finely chopped shallots
- ½ cup niçoise olives, pitted and roughly chopped
- ¼ cup torn fresh basil

1. In a medium bowl whisk together olive oil, malt vinegar, lemon juice, soy sauce, and cayenne pepper. Pour half the mixture into a shallow baking dish. Season steaks with salt and pepper; add to the baking dish, turning to coat the steaks; set aside.

2. Meanwhile, for the fig tapenade, to the medium bowl add figs, shallots, olives, and basil. Stir to combine; set aside.

3. For a gas or charcoal grill, grill steaks on the rack of a covered grill directly over medium heat to desired doneness, turning once halfway through grilling. Allow 8 to 12 minutes for medium-rare (145°) or 10 to 15 minutes for medium (160°F). Serve steaks with fig tapenade. Makes 4 servings.

EACH SERVING *665 cal, 31 g fat, 221 mg chol, 648 mg sodium, 22 g carb, 4 g fiber, 78 g pro.*

PORK SANDWICH
WITH TARRAGON
APPLE SLAW

Rosemary Cod with Plum-Tomato Sauce

"Don't be afraid of fish sauce," Stephanie says. "It doesn't overpower a dish when you add just a little bit, and you get this awesome salty, funky flavor. You'll find the best stuff at Asian markets. Look for fish sauce that's reddish brown and fairly clear."

PREP 20 min. STAND 30 min.
COOK 6 min.

 6 plums, halved, pitted, and chopped
 1 lb. tomatoes, chopped
 ½ cup malt vinegar
 2 Tbsp. lemon juice
 1 to 2 Tbsp. fish sauce
 2 Tbsp. olive oil
 2 tsp. finely chopped fresh rosemary plus 1 sprig fresh rosemary
 1 Tbsp. butter
 4 5- to 6-oz. cod fillets, ½ to ¾ inch thick
   Kosher salt and freshly ground black pepper

1. In a large bowl combine plums, tomatoes, vinegar, lemon juice, fish sauce, 1 Tbsp. of the oil, and the 2 tsp. rosemary. Let stand at room temperature for 30 minutes.
2. In a large skillet heat butter, remaining 1 Tbsp. olive oil, and the rosemary sprig over medium-high heat. Sprinkle fish with salt and pepper. Add fish to the skillet. Cook about 6 minutes or until fish flakes easily with a fork, turning once halfway through cooking. Remove and discard the rosemary sprig.
3. Transfer fish to a platter and spoon plum-tomato sauce over to serve. Makes 4 servings.
EACH SERVING *272 cal, 11 g fat, 69 mg chol, 584 mg sodium, 17 g carb, 3 g fiber, 27 g pro.*

Pork Sandwich with Tarragon Apple Slaw

"I love this sandwich on white bread because of that super soft texture. It lets the crunch of the pork cutlet and the apple shine through," Stephanie says. "And the slaw is so versatile. You could throw it on tacos or serve it with grilled chicken."

PREP 25 min. COOK 5 min.

 2 red-skinned apples, cored and cut into julienne strips
 2 Tbsp. lemon juice
 1 Tbsp. extra-virgin olive oil
 ¼ cup torn fresh tarragon
 ½ cup panko (Japanese-style bread crumbs)
 12 oz. boneless pork loin, cut into 4 equal pieces
 ½ cup all-purpose flour
 ½ tsp. salt
 ¼ tsp. ground black pepper
 2 eggs, beaten
   Vegetable oil
 8 thin slices white country bread
 2 Tbsp. mayonnaise
 2 Tbsp. Dijon-style mustard

1. For apple slaw, in a medium bowl toss apples with lemon juice, olive oil, and tarragon; set aside.
2. Place panko in food processor; pulse with a few on-off turns. Transfer to a shallow dish. Place each piece of pork between two pieces of plastic wrap. Pound to about ¼ inch thickness; set aside. In a shallow dish mix together flour, salt, and pepper. Place egg in another shallow dish. Coat pork slices with flour, then egg, and finally panko.
3. In a 10-inch skillet heat ¼ to ½ inch vegetable oil over medium heat. Cook pork about 3 minutes each side or until golden brown and no pink remains.
4. Serve pork and apple slaw between slices of white bread smeared with mayonnaise and mustard. Makes 4 servings.
EACH SERVING *613 cal, 31 g fat, 132 mg chol, 874 mg sodium, 58 g carb, 4 g fiber, 26 g pro.*

ROSEMARY COD
WITH PLUM-
TOMATO SAUCE

Delicious Every Day

Fresh and easy ideas for dinner.

CHEESY BUTTERNUT SQUASH CAVATAPPI BAKE

Cheesy Butternut Squash Cavatappi Bake

This dish is packed with vitamin A and has less fat than traditional macaroni and cheese yet doesn't sacrifice taste.

PREP 30 min. COOK 8 min.
BAKE 20 min. OVEN 375°F

- 3 cups peeled and cubed butternut squash
- 8 oz. dried cavatappi or other elbow macaroni
- 1 Tbsp. butter
- 8 oz. cremini or button mushrooms, sliced
- 3 green onions, thinly sliced
- 2 Tbsp. all-purpose flour
- 1 cup fat-free milk
- 6 oz. fontina cheese, shredded (1½ cups)
- 2 slices reduced-sodium bacon, cooked and crumbled (optional)

1. Preheat oven to 375°F. Lightly coat a 2-quart rectangular baking dish with nonstick cooking spray; set aside.
2. In a medium microwave-safe bowl combine squash and 2 Tbsp. water; cover with vented plastic wrap. Microwave on high for 4 minutes; stir. Microwave, covered, about 4 minutes more or until squash is tender. Carefully remove plastic wrap. Mash squash; set aside.
3. Meanwhile, cook pasta according to package directions; drain. In a medium saucepan heat butter over medium-high heat. Add mushrooms and green onions. Cook until tender, about 5 minutes. Sprinkle flour over mushroom mixture. Cook and stir for 1 minute. Add milk and ¼ tsp. each of salt and pepper. Cook and stir over medium heat until thickened and bubbly. Remove from heat; stir in squash. Add pasta. Gently fold to combine.
4. Transfer half the pasta mixture to the prepared baking dish. Sprinkle with half the cheese. Add remaining pasta mixture and cheese. Top with bacon, if desired. Bake, uncovered, 20 to 25 minutes or until heated through and cheese is melted. Top with additional green onions. Makes 6 servings.

EACH SERVING 334 cal, 12 g fat, 39 mg chol, 366 mg sodium, 42 g carb, 3 g fiber, 16 g pro.

HERB-CRUSTED COD WITH CAULIFLOWER MASH

Herb-Crusted Cod with Cauliflower Mash

Pick up cut-up veggies and prepare this meal in even less time.

START TO FINISH 30 min. OVEN 300°F

- 4½ cups cauliflower florets, baby gold potatoes, and/or peeled carrots, coarsely chopped
- 2 oz. semisoft cheese with garlic and fine herbs
- 4 skinless, boneless cod fillets (about 1¼ lb.)
- 1 egg
- ⅔ cup panko (Japanese-style bread crumbs)
- 2 Tbsp. snipped fresh dillweed
- 1 Tbsp. olive oil

1. For cauliflower mash, place vegetables in a Dutch oven. Add ½ tsp. salt and water to cover. Cover and bring to boiling. Reduce heat to medium. Cook, covered, 15 to 20 minutes or until tender. Drain vegetables, reserving some cooking water. Using a potato masher, mash vegetables to desired consistency, adding reserved water as needed. Stir in cheese. Season to taste with salt and pepper. Cover and keep warm.
2. Meanwhile, preheat oven to 300°F. Rinse fish and pat dry with paper towels. Cut fish into 8 equal pieces. In a shallow dish beat egg. In another shallow dish combine bread crumbs, dill, and ½ tsp. each salt and pepper. Dip fish pieces into egg, then into bread crumb mixture. Set aside.
3. In a large skillet heat olive oil over medium-high heat. Add half the fish. Cook 2 to 3 minutes on each side or until fish is golden brown and flakes easily with a fork. Drain on paper towels. Keep warm in oven while frying remaining fish. Serve with cauliflower mash. Makes 4 servings.

EACH SERVING 317 cal, 12 g fat, 122 mg chol, 778 mg sodium, 21 g carb, 4 g fiber, 31 g pro.

CHICKEN FRITTATA WITH CANTALOUPE TOMATO SALSA

Chicken Frittata with Cantaloupe-Tomato Salsa

Tomato and cantaloupe might seem like an unusual combination, but it works deliciously! With only three ingredients, this flavorful salsa might just become a staple recipe.

PREP **15 min.** COOK **8 min.**
BROIL **1 min.**

- 1 cup chopped cherry tomatoes
- 1 cup chopped cantaloupe
- 2 Tbsp. snipped fresh cilantro
- 8 eggs
- ½ cup milk or half-and-half
- ¼ tsp. salt
- 1 Tbsp. olive oil
- 1 4-oz. can diced green chiles
- 1 cup shredded cooked chicken
- ⅔ cup canned kidney beans, rinsed and drained
- 2 oz. Monterey Jack cheese, shredded
  Fresh cilantro leaves

1. For salsa, in a medium bowl combine tomatoes, cantaloupe, and cilantro; set aside.

2. In a medium bowl whisk together eggs, milk, and salt; set aside.

3. In a 12-inch broiler-proof nonstick skillet heat oil over medium heat. Add chiles. Cook and stir for 3 minutes. Scatter chicken and beans evenly in skillet.

4. Preheat broiler. Pour egg mixture over chicken and beans. Cook over medium heat. As mixture sets, run a spatula around edge of skillet, lifting egg mixture so uncooked portion flows underneath. Continue cooking and lifting edges until egg is almost set (surface will be moist). Sprinkle with cheese.

5. Place skillet under broiler 4 to 5 inches from heat. Broil 1 to 2 minutes or just until top is set and cheese is melted. Top with salsa and fresh cilantro leaves. Makes 4 servings.

EACH SERVING *370 cal, 21 g fat, 418 mg chol, 605 mg sodium, 15 g carb, 3 g fiber, 31 g pro.*

Dinner on a Dollar

Get inspired by the flavors of the Mediterranean with this tangy, no-cook bean and tuna salad.

White Bean Tuna Salad

A salad of fiber-rich beans and protein-packed tuna gets plenty of bright flavor from an easy-to-make vinaigrette. To make sure the dressing sticks, drain the tuna well and pat your greens dry. Any excess water will leave all the flavor on the bottom of the plate instead of on your fork.

START TO FINISH **20 min.**

- 1   15-oz. can cannellini beans, rinsed and drained
- 2   5-oz. cans tuna packed in water, drained
- 2   cups lightly packed arugula
- ½   small red onion, thinly sliced
- ¼   cup fresh flat-leaf Italian parsley, chopped
- ¼   cup red wine vinegar
- 3   Tbsp. extra-virgin olive oil
- ½   tsp. dried leaf oregano, crushed
- ¼   tsp. salt
- ¼   tsp. ground black pepper
- ½   lemon
      Toasted baguette slices (optional)

1. In a large bowl combine beans, tuna, arugula, red onion, and parsley.
2. For vinaigrette, in a screw-top jar combine vinegar, oil, oregano, salt, and pepper. Shake well to combine.
3. Pour vinaigrette over tuna mixture; toss gently to combine. Squeeze juice from half a lemon over the salad. Serve with toasted baguette slices, if desired. Makes 4 servings.

EACH SERVING *274 cal, 13 g fat, 30 mg chol, 644 mg sodium, 15 g carb, 5 g fiber, 22 g pro.*

WHITE BEAN TUNA SALAD

MEDLEY OF
ROASTED ROOT
VEGETABLES

october

SAVOR THE SEASON With cooler temps, earthy root vegetables take center stage in main dishes and sides. This fall, serve seasonal produce, succulent roasted chicken, and perfectly spiced gingersnaps.

255

257

263

Good Roots

Beneath the soil lies a wealth of vegetables to explore. Here are seven recipes that make the most of these buried treasures.

Sweet Potato-Topped Turkey Pot Pie

For faster preparation, make the mashed sweet potato topping up to 2 days ahead and use purchased rotisserie chicken and chicken stock.
PREP 45 min. BAKE 20 min.
OVEN 400°F

Sweet Potato Topping
- 2 lb. orange-flesh sweet potatoes, peeled and cut into 1-inch cubes
- 2 tsp. kosher salt
- 3 Tbsp. unsalted butter, melted
- ¼ tsp. freshly grated nutmeg
  Freshly ground black pepper

Turkey Filling
- 2 Tbsp. unsalted butter
- 2 Tbsp. canola oil
- 1 large yellow onion, diced
- ¾ cup diced celery
- ¾ cup peeled and diced carrots
- 1 tsp. kosher salt
- 3 Tbsp. all-purpose flour

- 1½ cups homemade chicken or turkey stock or canned low-sodium chicken broth
- ½ cup whipping cream or half-and-half
- 2½ cups shredded roast turkey or chicken
- 2 Tbsp. finely chopped fresh flat-leaf parsley
- 1 Tbsp. finely chopped fresh sage
- 1 Tbsp. minced fresh thyme

  Small sage or thyme leaves

1. For Sweet Potato Topping, in a saucepan combine sweet potatoes, 1 tsp. of the salt, and enough water to cover by 1 inch. Cover partially. Bring to boiling over medium-high heat. Reduce heat to medium. Simmer until potatoes are fork-tender, about 10 minutes.
2. Drain potatoes; return to warm pan. Stir over low heat for 1 minute. Using a potato masher, mash potatoes. Stir in melted butter, nutmeg, the remaining 1 tsp. salt, and freshly ground black pepper. Set aside.

3. Position a rack in center of oven. Preheat oven to 400°F.
4. For Turkey Filling, in a large saucepan melt butter with oil over medium heat. Add onion, celery, and carrots. Cook and stir about 2 minutes. Add salt. Cover partially. Reduce heat to medium-low. Cook about 12 minutes or until vegetables are very tender.
5. Sprinkle flour over vegetables. Stir to combine. Slowly stir in stock. Simmer, stirring occasionally until smooth and thickened, about 2 minutes. Stir in cream; bring to a simmer. Add turkey, parsley, sage, and thyme. Stir to combine; return to a simmer. Remove from heat. Spoon into a 2½- to 3-quart rectangular baking dish. Using a rubber spatula, spread and mound Sweet Potato topping over filling, leaving some filling visible. Bake about 20 minutes or until bubbly. Sprinkle a few sage or thyme leaves on top before serving. Makes 5 servings.
EACH SERVING *515 cal, 29 g fat, 134 mg chol, 1,230 mg sodium, 39 g carb, 26 g pro.*

MEET DIANE
No one knows root vegetables better than James Beard award-winning author Diane Morgan, who created this batch of delicious recipes. Her latest cookbook, *Roots,* is loaded with enticing recipes and a wealth of facts—from the history of roots to their storage. Diane's path into food writing began in the kitchen. From summers spent in a small restaurant to years working in one of the country's foremost cooking schools, Diane discovered her talent and passion for teaching and cooking.

From salads to main dishes, raw to roasted, even the most familiar root vegetables can impress with a fresh new spin.

KID FRIENDLY | LOW FAT

Pan-Roasted Pork Tenderloin with Carrots, Chickpeas, and Cranberries

"These days, there are many varieties of carrots found at grocery stores and farmer's markets," Diane says. "This recipe is a good opportunity to explore your options and try a new carrot."

PREP **25 min.** COOK **15 min.**
ROAST **10 min.** STAND **10 min.**
OVEN **400°F**

- 2 1-lb. pork tenderloins, trimmed of fat
- 3 Tbsp. extra-virgin olive oil
- 2 lb. carrots, larger halved lengthwise, smaller left whole
- ½ cup canned chickpeas, drained, rinsed, and dried
- ½ cup fresh orange juice
- ½ cup water
- 2 Tbsp. unsweetened dried cranberries
- 1 Tbsp. firmly packed light brown sugar
- 1 star anise pod
- ¼ tsp. smoked paprika
- 1 Tbsp. unsalted butter
- 1 Tbsp. finely chopped fresh flat-leaf parsley
- 1 Tbsp. finely chopped fresh oregano

1. Place rack in center of oven. Preheat oven to 400°F.
2. Season pork generously on all sides with salt and pepper. Set aside. In a 12-inch ovenproof skillet heat oil over medium-high heat. Add pork. Sear on all sides until browned, about 6 minutes. Transfer pork to a large plate; set aside.
3. Add carrots to pan. Cook and stir until browned at the edges, about 5 minutes. Add chickpeas and ½ tsp. salt. Cook 1 minute more. Using a spatula, make two wide channels through vegetables. Place pork tenderloins in the channels to rest directly on the pan, surrounded by the carrots.
4. Transfer pan to oven. Roast 10 to 15 minutes or until an instant-read thermometer inserted into center of a tenderloin registers 145°F. The center should be rosy when cut into with a knife. Transfer pork to a carving board; tent loosely with foil. Let rest for 10 minutes.
5. Carefully place the hot pan with carrots and chickpeas over medium heat. Add orange juice, the water, cranberries, brown sugar, star anise, and paprika; mix well. Simmer, stirring occasionally, until sauce is reduced by half, about 3 minutes. Stir in butter, parsley, and oregano. Season to taste with salt.
6. To serve, cut pork on a slight diagonal into 1-inch-thick slices. Serve with roasted carrots and chickpeas. Makes 6 servings.
EACH SERVING *330 cal, 12 g fat, 98 mg chol, 428 mg sodium, 23 g carb, 4 g fiber, 32 g pro.*

DIANE'S ROOT BASICS
● Store root vegetables in the refrigerator up to 1 month wrapped in paper towels (to wick away moisture) and placed in a loosely closed plastic bag.

● Buy root vegetables with tops attached, especially carrots and beets. The greens are delicious too; just remove them and store separately in the refrigerator.

● Think beyond the ordinary. Roast radishes or enjoy a baked sweet potato for breakfast. There is more than one way to eat root vegetables.

● Plan for leftovers. Serve mashed rutabagas for dinner, then for breakfast the next day, top warmed up leftovers with a poached egg.

CARROT

RAW BEET SLAW
WITH FENNEL,
TART APPLE, AND
PARSLEY

Raw Beet Slaw with Fennel, Tart Apple, and Parsley

"Beets are terrific raw," Diane says. "Their crisp texture along with the tangy flavors from the dressing make this salad a fun alternative to coleslaw and an easy appetizer." Diane uses a mandoline to get uniform matchsticks and recommends wearing gloves to prevent the beet juice from staining your hands.

START TO FINISH **20 min.**

- 3 Tbsp. extra-virgin olive oil
- 1 Tbsp. fresh lemon juice
- 1 Tbsp. freshly grated lemon or orange zest
- ½ tsp. honey
- ½ tsp. kosher salt
- ⅛ tsp. freshly ground black pepper
- 1 medium red beet, peeled and cut into matchsticks
- ½ fennel bulb, trimmed, halved lengthwise, cored, and cut into matchsticks
- ½ medium crisp-tart apple, such as Granny Smith, cored and cut into matchsticks
- ½ cup firmly packed chopped fresh flat-leaf parsley

1. For dressing, in a small bowl whisk together oil, lemon juice, lemon zest, honey, salt, and pepper.
2. In a medium bowl combine beet, fennel, apple, and parsley. Pour dressing over. Toss gently to coat. Serve immediately, or cover and chill up to 8 hours. (If chilled, remove from refrigerator and let stand 30 minutes before serving.) Makes 4 servings.

EACH SERVING *127 cal, 10 g fat, 282 mg sodium, 9 g carb, 2 g fiber, 1 g pro.*

CREAM OF CELERY ROOT SOUP

Cream of Celery Root Soup

"If there's one new root to add to the routine, it's celery root. It's starchy with a faint celery flavor and can be eaten raw or cooked," Diane says.

PREP **30 min.** COOL **10 min.**
COOK **35 min.**

- 10 white peppercorns
- 1 bay leaf
- 4 sprigs fresh flat-leaf parsley
- 4 sprigs fresh thyme
- 2 Tbsp. unsalted butter
- 1 large leek, white and light green parts only, halved lengthwise and thinly sliced crosswise (1 cup)
- 1 large clove garlic, minced
- 4 cups water
- 1 large celery root (about 1½ lbs.), trimmed, peeled, and cut into ½-inch cubes (5 cups)
- 2 tsp. kosher salt
- ¼ tsp. freshly ground white pepper
- ⅓ cup whipping cream
- ¼ cup crème fraîche or sour cream
- 2 Tbsp. finely snipped fresh chives
  Pear slices (optional)

1. For bouquet garni*, place peppercorns, bay leaf, parsley, and thyme in center of an 8-inch square of cheesecloth. Bring up edges to form a bag; tie securely with kitchen string.
2. In a large saucepan melt butter over medium heat. Add leek. Cook and stir until softened, 6 to 8 minutes. Add garlic. Cook 1 minute more. Add water, celery root, salt, pepper, and bouquet garni. Bring to boiling. Reduce heat. Simmer, uncovered, until celery root is fork-tender, about 20 minutes. Remove from heat. Let cool 10 minutes.
3. Remove and discard bouquet garni. Working in batches, puree soup with an immersion blender or food processor. Return soup to low heat. Stir in cream. Heat through. (Do not boil.) Season with salt and white pepper. Thin soup with chicken broth, if desired.
4. To serve, top soup with crème fraîche, chives, and fresh pear slices, if desired. Makes 8 servings.
*A bunch of herbs and whole spices wrapped and tied in cheesecloth and used to flavor soups, then removed before serving.

EACH SERVING *134 cal, 10 g fat, 31 mg chol, 599 mg sodium, 11 g carb, 2 g fiber, 2 g pro.*

GINGER CIDER SPRITZER

Medley of Roasted Root Vegetables

"There shouldn't be anything intimidating about roasting root vegetables," Diane says. "In fact, roasting is one of the easiest, most delicious ways to try out a new vegetable. Follow the recipe once or twice and then find ways to make it your own. Change the herbs, add a vinaigrette, or top the vegetables with a poached or fried egg for a complete meal."

PREP **30 min.** ROAST **45 min.**
OVEN **400°F**

- 3 lbs. assorted root vegetables (carrots, parsnips, beets, fingerling or new potatoes, celery root, turnips, rutabagas, and Jerusalem artichokes), peeled and cut into even-size chunks
- 8 shallots, halved lengthwise
- ¼ cup extra-virgin olive oil
- 2 Tbsp. chopped fresh herbs, such as thyme, parsley, dill, rosemary, and/or sage
- 2 tsp. kosher salt
- 1 tsp. freshly ground black pepper

1. Place rack in center of oven. Preheat oven to 400°F.
2. In a large roasting pan or baking dish gently toss vegetables and shallots with oil, herbs, salt, and pepper. Roast, uncovered, stirring once or twice, until vegetables are fork-tender and browned, about 45 minutes. Serve immediately, or cover and keep warm up to 1 hour before serving. Makes 6 servings.
Make ahead The roasted vegetables can be made up to 1 day in advance. Cover and refrigerate. Let stand at room temperature 2 hours. Reheat in a 350°F oven until hot, about 20 minutes.
EACH SERVING *216 cal, 9 g fat, 0 mg chol, 760 mg sodium, 32 g carb, 7 g fiber, 4 g pro.*

KID FRIENDLY | LOW FAT
Ginger Cider Spritzer

Large pieces of ginger with several knobby branches are called hands. "If you don't need a whole hand of ginger, it's perfectly acceptable to break off the amount you want to purchase," Diane says. Freeze any remaining ginger.
PREP **30 min.** COOK **5 min.**
COOL **30 min.**

- 2 Tbsp. Ginger Syrup
- ¼ cup apple cider, chilled
- ½ cup club soda, chilled

1. For each spritzer, to a 16-oz. ice-filled glass add Ginger Syrup, apple cider, and club soda. Stir to combine. Serve immediately. Makes 1 serving.
Note For a warm Ginger Cider Spritzer, substitute water for the club soda and heat through.
Ginger Syrup In a small saucepan combine ½ cup grated fresh ginger, 1 cup packed brown sugar, and 1 cup water. Bring to boiling over high heat, stirring constantly until sugar dissolves. Reduce heat; simmer for 5 minutes or until sugar is completely dissolved. Remove from heat; let steep until cool, about 30 minutes. Strain through a fine-mesh sieve placed over a container with a tight-fitting lid. Cover and refrigerate until well chilled. Makes 1½ cups syrup. Store syrup in the refrigerator up to 2 weeks.
EACH SERVING *100 cal, 0 g fat, 0 mg chol, 37 mg sodium, 25 g carb, 0 g fiber, 0 g pro.*

MEDLEY OF
ROASTED ROOT
VEGETABLES

Sugar and spice is definitely nice when the spice has the zing of ginger root. This aromatic root pairs well with the bold flavors of molasses and nutmeg.

KID FRIENDLY

Old-Fashioned Gingersnaps

"These heavily spiced gingersnap cookies are incredibly fragrant and will perfume your kitchen as you bake," Diane says. "Bake them 10 minutes for a soft chewy cookie or 12 minutes for more of the traditional crunchy snap."

PREP **40 min.** CHILL **1 hr.**
BAKE **10 min. per batch** OVEN **350°F**

- 2 cups all-purpose flour
- 2 tsp. baking soda
- 2 tsp. ground ginger
- 1 tsp. ground cinnamon
- ½ tsp. freshly grated nutmeg
- ½ tsp. ground allspice
- ½ tsp. kosher salt
- ½ cup unsalted butter, melted and cooled
- ¼ cup unsulfured dark molasses (not blackstrap)
- ½ cup firmly packed light brown sugar
- ⅓ cup granulated sugar
- 3 Tbsp. peeled and grated fresh ginger
- 1 large egg, beaten
- ½ cup coarse sugar, such as turbinado
- 1 recipe Orange Whipped Cream (optional)

1. Position oven racks in upper and lower thirds of oven. Preheat oven to 350°F. Line two baking sheets with parchment paper; set aside.
2. In a medium bowl whisk together flour, baking soda, the 2 tsp. ground ginger, cinnamon, nutmeg, allspice, and salt; set aside.
3. In a large bowl whisk together melted butter, molasses, brown sugar, granulated sugar, the 3 Tbsp. grated ginger, and egg. Add the flour mixture. Stir to combine. Cover and chill 1 hour.
4. Place turbinado sugar in a small shallow bowl; set aside. Using a tablespoon, scoop out a ball of dough. Roll dough between your palms to a 1-inch-diameter ball. Continue with remaining dough, then roll balls in turbinado sugar to evenly coat. Space balls 2 inches apart on prepared baking sheets.
5. Bake 10 to 12 minutes or until edges are crisp and centers are chewy. Switch baking sheets between racks and rotate them front to back halfway through. Remove from oven. Using a spatula, transfer cookies to wire racks to cool. Serve with Orange Whipped Cream, if desired. Makes 40 cookies.

Make ahead Store cookies between sheets of waxed paper in an airtight container at room temperature up to 5 days or freeze up to 2 weeks.
EACH COOKIE *78 cal, 3 g fat, 11 mg chol, 91 mg sodium, 13 g carb, 0 g fiber, 1 g pro.*
Orange Whipped Cream In a chilled mixing bowl beat 1 cup whipping cream, 1 Tbsp. sugar, and 1 tsp. finely shredded orange peel until soft peaks form.

Home Cooking

ROAST CHICKEN Learn simple techniques to perfecting this classic dish. Meat and poultry guru Ariane Daguin shows how.

Classic Roast Chicken

Growing up in France, Ariane Daguin experienced roast chicken as a tradition on the farm where her family raised poultry. She was an early leader in the farm-to-table movement, and her company D'Artagnan (dartagnan.com), sells organic poultry, meat, pâtés, sausages, and wild mushrooms.

PREP 20 min. CHILL overnight
ROAST 55 min. STAND 5 min.
OVEN 475°F/375°F

- 1 3½- to 4-lb. whole broiler chicken
- 3 cups assorted vegetables, such as carrots, celery, onions, parsnips, beets, or other root vegetables
- 2 Tbsp. softened butter
- 2 cups chicken broth

1. Rinse chicken; thoroughly pat dry inside and out with paper towels. Chill, uncovered, overnight in refrigerator.
2. Place rack in bottom third of oven. Preheat oven to 475°F. Gently run your fingers between skin and breast meat. Sprinkle salt and pepper over top of skin.
3. Tuck wings under breasts. Loop a long piece of kitchen string around drumsticks in a figure-eight pattern; pull tightly. Pull string up around thighs and breast; tie at neck. Place chicken, breast side up, on a rack in a shallow roasting pan. Toss vegetables with butter. Place in pan around chicken.
4. Roast 15 minutes; reduce heat to 375°F. Roast 40 to 60 minutes more or until drumsticks move easily in sockets, chicken is no longer pink inside, and thermometer inserted into center of an inside thigh muscle registers 175°F. Remove chicken from oven. Cover; let stand at least 5 minutes. Transfer chicken and vegetables to a serving platter.
5. For pan sauce, place roasting pan over a burner on a stovetop; stir in chicken broth, scraping up any browned bits in the pan. Bring to boiling; boil gently until reduced by about half. Serve pan sauce with chicken. Makes 6 servings.

EACH SERVING *234 cal, 8 g fat, 92 mg chol, 334 mg sodium, 7 g carb, 2 g fiber, 33 g pro.*

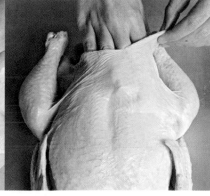

DRY AND CHILL
Do this the night before to completely dry out the skin. "This results in a golden, crackling finish," Ariane says.

SEPARATE THE SKIN
This also aids in crisping. "Be gentle, but it's not the end of the world if you break the skin," Ariane says.

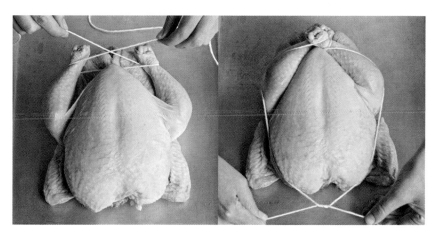

TIE IT UP
Trussing (securing the bird with kitchen string to make it compact) allows for even cooking. Loop string around drumsticks in a figure-eight pattern then pull in legs.

PULL TIGHT
Pull the string around the thighs and breast and tie a knot at the neck. "Anything goes when trussing," Ariane says. "Just keep it simple."

USE A SHALLOW PAN
"A deep pan will trap steam between the chicken and pan, creating soggy skin," Ariane says. Elevate on a rack for air circulation. Adding veggies enhances the flavor.

LET IT REST
Tenting the bird with foil for at least 5 minutes allows the juices to integrate. "It makes the meat succulent," Ariane says.

"The perfect roast chicken has crispy golden skin and juicy, tender meat that's bursting with flavor."

LEMON HERB-STUFFED CHICKEN

SPICE-RUBBED CHICKEN

ROASTED GARLIC BUTTERED CHICKEN

Add variety with these three easy flavor change-ups.

Lemon Herb-Stuffed Chicken

"Don't be afraid to overstuff," Ariane says. "The herbs will release their natural oils and flavor the chicken from the inside out."

To prepare Stuff chicken cavity with 2 to 3 lemon wedges, a handful of fresh herbs (such as rosemary, sage, thyme, oregano, and/or parsley), and a few halved garlic cloves. Finish pan juices with ½ tsp. herbes de Provence.

Spice-Rubbed Chicken

Dried mushrooms are available at just about any grocery store and are a perfect way to try a mushroom you haven't before—at much less cost. "Dried mushrooms are very aromatic and earthy," Ariane says. "Grinding them into a powder intensifies their flavor, which is lovely with a bit of heat."

To prepare Place ¼ cup dried mushrooms (such as porcini, chanterelle, or a mix) in a spice grinder or food processor. Grind to a fine powder. Transfer to a small bowl. Add 1 Tbsp. chili powder. Stir to combine. Before trussing, rub 2 Tbsp. of the mixture all over chicken skin and sprinkle in chicken cavity. Finish pan juices with 1 tsp. spice mixture; store remaining spice mixture.

Roasted Garlic Buttered Chicken

"Butter enhances whatever it's flavored with as it cooks," Ariane says. Roasting garlic makes it more aromatic and imparts a bit of sweetness.

To prepare Cut off top ½ inch of garlic bulb, leaving bulb whole; remove any loose outer layers. Place in custard cup; drizzle with 1 Tbsp. olive oil. Wrap with foil. Roast in a 400°F oven for 25 minutes or until soft. Cool. Squeeze out garlic cloves; mash into ¼ cup softened butter. Before trussing, gently rub 2 Tbsp. garlic butter under chicken skin. Chill remaining butter.

Delicious Every Day

Fresh and easy ideas for dinner.

PORK CHOPS WITH MAPLE APPLES

PUMPKIN SOUP WITH LENTILS

Pork Chops with Maple Apples

Cooking pork chops to the correct temperature ensures the best flavor, plus it confirms the meat is safely done. For an accurate temperature, insert a meat thermometer through the side of the chop into the center. Allowing the pork to rest while you prepare the apples gives it time to continue cooking. Don't skip this step!

PREP **15 min.** COOK **15 min.**

- 4 pork loin chops, cut ¾ inch thick
- 1 Tbsp. olive oil
- 2 cooking apples, cored and thinly sliced
- 1 small red onion, cut into thin wedges
- 2 cloves garlic, minced
- ¼ cup apple juice
- ⅓ cup whipping cream
- 1 Tbsp. pure maple syrup
- 2 tsp. snipped fresh thyme or 1 tsp. dried thyme

1. Trim excess fat from pork chops. Sprinkle with salt and pepper. In a 12-inch nonstick skillet heat oil over medium-high heat. Add pork chops. Cook for 8 to 12 minutes or until an instant-read thermometer registers 145°F, turning once halfway through cooking. Remove from skillet. Cover with foil. Let stand 3 minutes.
2. Add apples, onion, and garlic to skillet. Cook for 2 minutes, stirring occasionally. Add apple juice. Cook about 4 minutes more or until most liquid has evaporated and apples are crisp-tender.
3. Meanwhile, stir together whipping cream, maple syrup, and thyme. Pour over apples in skillet. Cook and stir 1 to 2 minutes or until heated through and sauce begins to thicken.
4. Serve maple apples with pork chops. Sprinkle with additional fresh thyme, if desired. Makes 4 servings.
EACH SERVING *369 cal, 17 g fat, 108 mg chol, 234 mg sodium, 21 g carb, 3 g fiber, 33 g pro.*

Pumpkin Soup with Lentils

Canned pumpkin is versatile. This easy-to-make soup brings together rich pumpkin, ginger, curry, and cumin for a comforting dish that's high in vitamin A and packed with flavor. To make this soup vegetarian, swap vegetable broth for the chicken stock.

PREP **15 min.** COOK **27 min.**

- 1 small sweet onion, cut into wedges
- 1 yellow sweet pepper, seeded and sliced
- ½ cup lentils, rinsed and well drained
- 1 Tbsp. olive oil
- 2 tsp. grated fresh ginger
- 1 tsp. curry powder
- 1 tsp. ground cumin
- 1 26-oz. box chicken stock
- 1 15-oz. can pumpkin puree

1. In a 4- to 5-quart Dutch oven cook onion, sweet pepper, and lentils in hot oil over medium-high heat for 2 minutes. Whisk in ginger, curry powder, cumin, stock, and pumpkin puree. Bring to boiling; reduce heat to medium-low. Simmer, covered, for 25 minutes or until lentils are tender. Season to taste with salt and pepper before serving. Makes 4 servings.
EACH SERVING *189 cal, 4 g fat, 0 mg chol, 548 mg sodium, 29 g carb, 11 g fiber, 11 g pro.*

Beef Nachos with Blender Salsa

Yes, you can have nachos for dinner! The trick is to include enough nutritious and filling ingredients to make a meal. This tasty combination of protein-rich ground beef and kidney beans satisfies even your hungriest amigos.

PREP **15 min.** COOK **10 min.**
BROIL **4 min.**

12 oz. ground beef
 1 cup canned kidney beans, rinsed
    and drained
½ tsp. salt
½ tsp. ground black pepper
 1 bunch green onions, sliced
⅔ cup coarsely chopped fresh
    cilantro
 1 14½-oz. can fire-roasted
    tomatoes, undrained
 2 tsp. chili powder
1½ tsp. garlic powder
 1 tsp. ground cumin
 4 cups corn tortilla chips
 1 cup shredded cheddar cheese

1. Preheat broiler. In a large skillet cook ground beef over medium heat until browned, breaking up any large pieces. Drain off fat. Stir in kidney beans, salt, and pepper. Heat through. Remove from heat. Cover and set aside.
2. Meanwhile, set aside 2 Tbsp. green onions and 2 Tbsp. cilantro. For salsa, in a blender combine remaining green onions, cilantro, tomatoes, chili powder, garlic powder, and cumin. Blend until smooth. Set aside.
3. On a baking sheet arrange chips in a single layer. Sprinkle with cheese. Broil 5 to 6 inches from heat for 2 to 3 minutes or until cheese is melted. Top with ground beef mixture and about half the salsa. Broil 2 to 3 minutes or until heated through.
4. To serve, top nachos with reserved green onions and cilantro. Makes 4 servings.
EACH SERVING *471 cal, 26 g fat, 86 mg chol, 1,019 mg sodium, 31 g carb, 6 g fiber, 29 g pro.*

Dinner on a Dollar

Elevate eggs to dinner status with sweet potatoes and a hint of cumin in this fast and flavorful skillet meal.

Savory Egg and Sweet Potato Scramble

Spinach is a nutritious green to have on hand, but it has a tendency to wilt quickly. Next time you have some to be used pronto, stir it into a dinner scramble with sweet potatoes for a weeknight-friendly meal.
START TO FINISH **35 min.**

    8 eggs
    ⅓ cup milk
    ½ tsp. cumin
    ¼ tsp. salt
    ¼ tsp. ground black pepper
    1 Tbsp. butter
    2 medium sweet potatoes, peeled,
       quartered lengthwise, and thinly
       sliced
    1 green onion, sliced
    2 cups baby spinach
       Bottled hot pepper sauce
       (optional)

1. In a medium bowl whisk together eggs, milk, cumin, salt, and pepper. Set aside.
2. In a large skillet melt butter over medium heat. Add sweet potatoes and green onion. Cook, stirring occasionally, until potatoes are almost tender, about 8 minutes. Add spinach. Cook until slightly wilted, about 1 minute.
3. Pour egg mixture over vegetables in skillet. Cook, without stirring, until mixture begins to set on bottom and around edges. Lift and fold partially cooked egg mixture, allowing the uncooked portion to flow underneath. Continue cooking for 2 to 3 minutes or until egg mixture is cooked through but still moist. Remove from heat and serve at once. Pass hot pepper sauce, if desired. Makes 4 servings.
EACH SERVING *258 cal, 13 g fat, 381 mg chol, 390 mg sodium, 20 g carb, 3 g fiber, 15 g pro*

MAPLE PUMPKIN
PIE WITH SALTED
PECAN BRITTLE

november

THANKSGIVING Add to your holiday repertoire of favorite dishes with options for succulent turkey and gravy, creamy mashers, fresh takes on stuffings, and decadent desserts. Be inspired all season.

279

280

294

BACON-WRAPPED
TURKEY

Mix & Match Thanksgiving

Save space next to holiday favorites for artfully inspired flavor. These dishes cozy right up to Thanksgiving classics to create an unforgettable feast.

Bacon-Wrapped Turkey

PREP 40 min. ROAST 3 hr.
STAND 15 min. OVEN 325°F

- 10 slices applewood-smoked bacon
- 1 medium onion, finely chopped
- 2 Tbsp. finely snipped fresh sage or 2 tsp. dried sage, finely crushed
- 1 12- to 14-lb. fresh or thawed turkey
  Kosher salt and ground black pepper
- 2 to 3 sprigs fresh sage
- 1 medium sweet onion, cut in wedges
- 1 recipe Bacon-Onion Gravy (optional)

1. Preheat oven to 325°F. Finely chop 2 slices of the bacon. In a medium bowl stir together the chopped bacon, chopped onion, and the snipped or crushed sage; set aside.
2. Remove neck and giblets from turkey; discard. Rinse turkey; pat dry with paper towels. Starting at neck end of turkey, loosen skin by sliding your fingers underneath, separating skin from meat. Rub onion mixture under skin, over breast, and toward thighs.
3. Sprinkle kosher salt and pepper inside body cavity. Insert sage sprigs and sweet onion wedges. Pull neck skin to back; fasten with a small skewer. Tuck wings under breast. Loop kitchen string around drumsticks; tie securely

to tail. Place turkey, breast side up, on a rack in a shallow roasting pan. Sprinkle turkey with salt and pepper. Weave remaining 8 strips of bacon in a lattice pattern over breast. Tuck additional fresh sage leaves into lattice. Insert an oven-going meat thermometer into center of an inside thigh muscle, avoiding bone. Cover loosely with foil.
4. Roast 2¾ hours. Remove foil. Roast 15 to 45 minutes more, or until thermometer reaches 175°F. Remove turkey from oven.
5. Cover turkey with foil; let stand 15 minutes. Remove and discard onion and sage from turkey. Serve with Bacon-Onion Gravy, if desired. Makes 8 servings plus leftovers.
EACH 4-OZ. SERVING *557 cal, 29 g fat, 270 mg chol, 519 mg sodium, 1 g carb, 0 g fiber, 73 g pro.*

Basic Pan Gravy

START TO FINISH 15 min.

   Pan drippings from roasted turkey
   Melted butter
- 1 cup turkey or chicken broth
- ¼ cup all-purpose flour

1. Pour pan drippings from roasted turkey into a 2-cup glass measure. Scrape browned bits from bottom of pan into cup. Skim and reserve fat from drippings. If necessary, add enough

melted butter to reserved fat to equal ¼ cup. Add enough broth to drippings in measuring cup to equal 2 cups total.
2. Pour the ¼ cup fat into a medium saucepan (discard remaining fat). Stir in flour. Cook and stir over medium heat 1 minute. Add drippings mixture, stirring until smooth. Cook and stir over medium heat until bubbly, about 1 minute. Season to taste with salt and pepper. Makes 8 servings.
EACH SERVING *74 cal, 7 g fat, 7 mg chol, 288 mg sodium, 3 g carb, 0 g fiber, 1 g pro.*

Bacon-Onion Gravy Prepare Basic Gravy as directed in Step 1. In a large saucepan cook 2 slices of bacon over medium heat until crisp. Remove bacon from saucepan; drain. Crumble once cooled. Set aside. Reserve 1 Tbsp. bacon drippings in saucepan. Add ¼ cup chopped onion. Cook and stir 2 minutes. Add 2 tsp. cider vinegar; cook until evaporated. Add the ¼ cup fat to saucepan. Stir in ¼ cup flour. Cook and stir over medium heat 1 minute. Add drippings mixture; stir until smooth. Cook and stir over medium heat until bubbly, about 1 minute. Stir in bacon. Season to taste with salt and pepper. Makes 12 servings.
EACH SERVING *67 cal, 6 g fat, 10 mg chol, 162 mg sodium, 3 g carb, 0 g fiber, 1 g pro.*

Cranberry BBQ Turkey

Bold flavors come from a heady spice rub of brown sugar, cumin, chili, and paprika. For a final kick of sweet heat, brush on barbecue sauce—made from cranberry sauce, cranberry-pomegranate juice, chili sauce, and fresh herbs.

PREP 40 min. ROAST 3 hr.
STAND 15 min. OVEN 325°F

    2 Tbsp. packed dark brown sugar
    2 tsp. garlic powder
    2 tsp. sweet paprika
    1 tsp. ground black pepper
    1 tsp. chili powder
    ½ tsp. kosher salt
    ½ tsp. ground cumin
    ½ tsp. dry mustard
    1 12- to 14-lb. fresh or thawed
       turkey
       Olive oil
    1 recipe Cranberry BBQ Sauce
       Kumquats (optional)

1. Preheat oven to 325°F. For spice mix, in a small bowl stir together brown sugar, garlic powder, paprika, black pepper, chili powder, salt, cumin, and dry mustard. Set spice mixture aside.
2. Remove neck and giblets from turkey; discard. Rinse turkey; pat dry with paper towels. Starting at neck end, loosen skin by sliding your fingers underneath, separating skin from meat. Rub spice mixture under skin, over breast, and toward thighs.
3. Rub 2 Tbsp. olive oil over turkey. Pull neck skin to back; fasten with a small skewer. Tuck wings under breast. Loop kitchen string around drumsticks; tie securely to tail. Place turkey, breast side up, on a rack in a roasting pan. Insert an oven-going meat thermometer into center of an inside thigh muscle, avoiding bone. Cover loosely with foil.
4. Roast 2¾ hours. Remove foil. Roast 15 to 45 minutes more, or until thermometer reaches 175°F. Generously brush turkey with ½ cup

Cranberry BBQ Sauce the last 15 minutes. Remove from oven.
5. Cover turkey with foil. Let stand 15 minutes. Remove foil. Sprinkle with fresh oregano. Serve with remaining Cranberry BBQ Sauce and kumquats. Makes 8 servings plus leftovers.
Cranberry BBQ Sauce In a medium saucepan cook 1 large finely chopped onion in 1 Tbsp. olive oil over medium heat, about 6 minutes. Add one 14-oz. can whole cranberry sauce, 1 cup cranberry-pomegranate juice, ⅔ cup chili sauce, 1 Tbsp. balsamic vinegar, and 1 tsp. dry mustard. Bring to boiling; reduce heat. Simmer, uncovered, 25 minutes or until thickened. Stir in 2 Tbsp. snipped fresh oregano; cook 1 minute more. Makes 2½ cups.
EACH 4-OZ. SERVING 427 cal, 15 g fat, 174 mg chol, 819 mg sodium, 24 g carb, 1 g fiber, 48 g pro.

KID FRIENDLY

Cilantro and Lime Rubbed Turkey

Herby, citrusy, and incredibly bright, this turkey is flavored with an herb- and lime-zest mixture tucked under the skin. Sprinkle fresh cilantro right before serving.

PREP 45 min. ROAST 3 hr.
STAND 15 min. OVEN 325°F

    ½ cup firmly packed cilantro leaves
    ½ cup firmly packed Italian flat-leaf
       parsley leaves
    1 Tbsp. butter, melted
    1 Tbsp. chopped shallot
    1 tsp. finely shredded lime peel
    1 12- to 14-lb. fresh or thawed
       turkey
       Kosher salt
    4 sprigs fresh cilantro
    2 carrots, cut into 3-inch pieces
    1 medium onion, quartered
       Butter
    2 Tbsp. honey
    1 recipe Basic Pan Gravy, page 267

1. Preheat oven to 325°F. In a food processor combine cilantro, parsley, butter, shallot, and lime peel. Add ½ tsp. salt and ¼ tsp. pepper. Cover and process with on/off pulses until a chunky paste forms. Set aside.
2. Remove neck and giblets from turkey; discard. Rinse turkey; pat dry with paper towels. Starting at neck end of turkey, loosen skin by sliding your fingers underneath, separating skin from meat. Rub half the herb mixture under skin, over breast, and toward thighs.
3. Sprinkle body cavity with kosher salt and pepper. Insert cilantro sprigs, carrots, and onion. Pull neck skin to back; fasten with a small skewer. Tuck wings under breast. Loop kitchen string around drumsticks; tie securely to tail. Place turkey, breast side up, on a rack in a roasting pan. Brush melted butter over turkey. Insert an oven-going meat thermometer into center of an inside thigh muscle, avoiding bone. Cover loosely with foil.
4. Roast 2¾ hours. Meanwhile, in a small saucepan melt ¼ cup butter. Stir in honey and remaining herb mixture; set aside. Remove foil. Roast 15 to 45 minutes more or until thermometer reaches 175°F, occasionally brushing with honey-butter mixture. Remove from oven.
5. Cover turkey with foil; let stand 15 minutes. Remove and discard vegetables from inside turkey. Top with fresh cilantro. Serve with Basic Pan Gravy. Makes 8 servings plus leftovers.
EACH 4-OZ. SERVING 544 cal, 27 g fat, 277 mg chol, 525 mg sodium, 7 g carb, 1 g fiber, 70 g pro.

CRANBERRY
BBQ TURKEY

CILANTRO AND
LIME RUBBED
TURKEY

Spiced Turkey with Cherry-Pear Glaze

Stuffing the bird with lemons, pears, and a mix of aromatic spices seasons it from the inside out. Combining the ingredients in the cherry-pear glaze ensures that flavors come through in every slice.

PREP **25 min.** ROAST **3 hr.**
STAND **15 min.** OVEN **325°F**

1 12- to 14-lb. fresh or thawed turkey
Kosher salt and ground black pepper
2 medium pears, quartered
2 lemons, quartered
2 3-inch cinnamon sticks
2 ½-inch-thick slices fresh ginger
8 whole allspice
1 recipe Cherry-Pear Glaze

1. Preheat oven to 325°F. Remove neck and giblets from turkey; discard. Rinse turkey; pat dry with paper towels. Sprinkle body cavity with kosher salt and pepper. Fill cavity with pears, lemons, cinnamon sticks, ginger, and allspice. Pull neck skin to back; fasten with a small skewer. Tuck wings under breast. Loop kitchen string around drumsticks; tie securely to tail. Place turkey, breast side up, on a rack in a roasting pan. Brush olive oil over turkey. Sprinkle with additional salt and pepper. Insert an oven-going meat thermometer into center of an inside thigh muscle, avoiding bone. Cover loosely with foil.

2. Roast 2¾ hours. Remove foil. Roast 15 to 45 minutes more, or until thermometer reaches 175°F. The last 20 minutes of roasting generously brush turkey with about ½ cup of the Cherry-Pear Glaze Remove from oven.

3. Cover turkey with foil; let stand 15 minutes. Transfer turkey to a cutting board. Remove and discard fruits and spices from inside turkey. Serve with remaining Cherry-Pear Glaze. Makes 8 servings plus leftovers.

Cherry-Pear Glaze In a medium saucepan combine 3 cups pear juice, two cinnamon sticks, two ½-inch slices fresh ginger, and 6 whole allspice. Bring to boiling; reduce heat. Simmer, uncovered, about 30 minutes or until reduced to 1½ cups. Using a slotted spoon, remove spices; discard. Stir in ½ cup cherry preserves, 2 Tbsp. red wine vinegar, and ¼ tsp. salt. Makes 2 cups.

EACH 4-OZ. SERVING *516 cal, 19 g fat, 249 mg chol, 364 mg sodium, 19 g carb, 1 g fiber, 69 g pro.*

LET'S TALK TURKEY

• Recommendations vary, but it's better to err on the side of caution when thawing a turkey. Refrigerate the turkey for 24 hours per each 3½–4 lbs. For a 12-lb. turkey, about 3 days.

• When buying a bird, allow 1 lb. per serving. A 12-lb. turkey should feed 10 to 12 guests.

• To get an accurate temperature reading, ensure your thermometer is correctly calibrated (look for directions on packaging). Insert the thermometer into the thickest part of the thigh, avoiding bone. The turkey is done when the temperature reaches 175°F. If the bird is stuffed, stuffing should reach 165°F.

• Cover turkey with foil before putting it in the oven. When 45 minutes of roasting time remains, remove the foil so the skin can brown and crisp.

• After the turkey is roasted to 175°F, remove from oven, cover with foil, and allow to rest in the roasting pan for 15 to 20 minutes. Resting or standing before carving allows juices to redistribute for better flavor. Remove stuffing from bird before carving.

Whip up kitchen magic by prepping a few dishes a day ahead. With a head start, there's no worry about serving dinner on time.

KID FRIENDLY

Sour Cream and Corn Mashers

Sautéed corn gets stirred into mashed potatoes with a swirl of sour cream for tangy flavor and surprise texture. The cornflake and smoky paprika topping adds delicious crunch.

PREP 25 min. COOK 15 min.
BAKE 5 min. OVEN 450°F

- 2 lbs. russet potatoes, peeled and chopped
- 1 tsp. olive oil
- 1 cup fresh or frozen corn kernels, thawed
- 6 green onions, cut into 1-inch pieces
- 1 clove garlic, minced
- ½ cup sour cream
- 2 Tbsp. butter
- ½ tsp. kosher salt
- ¼ tsp. freshly ground black pepper
- 2 cups cornflakes, crushed
- 1 tsp. smoked paprika
- 3 Tbsp. butter, melted

1. Preheat oven to 450°F. In a large saucepan cook potatoes in lightly salted boiling water, covered, 15 minutes or until tender; drain. Return to saucepan.
2. Meanwhile, heat oil in a large skillet over medium heat. Add corn, green onions, and garlic. Cook and stir 5 minutes or until vegetables are tender; set aside.
3. Mash potatoes with potato masher until smooth. Stir in sour cream, the 2 Tbsp. butter, salt, and pepper. Stir in corn mixture.

4. Transfer to a 1½-quart baking dish. Top with cornflakes and sprinkle with paprika. Drizzle with the 3 Tbsp. butter. Bake 5 minutes or just until browned. Makes 8 servings plus leftovers.
Make ahead Prepare as above through Step 3. Transfer potato mixture to a storage container. Cover and chill up to 24 hours. To serve, transfer mixture to a large saucepan; heat through. Continue with Step 4.
EACH ½-CUP SERVING *163 cal, 8 g fat, 20 mg chol, 205 mg sodium, 21 g carb, 2 g fiber, 3 g pro.*

KID FRIENDLY

White Cheddar Mashed Sweet Potatoes

Take advantage of make-ahead-friendly sweet potatoes, and do the prep a day in advance. Play up the savory side by adding a handful of white cheddar and a topping of fried sage on the big day.

PREP 15 min. COOK 20 min.

- 2 lb. sweet potatoes, peeled and chopped
- ½ cup half-and-half or light cream
- ¼ cup butter
- 3 oz. white cheddar cheese, shredded
- 1 tsp. snipped fresh sage
- ½ tsp. salt
- ¼ tsp. ground pepper
- 2 medium cooking apples, cored and sliced

- 2 Tbsp. butter
- ¼ cup olive oil
- 8 whole sage leaves

1. In a large saucepan cook potatoes in lightly salted boiling water, covered, 15 minutes or until tender; drain. Return to saucepan. Add half-and-half and butter. Mash potatoes with a potato masher until smooth. Stir in cheese, snipped sage, salt, and pepper.
2. Meanwhile, in a large skillet cook apples in the 2 Tbsp. butter over medium heat 7 to 10 minutes or until lightly browned, stirring occasionally. Remove from skillet. Cover; keep warm.
3. In the same skillet heat olive oil over medium heat. Fry sage leaves for 30 to 60 seconds or until crisp.
4. To serve, transfer potato mixture to a serving bowl. Top with apple mixture and fried sage leaves. Makes 8 servings plus leftovers.
Make ahead Prepare as above through Step 1. Transfer potato mixture to a storage container. Cover and chill up to 24 hours. Transfer to a large saucepan; heat through. Continue with Step 2.
EACH ½-CUP SERVING *213 cal, 15 g fat, 29 mg chol, 192 mg sodium, 17 g carb, 3 g fiber, 3 g pro.*

SOUR CREAM AND CORN MASHERS

WHITE CHEDDAR MASHED SWEET POTATOES

LEMON GARLIC
MASHED POTATOES

Lemon Garlic Mashed Potatoes

Silky olive oil and starchy reserved water from cooking transform these potatoes into edible clouds. A sprinkle of capers, lemon peel, and fresh parsley delivers the vibrant finish.

PREP 20 min. COOK 20 min.

- 3 lb. Yukon gold potatoes, scrubbed and cut into chunks
- 4 cloves garlic, halved
- 3 Tbsp. olive oil
- 2 Tbsp. butter
- ¼ tsp. salt
- ¼ tsp. freshly ground black pepper
- 2 Tbsp. capers, drained and chopped
- ⅓ cup fresh Italian flat-leaf parsley
- 2 tsp. finely shredded lemon peel
- 1 lemon half

1. In a large saucepan cook potatoes and garlic in lightly salted boiling water, covered, 20 to 25 minutes or until tender.

2. Drain potatoes, reserving 1 cup water. Mash potatoes with a potato masher until smooth. Add 2 Tbsp. of the olive oil, the butter, salt, pepper, and enough of the reserved water to reach desired consistency. Stir to combine.

3. Transfer potatoes to a serving dish. Top with capers, parsley, and lemon peel. Drizzle with remaining olive oil. Squeeze lemon juice over before serving. Makes 8 servings plus leftovers.

Make ahead Prepare through Step 2. Transfer potato mixture to a storage container. Cover and chill up to 24 hours. Transfer potato mixture to a large saucepan; heat through. Continue with Step 3.

EACH ½-CUP SERVING *98 cal, 4 g fat, 4 mg chol, 130 mg sodium, 15 g carb, 2 g fiber, 2 g pro.*

CARAMELIZED ONION AND CARROT STUFFING

Caramelized Onion and Carrot Stuffing

The rich, deep sweetness of caramelized onions and roasted carrots epitomizes classic Thanksgiving flavors. A hint of tanginess emerges from the sourdough bread.

PREP 30 min. COOK 20 min.
BAKE 45 min. OVEN 325°F

- ¼ cup olive oil
- 2 large sweet onions, coarsely chopped
- 4 medium carrots, cut in chunks and/or sliced
- ⅓ cup butter
- ¼ cup torn fresh sage or 1 Tbsp. dried sage, crushed
- ½ tsp. kosher salt
- ½ tsp. freshly ground black pepper
- 12 cups dry sourdough and/or wheat bread cubes
- 1 to 1½ cups chicken broth

1. In a 4- to 5-quart Dutch oven heat oil over medium-low heat. Add onions and carrots. Cook, covered, for 15 minutes or until vegetables are tender, stirring occasionally. Uncover; increase heat to medium-high and cook 5 to 8 minutes more or until onions are golden brown, stirring frequently. Remove from heat. Add butter. Stir until melted. Add sage, salt, and pepper. Add bread; toss to combine. Drizzle with broth to moisten; toss lightly to combine.

2. Place stuffing in a 3-quart casserole. Bake, covered, alongside turkey for 45 to 60 minutes or until heated through. Top with fresh sage, if desired. Makes 8 servings plus leftovers.

Make ahead Prepare as above through Step 1. Transfer stuffing to the casserole. Cover and chill up to 24 hours. Bake, covered, 60 minutes.

Note Stuffing can be used in one 12- to 14-lb. turkey.

EACH ½-CUP SERVING *161 cal, 7 g fat, 11 mg chol, 306 mg sodium, 19 g carb, 1 g fiber, 4 g pro.*

Need to take a dish? Stuffings and dressings have take-it-then-bake-it potential. Assemble at home then pop it in the oven when you arrive at your destination. Voilà! Piping hot and delicious.

KID FRIENDLY

Double-Corn Cornbread Dressing

Fresh corn and hearty homemade cornbread—two times the corn—plus spinach and a sprinkle of crushed red pepper make for a mouthwatering version of traditional cornbread stuffing.

PREP 30 min. BAKE 1 hr. + 10 min.
COOK 6 min. OVEN 400°F/325°F

- 1½ cups cornmeal
- 1¼ cups all-purpose flour
- 3 Tbsp. sugar
- 4 tsp. baking powder
- 1 tsp. salt
- 1½ cups milk
- 3 eggs
- ⅓ cup butter, melted
- 3 cups fresh or frozen corn kernels, thawed
- 1 large red onion, cut into wedges
- ½ cup butter
- ½ tsp. crushed red pepper
- 6 cups fresh spinach
- 1¾ to 2¾ cups chicken broth
- Italian flat-leaf parsley

1. For cornbread, preheat oven to 400°F. Grease a 13×9×2-inch baking pan; set aside. In a large bowl stir together cornmeal, flour, sugar, baking powder, and salt; set aside.
2. In a medium bowl whisk together milk, eggs, and the ⅓ cup melted butter. Stir milk mixture into cornmeal mixture just until moistened. Pour batter into prepared pan.
3. Bake 20 minutes or until edges are golden. Cool cornbread on a wire rack 30 minutes. Cut into 1-inch cubes. Makes about 10 cups.
4. For Double-Corn Cornbread Dressing, preheat oven to 325°F. Spread cool cornbread cubes on a baking pan. Bake, uncovered, 10 to 15 minutes, stirring once. Cool on a wire rack.
5. In a large skillet cook corn and onion in the ½ cup butter over medium-high heat for 6 to 8 minutes or until browned. Stir in crushed red pepper, ½ tsp. salt, and ¼ tsp. pepper. In an extra-large bowl combine cornbread cubes, corn mixture, and spinach. Drizzle with broth to moisten; toss lightly to combine.

6. Spoon into a 3-quart baking dish. Bake, uncovered, 40 minutes or until top is browned and dressing is heated through. Top with chopped Italian flat-leaf parsley. Makes 8 servings.
Make ahead Prepare through Step 5. Transfer dressing to a baking dish. Cover and chill up to 24 hours. Bake, covered, for 50 to 60 minutes or until heated through.
EACH ½-CUP SERVING *136 cal, 7 g fat, 36 mg chol, 319 mg sodium, 17 g carb, 1 g fiber, 3 g pro.*

CREAMY BARLEY AND
CHARD DRESSING

Creamy Barley and Chard Dressing

Grains in a dressing? You bet! Make the most of barley's nutty flavor and toothsome texture by precooking it in chicken broth before tossing with greens and squash. For creaminess, mix in Parmesan cheese right before baking.

PREP **1 hr.** COOK **10 min.**
BAKE **25 min.** OVEN **325°F**

- 1¼ cups pearled barley (not quick-cooking)
- 4 cups chicken broth
- ¾ tsp. cracked black pepper
- 2 cups chopped onion
- 1½ lb. winter squash, peeled, seeded, and cut into 1-inch pieces
- ½ cup butter
- 5 cups chopped Swiss chard or spinach
- 1 cup walnuts, toasted and chopped (see tip, page 35)
- 1½ cups finely shredded Parmesan cheese

1. Preheat oven to 325°F. Cook barley according to package directions using chicken broth in place of water and adding cracked black pepper.
2. Meanwhile, in a large skillet cook onion and squash in butter over medium heat, covered, just until tender, stirring occasionally, about 10 minutes. Remove from heat. Stir in cooked barley, chard, walnuts, and Parmesan cheese.
3. Transfer to a 3-quart rectangular baking dish. Bake, uncovered, 25 to 30 minutes or until heated through. Makes 8 servings.
Make ahead Prepare through Step 2. Transfer dressing to a baking dish. Cover and chill up to 24 hours. Bake, uncovered, for 40 minutes or until heated through.
EACH ½-CUP SERVING *189 cal, 12 g fat, 19 mg chol, 374 mg sodium, 17 g carb, 4 g fiber, 6 g pro.*

HARVEST FRUIT AND CHEESE STUFFING

Harvest Fruit and Cheese Stuffing

Take a cue from a tantalizing cheese plate and combine dried cherries and crisp pears with sharp white cheddar for a richly flavored stuffing. Make the stuffing with the whole wheat bread or swap in a favorite for your version.

PREP **45 min.** BAKE **45 min.**
OVEN **325°F**

- 3 medium leeks, halved, rinsed, and sliced
- 1 cup thinly sliced celery
- ½ cup butter
- ¼ tsp. freshly ground black pepper
- ⅛ tsp. ground cloves
- 8 cups dry whole wheat bread cubes
- 3 large firm ripe pears, cut in wedges
- ½ cup dried cherries, coarsely chopped
- ½ cup dried apricots, chopped
- 1½ cups chicken broth
- 8 oz. white cheddar cheese, shredded (2 cups)

1. Preheat oven to 325°F. In a large skillet cook leeks and celery in butter until tender, about 5 minutes. Stir in pepper and cloves.
2. In an extra-large bowl combine leek mixture, bread cubes, pears, cherries, and apricots. Drizzle with broth; toss to combine. Stir in cheese.
3. Transfer to a 3-quart casserole. Bake, covered, 45 to 60 minutes or until heated through. Makes 8 servings.
Make ahead Prepare through Step 2. Transfer stuffing to a casserole. Cover and chill up to 24 hours. Bake, covered, for 60 minutes or until heated through.
Note Stuffing can be used in one 12- to 14-lb. turkey.
EACH ½-CUP SERVING *167 cal, 9 g fat, 24 mg chol, 250 mg sodium, 17 g carb, 3 g fiber, 6 g pro.*

Can't live without green bean casserole? That's OK. Just add to the mix with these big-flavor sides. One might become a new favorite.

KID FRIENDLY

Maple-Glazed Squash with Pancetta

Bacon lovers will squeal over crispy bits of pancetta peeking between slices of squash and clementines. The squash cooks in the tasty drippings, adding rich flavor to the whole dish.

PREP 30 min. COOK 21 min.

- 3 oz. pancetta, chopped
- 2 Tbsp. butter
- 2 1½-lb. butternut squash, halved lengthwise, peeled, seeded, and cut crosswise into ¼-inch slices
- ½ cup water
- 3 Tbsp. maple syrup
- ½ tsp. salt
- ½ cup unpeeled* tiny clementines, cut into ½-inch wedges and seeded
- ½ cup orange juice
  Cracked black pepper

1. In a large skillet cook and stir pancetta over medium heat for 5 to 7 minutes or until crisp. Using a slotted spoon, transfer to paper towels to drain. Set aside. Reserve drippings in skillet.
2. Add butter to skillet with pancetta drippings. Add squash. Cook over medium-high heat 4 to 5 minutes, just until squash starts to soften, turning occasionally. Carefully add the water, maple syrup, and salt. Reduce heat.

Simmer, covered, 8 minutes, turning occasionally. Stir in clementines and orange juice. Increase heat to medium-high. Cook, uncovered, 4 to 6 minutes, turning squash occasionally, until orange juice has reduced slightly and squash is tender. Remove from heat.
3. Transfer to a serving dish. Sprinkle with cracked black pepper. Top with pancetta. Makes 8 servings.
*Clementine peels are so thin, they soften during cooking.
EACH SERVING *168 cal, 6 g fat, 11 mg chol, 239 mg sodium, 28 g carb, 4 g fiber, 4 g pro.*

Brown Butter Brussels Sprouts and Apples

Butter becomes fragrant and nutty when cooked low and slow on the stovetop. Infuse it with fresh thyme to coat crisp-tender Brussels sprouts that look as good as they taste.

PREP 15 min. COOK 18 min.
STAND 3 min.

- 2 lb. Brussels sprouts
- ¼ cup butter
- ½ tsp. salt
- 2 small Braeburn or other cooking apples, cored and cut into thin slices
- 2 Tbsp. fresh thyme leaves
- ¼ cup walnuts, toasted and chopped (see tip, page 35)
  Crushed red pepper (optional)

1. Line a baking pan with paper towels; set aside. Remove wilted outer leaves from Brussels sprouts; wash and halve.
2. In a large saucepan cook Brussels sprouts in boiling water, covered, 1 to 2 minutes; drain. Immediately plunge Brussels sprouts in ice water. Let stand for 3 minutes or until cool; drain. Transfer to prepared baking pan. Pat dry with paper towels.
3. Meanwhile, in a large skillet melt butter over low heat. Cook, stirring often, until the butter begins to brown, about 10 to 12 minutes. Add Brussels sprouts and salt. Cook, turning occasionally, about 5 minutes. Add apples and thyme. Cook 2 minutes more or until Brussels sprouts are browned and apple is just tender. Transfer to a serving bowl. Sprinkle with toasted walnuts and, if desired, crushed red pepper. Makes 8 servings.
EACH SERVING *143 cal, 9 g fat, 15 mg chol, 221 mg sodium, 16 g carb, 5 g fiber, 4 g pro.*

MAPLE-GLAZED SQUASH WITH PANCETTA

BROWN BUTTER BRUSSELS SPROUTS AND APPLES

ROASTED CAULIFLOWER WITH CRANBERRIES

Roasted Cauliflower with Cranberries

Dress up cauliflower by roasting it with cranberries that almost burst as they cook. A sweet and tangy balsamic drizzle makes the dish a crowd-pleaser.

PREP 15 min. ROAST 30 min. OVEN 450°F

- 2 medium heads cauliflower (1½ to 2 lbs. each), broken into florets
- 1 large yellow or red onion, cut into wedges
- 3 Tbsp. olive oil
- 1 tsp. kosher salt, divided
- 1½ cups fresh or frozen cranberries
- ¼ cup balsamic vinegar
- ¼ cup honey
- ¼ tsp. freshly cracked pepper
  Mint leaves

1. Preheat oven to 450°F. Place cauliflower and onion in a baking pan. Drizzle with olive oil and sprinkle with ½ tsp. of the salt. Stir to coat. Spread in an even layer. Roast, uncovered, 30 minutes or until tender, stirring in cranberries halfway through cooking time.
2. Meanwhile, in a small saucepan whisk together balsamic vinegar, honey, the remaining salt, and pepper. Simmer, uncovered, until sightly thickened, about 10 minutes. Pour over cauliflower mixture; stir to coat. Transfer to a serving dish. Sprinkle with mint. Makes 8 servings.

EACH SERVING *135 cal, 5 g fat, 0 mg chol, 281 mg sodium, 21 g carb, 4 g fiber, 3 g pro.*

GARLICKY CRUMB-COATED BROCCOLINI

Garlicky Crumb-Coated Broccolini

Broccolini doused in buttery, cheesy bread crumbs will win over even those who shun veggies. Green olives and yellow bell pepper add delectable sweetness and a salty pop.

PREP 20 min. COOK 5 min. ROAST 15 min. OVEN 425°F

- 2 lbs. Broccolini or broccoli, trimmed
- 1 cup soft bread crumbs
- ¼ cup olive oil
- ¼ cup butter
- 3 Tbsp. finely chopped fresh garlic
- ½ cup grated Parmesan cheese
- ⅓ cup chopped pitted green olives
- ⅓ cup finely chopped yellow sweet pepper
- 1 Tbsp. finely shredded lemon peel
  Lemon wedges

1. Preheat oven to 425°F. Arrange Broccolini in a roasting pan. Sprinkle with bread crumbs.
2. In a small saucepan heat olive oil, butter, and garlic over low heat. Cook and stir about 5 minutes. Drizzle oil mixture over Broccolini. Sprinkle with Parmesan.
3. Roast, uncovered, 15 to 20 minutes or just until Broccolini is tender. Sprinkle with olives, sweet pepper, and lemon peel to serve. Pass lemon wedges. Makes 8 servings.

EACH SERVING *198 cal, 15 g fat, 20 mg chol, 281 mg sodium, 12 g carb, 4 g fiber, 6 g pro.*

Combine pumpkin with pureed sweet potatoes for an extra layer of flavor in a flaky peanut crust. The real fun is in the can't-stop-snacking-on-it topping: a playfully sweet, salty, nutty streusel made with crunchy cheese crackers.

Sweet Potato-Pumpkin Pie with Streusel Crunch

PREP 45 min. BAKE 2 hr. + 10 min.
CHILL 4 hr. COOL 30 min.
OVEN 375°F

- 1 recipe Peanut Piecrust
- 1¾ lb. sweet potatoes, scrubbed
- 1 15-oz. can pumpkin puree
- ¾ cup granulated sugar
- ½ tsp. salt
- ½ tsp. ground cinnamon
- ¼ tsp. ground nutmeg
- 4 eggs, lightly beaten
- 1 cup buttermilk
- ½ cup whipping cream
- 1 recipe Streusel Crunch

1. Prepare Peanut Pie Crust; set aside.
2. Preheat oven to 375°F. Line a baking sheet with foil. Place sweet potatoes on prepared baking sheet. Bake about 1 hour or until fork tender. Remove from oven; cool. Peel sweet potatoes; discard skin. Transfer to a food processor. Cover and process until smooth. Makes 2 cups.
3. For filling, in a large mixing bowl combine sweet potato and pumpkin purees, sugar, salt, cinnamon, and nutmeg. Stir to combine. Add eggs; beat lightly until combined. Stir in buttermilk and cream.
4. Pour filling into prepared crust. Cover edge of piecrust with foil. Bake in the 375°F oven for 50 minutes. Remove foil. Bake 20 minutes more or until center jiggles slightly when gently shaken. Cool on a wire rack at least 30 minutes. Cover and chill for 4 to 24 hours before serving. To serve, sprinkle with Streusel Crunch. Makes 10 servings.

Peanut Piecrust Place 1½ cups flour, ½ tsp. salt, and ½ cup salted peanuts in the bowl of a food processor. Cover; pulse to combine. Add ½ cup cold cut-up butter. Pulse until pieces are pea size. With processor running, pour in ¼ cup ice water, 1 Tbsp. at a time, just until dough starts to come together. Gather pastry in a ball, kneading gently until it holds together. Slightly flatten pastry on a lightly floured surface. Roll from center to edges into a circle about 13 inches in diameter. Wrap pastry around rolling pin; unroll into a 10-inch deep-dish pie plate, easing it in without stretching. Trim to ½ inch beyond edge of pie plate. Fold extra pastry under. Crimp as desired.

Streusel Crunch Preheat oven to 250°F. Line a baking sheet with foil; set aside. In a small bowl combine ½ cup broken cheese crackers (such as Cheez-It), ¼ cup salted chopped peanuts, 2 Tbsp. melted butter, and 1 Tbsp. brown sugar. Stir to coat. Spread on prepared baking sheet. Bake 25 minutes, stirring halfway through. Remove from oven; cool completely.
EACH SERVING *479 cal, 25 g fat, 122 mg chol, 544 mg sodium, 56 g carb, 5 g fiber, 10 g pro.*

Velvety, not-too-sweet maple in this classic pie is just enough tweak to make even traditionalists beg for seconds. Prepare the sparkling pecan brittle up to a week ahead, then sprinkle on just before serving.

KID FRIENDLY

Maple Pumpkin Pie with Salted Pecan Brittle

PREP 45 min. BAKE 55 min.
CHILL 2 hr. OVEN 375°F

- 1 recipe Single-Crust Pie Pastry
- 1 15-oz. can pumpkin puree
- ⅔ cup pure maple syrup
- ¼ cup packed brown sugar
- 1 tsp. vanilla bean paste or vanilla extract
- ½ tsp. salt
- 3 eggs, slightly beaten
- ¾ cup milk
- 1 recipe Salted Pecan Brittle

1. Prepare Pastry for Single-Crust Pie. Preheat oven to 375°F.
2. For filling, in a large bowl combine pumpkin, maple syrup, brown sugar, vanilla, and salt. Add eggs; beat lightly with a fork until combined. Gradually add milk. Stir to combine.
3. Carefully pour filling in pastry shell. To prevent overbrowning, cover edge of pie crust with foil. Bake for 30 minutes. Remove foil. Bake 25 to 30 minutes more or until a knife inserted near center comes out clean. Cool on wire rack. Cover; chill 2 hours. To serve, top with Salted Pecan Brittle. Makes 10 servings.

Single-Crust Pie Pastry Stir together 1¼ cups flour and ¼ tsp. salt. Using a pastry blender, cut in ⅓ cup shortening until pieces are pea size. Sprinkle 1 Tbsp. cold water over part of the mixture; gently toss with a fork. Push moistened dough to the side of the bowl. Repeat moistening dough, using 1 Tbsp. of the water at a time, until all the dough is moistened (about 5 Tbsp. total). Form dough into a ball. Using your hands, slightly flatten pastry on a lightly floured surface. Roll pastry from center to edges into a circle about 12 inches in diameter. Wrap pastry around rolling pin; unroll into a 9-inch pie plate, easing it in without stretching. Trim pastry to ½ inch beyond edge of pie plate. Fold extra pastry under. Crimp as desired.

Salted Pecan Brittle Line a baking pan with foil and coat with nonstick cooking spray; set aside. In a small saucepan combine ¾ cup sugar and ¼ cup water. Stir over medium heat until sugar is dissolved. Bring to boiling. Boil, without stirring, until mixture turns a dark amber color, about 10 minutes. Stir in ¾ cup toasted chopped pecans and ½ tsp. sea salt. Remove from heat; immediately pour onto prepared baking pan, spreading evenly. Immediately sprinkle with ½ tsp. sea salt. Cool completely. Break into pieces. Store in a covered container at room temperature up to 1 week.
EACH SERVING *560 cal, 30 g fat, 113 mg chol, 566 mg sodium, 68 g carb, 3 g fiber, 7 g pro.*

TWICE AS NICE
Turns out there's more than one way to bake a pie. Here's how to make Maple Pumpkin Pie in a springform pan.

● Prepare Single-Crust Pie Pastry. Roll the pastry out to about ⅛-inch thickness and 12 inches in diameter. Drape pastry over an upturned 8-inch cake pan. Some of the dough will hang over the sides. Place a springform pan over the cake pan, then invert. Remove cake pan. Gently pat the pastry into the springform pan and about 2 inches up the sides. Crimp pastry with a fork. Place pan on a baking sheet. Pour in prepared filling. Bake as directed.

● For the whipped cream topping, beat 1 cup cold whipping cream with 1 tsp. vanilla and 1 Tbsp. granulated sugar until soft peaks form. Spread evenly over pie. Top with Salted Pecan Brittle and drizzle maple syrup.

Home Cooking

EASY HOLIDAY BAKING Whether served to guests or nibbled between shopping trips, these six go-to desserts keep the season sweet.

Citrus Upside-Down Cake

If you like, leave the skins on the clementines. The thin skins become tender and less bitter when baked.

PREP 30 min. BAKE 45 min.
COOL 20 min. OVEN 350°F

1⅓ cups packed brown sugar
 ½ cup butter, melted
 ¼ cup water
 5 to 6 grapefruits, navel oranges, and/or clementines, peeled and thinly sliced
 2 cups all-purpose flour
 2 tsp. baking powder
 ½ tsp. ground cardamom
 4 eggs, room temperature
 2 cups granulated sugar
 1 cup milk
 ¼ cup butter, cut up
    Sprigs of thyme

1. Preheat oven to 350°F. In a medium bowl stir together the brown sugar, ½ cup melted butter, and the water until combined; spread evenly in a 13×9×2-inch baking pan. Place fruit slices on brown sugar mixture. Set aside.
2. In a medium bowl stir together flour, baking powder, and ground cardamom; set aside. In a large mixing bowl beat eggs with an electric mixer on high speed about 4 minutes or until thick. Reduce speed to medium. Gradually add granulated sugar, beating 4 to 5 minutes or until light and fluffy. Add flour mixture; beat on low to medium speed just until combined (mixture will be thick).

3. In a small saucepan heat and stir milk and ¼ cup butter until butter is melted; add to batter, beating until combined. Carefully pour batter into prepared pan over citrus slices.
4. Bake 45 minutes or until a wooden toothpick inserted near center comes out clean (avoid checking cake too early, which might cause it to sink in the center). Remove; cool on a wire rack at least 20 minutes. Loosen sides of cake; invert onto a serving platter. Spoon any remaining brown sugar mixture in pan over top of cake. Cool. Makes 20 servings.
EACH SERVING *277 cal, 8 g fat, 56 mg chol, 134 mg sodium, 49 g carb, 1 g fiber, 3 g pro.*

No need for decoration—warm shades of citrus glisten on top of spongy cake that's beautiful right out of the oven. Serve it as edible abstract art.

The "wow" is in the slice. Beautiful whole pears in a chocolate-spice olive oil cake will make jaws drop.

KID FRIENDLY

Chocolate-Cinnamon Pear Loaf Cake

The showstopping quality of this loaf comes from the recipe's easiest step—placing whole pears right into the batter, which rises up around them.

PREP 20 min. COOK 20 min.
BAKE 50 min. COOL 10 min.
OVEN 350°F

      2 cups water
    ¼ cup granulated sugar
      1 Tbsp. orange juice
      1 3-inch stick cinnamon
      3 8-oz. Bartlett pears, peeled and cored from bottom, leaving stems intact
1⅔ cups all-purpose flour
    ¾ cup packed brown sugar
    ⅓ cup unsweetened cocoa powder
      1 tsp. baking powder
      1 tsp. ground cinnamon
    ½ tsp. baking soda
    ½ tsp. salt
      1 egg
      1 cup buttermilk
    ½ cup olive oil
      1 Tbsp. all-purpose flour
      1 Tbsp. unsweetened cocoa powder
    ¼ tsp. ground cinnamon
      3 oz. white baking chocolate

1. In a large saucepan combine the water, granulated sugar, orange juice, and cinnamon stick. Bring to boiling, stirring to dissolve sugar. Add pears. Return to boiling; reduce heat. Cover; simmer 20 to 25 minutes or until pears are tender. Remove from heat. Discard cinnamon stick. Drain well; cool pears.
2. Preheat oven to 350°F. Grease a 9×5×3-inch loaf pan; set aside. In a large bowl combine 1⅔ cups flour, brown sugar, ⅓ cup cocoa powder, baking powder, 1 tsp. cinnamon, baking soda, and salt. In a medium bowl whisk together egg, buttermilk, and olive oil. Add to flour mixture. Whisk until smooth.
3. Pour batter into prepared pan. In a small shallow dish combine 1 Tbsp. flour, 1 Tbsp. cocoa powder, and ¼ tsp. cinnamon. Roll pears in flour mixture to lightly coat. Place pears, stem sides up, into center of batter. Bake 50 to 55 minutes or until a toothpick inserted near center comes out clean. Remove; cool in pan on a wire rack 10 minutes. Remove from pan; cool completely.
4. In a small microwave-safe bowl microwave chocolate on high for 1 to 2 minutes or until melted, stirring every 30 seconds. Drizzle over loaf. Makes 10 servings.

EACH SERVING 352 cal, 15 g fat, 21 mg chol, 274 mg sodium, 53 g carb, 4 g fiber, 5 g pro.

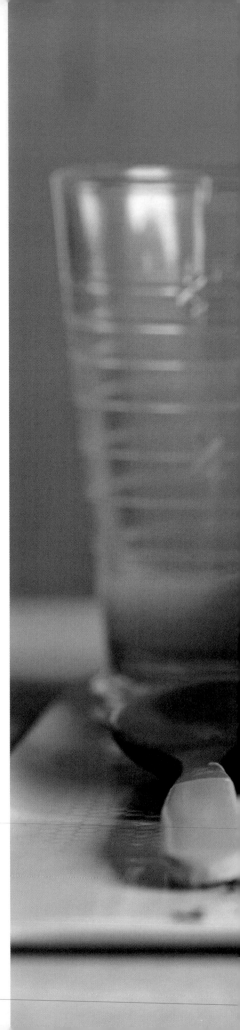

Beneath a blanket of rich pastry lies a whole apple stuffed with caramel and hazelnuts. Skip the crimp and simply lay the pastry over the no-fuss whole apple filling, pinching slightly at the corners.

Baked Apple Bowl Pies

Crunchy apples such as Granny Smiths, Braeburns, and Jonathans are all delicious in this recipe.

PREP 45 min.   BAKE 30 min.
STAND 20 min.   OVEN 350°F

- 2 cups all-purpose flour
- 3 Tbsp. sugar
- ½ tsp. salt
- ¼ cup butter
- ¼ cup shortening
- ⅓ cup milk
- 1 egg, separated
- 2 Tbsp. water
- 1 cup caramel ice cream topping
- ¼ cup chopped toasted hazelnuts*
- ½ tsp. apple pie spice
- 8 small baking apples, cored and peeled
- 2 Tbsp. butter, cut into 8 small pieces
- 1 lemon, cut in half
  Ground cinnamon
  Sage leaves (optional)

1. Preheat oven to 350°F. For pastry, in a large bowl combine the flour, 3 Tbsp. sugar, and salt. Cut in ¼ cup butter and shortening until pieces are pea size. In a small bowl combine milk, egg yolk, and 1 Tbsp. of the water. Add to flour mixture. Stir with a fork until combined. Gather and knead mixture gently until it forms a dough. Divide dough in half.

2. On a floured surface roll each dough half into an 8×8-inch square, about ⅛ inch thick. Using a pizza cutter, cut into four 4-inch squares. Cover; set aside.

3. In a small bowl combine ½ cup of the caramel topping, hazelnuts, and apple pie spice. Place each apple in a 6-oz. ramekin. Fill each apple center with caramel mixture. Dot each with 1 piece of butter. Squeeze lemon halves over apples. Lay a pastry square over each apple, pinching corners with fingers. Arrange ramekins in a foil-lined 15×10×1-inch baking pan. In a small bowl whisk together egg white and the remaining 1 Tbsp. water. Brush over pastry.

4. Bake 30 minutes or until pastry is golden brown and apples are tender. Remove; let stand in pan on wire rack 20 minutes. Serve warm with remaining caramel sauce and a sprinkle of cinnamon. Scatter with fresh sage leaves, if desired. Makes 8 servings.

Make ahead Cover apples with pastry squares, cover with plastic wrap, and chill up to 24 hours. Cover and chill egg white. When ready to bake, prepare egg white mixture and proceed as directed.

EACH SERVING *427 cal, 19 g fat, 47 mg chol, 292 mg sodium, 62 g carb, 4 g fiber, 5 g pro.*

***Tip** To toast hazelnuts, preheat oven to 350°F. Spread nuts in a single layer in a shallow baking pan. Bake for 8 to 10 minutes or until lightly toasted, stirring once to toast evenly. Cool nuts slightly. Place the warm nuts on a clean kitchen towel; rub with the towel to remove the loose skins.

No rolling or cutting necessary. Just pinch off portions of dough and pat them into rounds before laying them on the fruit filling.

KID FRIENDLY

Holiday Cobbler with Cinnamon Ice Cream

PREP 20 min. BAKE 35 min.
COOL 30 min. OVEN 375°F

1½ cups cranberries
½ cup dried red cherries
½ cup water
⅔ cup granulated sugar
3 Tbsp. all-purpose flour
2 lb. large plums, pitted and cut into chunks
1½ cups all-purpose flour
½ cup regular or quick-cooking rolled oats
2 Tbsp. packed brown sugar
1½ tsp. baking powder
½ tsp. salt
½ tsp. cream of tartar
6 Tbsp. butter
½ cup milk plus additional for brushing
   Purchased cinnamon ice cream

1. In a 10-inch cast-iron or other oven-going skillet combine cranberries, cherries, and the water. Stir in the granulated sugar and the 3 Tbsp. flour. Cook and stir over medium heat until hot and bubbly. Stir in plums. Set aside.
2. Preheat oven to 375°F. In a large bowl combine the 1½ cups flour, oats, brown sugar, baking powder, salt, and cream of tartar. Using a pastry blender, cut in butter until mixture resembles coarse crumbs. Make a well in center of flour mixture. Add milk all at once. Using a fork, stir just until moistened. Gently fold and press dough against the side of the bowl with your hands until it comes together.
3. Lightly flatten small portions of dough with your hands; lay on filling in skillet. Brush dough lightly with milk; sprinkle with additional brown sugar.

4. Bake 35 to 40 minutes or until topping is golden brown and filling is bubbly. (If necessary, cover with foil during last 10 minutes to prevent overbrowning.) Cool 30 minutes before serving. Serve with cinnamon ice cream. Makes 8 servings.
For a 9-inch deep-dish pie plate Prepare filling in a large saucepan; transfer to pie plate. Continue as directed.
EACH SERVING *526 cal, 19 g fat, 73 mg chol, 358 mg sodium, 85 g carb, 5 g fiber, 8 g pro.*

This fresh take on the traditionally dark, dense cake is studded with dried apples and apricots.

GINGERED
FRUITCAKE

Gingered Fruitcake

PREP 25 min.   BAKE 40 min.
COOL 10 min.   OVEN 350°F

- ¾ cup pecan halves, toasted (see tip, page 35)
- 2 cups all-purpose flour
- 1¼ cups sugar
- 1 Tbsp. baking powder
- ½ tsp. salt
- ½ cup milk
- ½ cup butter, softened
- 2 eggs
- 1 cup dried apples, chopped
- ⅔ cup dried apricots, chopped (not unsulphured)
- 2 Tbsp. grated fresh ginger
- 1 recipe Honey-Bourbon Butter (optional)

1. Preheat oven to 350°F. Grease and lightly flour a 9-inch springform pan.
2. Place ½ cup of the toasted pecans in a food processor; cover and process until finely ground; set aside.
3. In a large mixing bowl combine ground pecans, flour, sugar, baking powder, and salt. Add milk, butter, and eggs. Beat with an electric mixer on low speed until combined. Beat on medium speed for 1 minute. Fold in dried fruit and ginger. Transfer to prepared pan. Arrange remaining ¼ cup pecans on top of batter.
4. Bake about 40 minutes or until a wooden toothpick inserted near center comes out clean. Cool in pan on a wire rack 10 minutes. Remove sides of pan; cool completely. Remove bottom of pan.
5. To serve, pour Honey-Bourbon Butter over fruitcake, if desired. Makes 10 servings.

Honey-Bourbon Butter In a small saucepan melt ¼ cup butter. Add 2 Tbsp. bourbon and 1 Tbsp. honey. Stir until heated through.

To store Use bourbon or orange juice to moisten a large piece of 100-percent-cotton cheesecloth; wrap cake in cheesecloth. Place in a large resealable plastic bag or wrap in plastic wrap. Store in refrigerator up to 1 week.

EACH SERVING 451 cal, 20 g fat, 75 mg chol, 460 mg sodium, 64 g carb, 3 g fiber, 6 g pro.

Snickerdoodle Cheesecake

PREP 25 min.   STAND 30 min.
BAKE 40 min.   COOL 45 min.
CHILL 4 hr.   OVEN 350°F

- 2 8-oz. packages cream cheese
- 3 eggs, lightly beaten
- 1 10-oz. package shortbread cookies, finely crushed
- 1 Tbsp. sugar
- ¼ cup butter, melted
- 1 8-oz. carton sour cream
- 1 cup sugar
- 2 Tbsp. all-purpose flour
- 2 tsp. vanilla
- ½ tsp. ground cinnamon
- 1 Tbsp. sugar
- ½ tsp. ground cinnamon

1. Allow cream cheese and eggs to stand at room temperature 30 minutes. Meanwhile, preheat oven to 350°F. For crust, in a medium bowl stir together crushed cookies and 1 Tbsp. sugar. Stir in melted butter until combined. Press mixture onto bottom and 1½ inches up the sides of a 9-inch springform pan. Set aside.
2. In a large mixing bowl beat together cream cheese, sour cream, 1 cup sugar, flour, vanilla, and ½ tsp. cinnamon with an electric mixer on medium speed until smooth. Stir in eggs.
3. In a small bowl stir together 1 Tbsp. sugar and ½ tsp. cinnamon. Pour cream cheese mixture into pan, spreading evenly. Sprinkle with cinnamon-sugar mixture. Place springform pan in a shallow baking pan.
4. Bake 40 to 50 minutes or until a 2½-inch area around outside edge appears set when gently shaken. Cool in springform pan on a wire rack 15 minutes. Using a knife, loosen crust from sides of pan. Cool 30 minutes more. Remove sides of pan; cool cheesecake completely on wire rack. Cover and chill at least 4 hours before serving. Makes 12 servings.

EACH SERVING 412 cal, 27 g fat, 108 mg chol, 310 mg sodium, 39 g carb, 5 g pro.

Latke Basics

A Hanukkah classic, crisp and lacy potato pancakes are a welcome dish year round.

4-Step Potato Latkes

PREP 25 min. COOK 4 min. per batch

2	eggs, lightly beaten
2	cloves garlic, minced
¼	tsp. salt
1½	lbs. russet potatoes, peeled
2	Tbsp. vegetable oil

1. In a mixing bowl combine eggs, garlic, and salt. Using a box grater, finely shred potatoes. Add to egg mixture. Stir to combine.

2. Scoop out potato mixture ⅓ cup at a time. Using your hands, squeeze mixture over a separate bowl to remove excess liquid. Shape into 2½-inch patties.

3. In a 12-inch skillet heat oil over medium-high heat. Using a spatula, slide patties into pan. Cook about 4 minutes or until golden brown, turning once. Repeat with remaining potato mixture. Transfer to paper towels; drain. Keep warm.

4. Serve latkes with crème fraîche and fresh snipped dill or with applesauce, if desired. Makes 6 servings.

EACH SERVING *131 cal, 6 g fat, 62 mg chol, 223 mg sodium, 16 g carb, 1 g fiber, 4 g pro.*

Dinner on a Dollar

The savory-sweet topping of apples, onions, and ham turns on-hand pizza crust into an easy dinner.

Caramelized Onion and Apple Tart

Purchased pizza dough, your favorite homemade recipe, or even refrigerated pizza crust will work here, so use what you have on hand. Bake it on a pizza stone for an extra-crispy crust.

PREP 30 min. COOK 15 min.
BAKE 18 min. OVEN 450°F

- 2   Tbsp. butter
- 1   large red onion, thinly sliced
- 1   lb. pizza dough
- 2   oz. thinly sliced cooked ham
- 1   small red cooking apple, cored, quartered, and thinly sliced
- ⅔   cup shredded Swiss cheese
     Fresh snipped thyme

1. Place oven rack in lowest position. Preheat oven to 450°F. Lightly coat a large baking sheet with nonstick cooking spray; set aside.
2. For caramelized onions, in a large skillet melt butter over medium-low heat. Add sliced onion. Cook, covered, about 12 minutes or until tender, stirring occasionally. Uncover; cook and stir over medium-high heat for 3 to 5 minutes more. Remove from heat. Set aside.
3. On a lightly floured surface roll out pizza dough into a 13×9-inch rectangle. Transfer to prepared pan. Using your hands, shape dough to build up edges. Prick generously with a fork. Bake until puffed and lightly crisped, about 8 minutes. Remove from oven.
4. Top crust with ham, then layer on caramelized onions, apple slices, and cheese. Bake 10 minutes more or until crust is crispy and cheese is melted. Sprinkle with fresh thyme. Makes 6 servings.
EACH SERVING *304 cal, 10 g fat, 29 mg chol, 560 mg sodium, 41 g carb, 2 g fiber, 10 g pro.*

**WHITE CHOCOLATE
PEPPERMINT ICE CREAM**

december

HOLIDAYS From rich cookies (courtesy of Dorie Greenspan) to hidden cakes and snowballs, you'll have fun creating sweets to share. Then relax over a hearty no-fuss supper—Scott Peacock style.

305

315

321

Frosty

Powdery. Swirly. Fluffy and soft. There's a certain magic to the first snow. These nine sweet somethings bring the splendor indoors.

KID FRIENDLY

Coconut Snowballs

PREP 1 hr. BAKE 18 min.
COOK 7 min. OVEN 325°F

Coconut Milk Cake
- 4 eggs, separated, room temperature
- ¾ cup sugar
- ⅓ cup unrefined organic coconut oil, room temperature
- ¾ cup organic unsweetened coconut milk
- 1½ cups cake flour
- 2 tsp. baking powder
- ½ tsp. sea salt
- 1½ tsp. cream of tartar
- ½ tsp. vanilla

Meringue Frosting
- 5 egg whites
- 1 cup sugar
- 1½ cups unsalted butter, slightly colder than room temperature and cut into ½-inch cubes
- ½ tsp. vanilla
- 1½ tsp. vanilla bean paste
- 4 tsp. seedless raspberry or strawberry preserves
- 3 cups sweetened flake coconut

1. Preheat oven to 325°F. Grease and flour fifteen cups of 3-inch mini ball pans, or twenty cups of 2½ inch muffin pans, or forty-eight cups of 1¾-inch mini muffin pans. Set aside.

2. For Coconut Milk Cake, in a large bowl whisk together the egg yolks, ½ cup of the sugar, and coconut oil. Add coconut milk; whisk just until combined. In a large bowl sift together flour, baking powder, and salt. Sift flour mixture over egg yolk batter. Using a rubber spatula, fold in flour mixture until smooth.

3. In a medium mixing bowl beat egg whites and cream of tartar with an electric mixer on high speed until foamy. Slowly add remaining ¼ cup sugar; beat until medium-soft peaks form.

4. Add one-third of the egg whites to batter; stir until no streaks of white remain. Gently fold in remaining egg whites and vanilla until completely combined.

5. Spoon ⅓ cup batter into prepared mini ball cups, ¼ cup batter into 2½-inch into muffin cups, or a rounded tablespoon into 1¾-inch mini muffin cups. Bake ball pan for 18 to 20 minutes, 2½-inch muffin pan for 15 to 18 minutes, or 1¾-inch mini muffins 10 to 12 minutes or until a toothpick inserted near center comes out clean. Remove from oven. Cool

5 minutes on wire rack. Remove cakes from pans; cool completely on wire rack.

6. Meanwhile, for Meringue Frosting, in a large heatproof stainless-steel bowl combine egg whites and sugar. Set bowl over a large saucepan with simmering water (bottom of bowl should not touch the water). Beat egg white mixture with an electric mixer on high speed until light and fluffy and an instant-read thermometer registers 160°F, about 12 minutes. Remove bowl from saucepan. Continue beating until frosting doubles in volume and holds a peak, about 12 minutes. Reduce speed to medium-low. Slowly beat in butter, a few pieces at a time. Using a rubber spatula, fold in vanilla and vanilla bean paste.

7. For filling, in a small bowl combine 1 cup of the frosting and raspberry preserves. Place filling in a pastry bag fitted with a small round tip. Pipe filling in the center of the flat side of each cake. Use remaining frosting to attach pairs of cakes flat sides facing together. Using a small offset spatula, cover each cake ball with remaining frosting. Press coconut flakes in an even layer to cover each cake. Makes 14 servings (half of one 3-inch cake).

EACH SERVING *507 cal, 34 g fat, 105 mg chol, 239 mg sodium, 48 g carb, 2 g fiber, 5 g pro.*

MEET GESINE BULLOCK-PRADO
Noted cookbook author Gesine Bullock-Prado knows a thing or two about whipping up stunning desserts. For Gesine, baking is a meditative and comforting process that always results in something delicious and impressive. "When it comes to baking around the holidays, my No. 1 tip is to relax," Gesine says. "Holiday baking should be about joy. It should be a time to get into the holiday spirit while stretching some creative muscles."

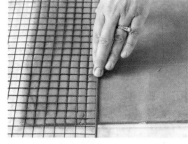

As a gift or displayed as a whimsical centerpiece, this edible village will spread holiday cheer.

KID FRIENDLY

Gingerbread Snow Globe City

Design and build a cookie community! Create buildings—short or tall—from warmly spiced gingerbread dough. Add a shimmery final dusting by rubbing baked cookies with powdered sugar before nestling the treats in a sugar-snow base.

PREP **1 hr.** CHILL **30 min.**
BAKE **20 min.** STAND **30 min.**
OVEN **350°F**

5 cups all-purpose flour
1 Tbsp. ground ginger
1 tsp. baking powder
1 tsp. salt
1 tsp. ground white pepper
1 tsp. ground cinnamon
½ tsp. ground nutmeg
1 cup butter, softened (2 sticks)
1 cup packed dark brown sugar
½ cup molasses
1 egg
½ cup milk
  Powdered sugar

1. In a large bowl whisk together the flour, ginger, baking powder, salt, white pepper, cinnamon, and nutmeg until well combined; set aside.
2. In an extra-large large bowl beat the butter, brown sugar, and molasses with an electric mixer on high speed until

light and fluffy. Add egg; beat until smooth. Add half the flour mixture; beat just until combined. Add milk; beat until combined. Add remaining flour mixture; beat just until combined. Using your hands, knead dough until smooth; divide in half. Wrap dough with plastic wrap; chill 30 minutes.
3. Preheat oven to 350°F. Roll each dough half on parchment paper to 15×10-inch rectangles. On one sheet, using a sharp knife, score three buildings and roof tops. Add brick and window scores. Score two shorter buildings and trees on the second sheet of rolled dough; add decorative score marks. Transfer each parchment sheet of dough to a large baking sheet.
4. Bake 10 minutes. Remove from oven. Carefully cut along scored lines; remove any scrap pieces from baking sheet.* Separate cut-out pieces. Bake 10 minutes more or until firm. Remove from oven. Cool completely on wire racks.
5. Sprinkle powdered sugar over cookies; gently rub in. Loosely cover with waxed paper; let stand at least 30 minutes or up to 24 hours. Arrange cookies in a large glass jar with about 2 inches of granulated sugar at the base. Makes 72 servings.
* Bake leftover cookie pieces separately.
EACH SERVING *76 cal, 3 g fat, 10 mg chol, 66 mg sodium, 12 g carb, 0 g fiber, 1 g pro.*

CONSTRUCTION TIPS
This gingerbread city is easy to make, following these construction tips.

• Use a wire rack to resemble brickwork on the gingerbread houses. Press rack into dough to make a visible impression. The straight edge of a bench scraper works as well.

• Carefully score dough with a sharp knife; do not slice all the way through. This step will make it easy to separate cookies for the next step. Score windows and other details during this step.

• Separate shapes by gently peeling dough along the scored line before baking the final 10 minutes.

Hidden Snowman Cake

PREP 1 hr. + 30 min.
BAKE 1 hr. + 45 min.
COOL 15 min. OVEN 350°F

Vanilla Cake
- 1½ cups all-purpose flour
- ½ tsp. salt
- ¼ tsp. baking powder
- ¼ tsp. baking soda
- ½ cup unsalted butter, softened (1 stick)
- 1½ cups granulated sugar
- ¼ cup canola oil
- 2 eggs
- ½ cup buttermilk or sour milk

Chocolate Cake
- 8 oz. bittersweet chocolate, very finely chopped
- 1 cup very hot brewed coffee
- ½ cup buttermilk or sour milk
- 1 tsp. vanilla
- 4 cups all-purpose flour
- ½ cup unsweetened cocoa powder
- 1 tsp. salt
- ¾ tsp. baking powder
- ½ tsp. baking soda
- 1½ cups unsalted butter, softened (3 sticks)
- 3 cups granulated sugar
- ¾ cup canola oil
- 6 eggs

Frosting
- 6 egg whites
- 1½ cups granulated sugar
- 2 Tbsp. light-color corn syrup
  Pinch of salt

1. For Vanilla Cake, preheat oven to 350°F. Grease a 13×9×2-inch baking pan. Line bottom of pan with parchment paper; grease paper and flour pan. Set aside.
2. In a medium bowl stir together flour, salt, baking powder, and baking soda; set aside. In a large mixing bowl beat butter and sugar with an electric mixer on high speed until light and fluffy, scraping down sides as necessary. Add oil; beat until combined. Add eggs, one at a time, beating well after each. To the batter, alternately add flour mixture with buttermilk, mixing on medium-low speed until smooth. Pour batter into prepared pan; spread evenly. Bake

25 to 30 minutes or until top springs back when lightly touched. Remove from oven. Transfer pan to wire rack; cool completely. Cover with plastic wrap. Freeze 30 minutes.
3. For Chocolate Cake, preheat oven to 350°F. Coat a 10-inch tube pan with nonstick cooking spray; set aside. Place chocolate in a medium heat-proof bowl. Pour over hot coffee; do not stir. Let stand 2 minutes. Whisk chocolate and coffee together until smooth; cool. Add buttermilk and vanilla; stir to combine. Set aside. In a large bowl whisk together flour, cocoa powder, salt, baking powder, and baking soda until combined, about 30 seconds; set aside.
4. In a large mixing bowl beat butter and sugar with electric mixer on high speed until light and fluffy, scraping sides of bowl as necessary. Add oil; beat 2 minutes more. Add eggs, one at a time, beating well after each addition. Alternately add flour mixture with chocolate mixture beating on medium-low speed until fully incorporated. Increase speed to medium high; beat 20 seconds. Set aside.
5. Using a 3-inch snowman cookie cutter, cut out 12 to 15 snowmen from vanilla cake; set aside.
6. Spread half the batter into prepared tube pan. Place snowmen cutouts, head down, about ½-inch apart into batter. Fill a pastry bag fitted with a large open round tip with some remaining batter. Pipe or spoon batter around snowmen, keeping them evenly spaced. Spoon remaining batter over snowman, within 1-inch of top of pan; carefully spread to cover. Transfer to a foil-lined baking sheet.
7. Bake 1 hour 20 minutes or until a long skewer inserted near center of cake comes out clean. Loosely cover cake with foil during the last 5 minutes of baking to prevent overbrowning, if necessary. Remove from oven. Cool 15 minutes on wire rack. Loosen sides and around the tube; turn cake out onto rack; invert bottom side up; remove pan. Cool completely.
8. Meanwhile, for Frosting, in a large heatproof stainless-steel bowl combine egg whites, sugar, corn syrup, and salt. Set bowl over a large saucepan with simmering water (bottom of bowl should not touch water). Beat

with an electric mixer on high speed until light and fluffy and an instant-read thermometer registers 160°F, about 12 minutes. Remove bowl from saucepan. Beat until stiff peaks form; Cool. Using a small offset spatula, frost top and sides of cooled cake. Makes 12 servings.
Note: Use remaining batter for cupcakes, spooning ¼ cup batter per paper bake cup lined pan. Bake 18 to 20 minutes at 350°F.
EACH SERVING *477 cal, 24 g fat, 79 mg chol, 197 mg sodium, 64 g carb, 2 g fiber, 6 g pro.*

FROSTY, DEMYSTIFIED

The secret to this cake is using two cake batters of different consistencies. One cake is inserted into the batter already baked!

- Freeze the dense, buttery cake for about 30 minutes to create sturdy cutouts.

- Nestle the cutouts into the batter, angling heads down. Gently spoon remaining batter between and over cutouts.

PINE CONES

WHITE CHOCOLATE PEPPERMINT ICE CREAM

Pine Cones

PREP 1 hr.　BAKE 15 min.
COOL 5 min.　OVEN 325°F

- 3 cups all-purpose flour
- 1 Tbsp. baking powder
- 1 tsp. salt
- ½ tsp. ground nutmeg
- 8 ounces (2 sticks) unsalted butter, softened
- 1 cup granulated sugar
- 1 cup packed brown sugar
- 5 eggs
- 1 Tbsp. vanilla bean paste
- 1½ cups buttermilk
- ½ cup whipping cream, whipped to stiff peaks
- 4 ounces (1 stick) unsalted butter, softened
- 2 8-ounce packages cream cheese, softened
- 4 cups powdered sugar
  Pinch salt
- ½ tsp. ground cinnamon
- 2 cups sliced almonds
  Edible white luster dust

1. Preheat oven to 325°F. Coat egg molds with nonstick spray for baking; set aside. In a large bowl combine the flour, baking powder, salt, and nutmeg; whisk for 30 seconds to evenly distribute leavening; set aside.
2. In large mixing bowl, beat butter and sugars until light and fluffy, about 5 minutes; scrape down bottom and sides of bowl. Add eggs, one at a time, mixing just to combine after each addition. Add the vanilla and mix until just combined. Scrape bottom and sides of bowl again; with the mixer on low, add half the flour mixture. Beat until combined. Add buttermilk, beat until combined. Add remaining flour mixture; beat until combined. Fold in whipped cream.
3. Divide batter among the egg molds (bake in batches), filling molds ⅔ full. Bake for 15 to 20 minutes or until cakes spring back when lightly touched. Cool in molds for 5 minutes. Remove and cool completely on wire racks.
4. In a large mixing bowl beat the butter and cream cheese until smooth. Add powdered sugar, salt, and cinnamon; beat on low speed until combined.

5. Frost the cakes with just enough icing to coat. Dip the rounded end of almond slices in luster dust, then arrange dipped sides up on frosted cakes in overlapping rows. Makes 12 servings.
EACH SERVING 462 cal, 25 g fat, 105 mg chol, 264 mg sodium, 54 g carb, 7 g pro.

White Chocolate-Peppermint Ice Cream

PREP 10 minutes　FREEZE 3 hr.

- 4 oz. white baking chocolate, chopped
- 1 cup sugar
- 3 cups half-and-half or light cream
- 1½ cups whipping cream
- 2 tsp. vanilla bean paste or vanilla
- ½ cup striped round peppermint candies, broken (about 15 candies)

1. Place white chocolate in a small microwave-safe bowl. Heat on 50% power (medium) for 1 to 1½ minutes or just until melted, stirring every 30 seconds. Place chocolate in a large bowl. Stir in the sugar. Gradually whisk in half-and-half and whipping cream. Whisk in vanilla.
2. Freeze in a 1½- to 2-quart ice cream freezer according to manufacturer's directions. Transfer ice cream to a 2-quart rectangular baking dish. Sprinkle with candies and swirl in with a spoon. Cover and freeze for 3 to 4 hours or until firm. Makes 10 servings.
Easy White Chocolate-Peppermint Ice Cream Place one 1.75-ounce container vanilla ice cream in an extra-large bowl. Let stand at room temperature until soft enough to stir. Stir in 4 ounces melted white chocolate and 2 teaspoons vanilla bean paste or vanilla. Spoon ice cream into a 2-quart rectangular baking dish. Sprinkle with ½ cup striped round peppermint candies, broken; swirl in with a spoon. Cover and freeze 3 to 4 hours or until firm.
EACH SERVING 390 cal, 25 g fat, 78 mg chol, 55 mg sodium, 39 g carb, 3 g pro.

Mile High Pie

PREP 40 min. FREEZE 20 min.
BAKE 18 min. + 50 min. OVEN 350°F

½ cup unsalted butter, softened (1 stick)
½ cup granulated sugar
½ tsp. vanilla
½ tsp. lemon zest
2 egg yolks
1½ cups all-purpose flour
½ tsp. salt
Nonstick cooking spray
4 tart apples, such as Granny Smith, peeled, cored, sliced ¼-inch thick, slices halved crosswise
3 ripe pears, such as Anjou, peeled, cored, sliced ¼-inch thick, slices halved crosswise
1 cup grated frozen purchased pound cake
½ cup all-purpose flour
¼ cup packed brown sugar
1 cup dried cranberries
2 tsp. finely shredded orange zest
½ 4-serving-size package instant vanilla pudding mix
½ cup whipping cream
2 Tbsp. orange juice
½ 17-oz. package frozen puff pastry sheets, thawed (1 sheet)
1 egg
1 recipe Icing

1. For crust, in a large mixing bowl beat the butter and sugar with an electric mixer on medium-high speed until light and fluffy. Add vanilla and lemon zest; beat just until combined, scraping down sides of bowl as necessary. Add egg yolks; beat until combined. Add flour and salt; beat just until dough comes together. Using your hands, knead dough until flour is fully incorporated.
2. Coat a 9-inch fluted tart pan with removable bottom with nonstick cooking spray. Press dough into bottom and sides of pan. Cover with plastic wrap; freeze 20 minutes.
3. Preheat oven to 350°F. Bake pastry 18 minutes or just until edges start to brown and bottom appears dry. Remove from oven. Cool on wire rack.
4. For filling, in an extra-large bowl toss together apples, pears, cake crumbs,

flour, brown sugar, cranberries, and orange zest; set aside. In a small bowl whisk together for 1 minute instant pudding, cream, and orange juice. Let stand 3 minutes. Add pudding mixture to apple mixture; toss to coat. Mound filling into prepared crust, leaving about ½ inch around edge.
5. Unfold puff pastry. On a lightly floured surface roll out to a 12-inch square. Drape pastry over filling. Tuck extra dough between filling and bottom crust; trim excess. In a small bowl combine 1 egg and 1 Tbsp. water. Using a pastry brush, brush puff pastry with egg mixture. Transfer pie to a foil-lined baking sheet. Bake 50 minutes or until top crust is golden brown. Remove from oven. Cool completely on a wire rack.
7. For Icing, whisk together 1 cup powdered sugar and 4 Tbsp. milk until smooth. Spoon icing over pie. Let icing stand until it sets. Top with a Maraschino cherry, if desired. Makes 10 servings.

EACH SERVING *633 cal, 27 g fat, 116 mg chol, 300 mg sodium, 95 g carb, 5 g fiber, 7 g pro.*

Salty-Sweet Snowflakes

PREP 1 hr. 10 min.
CHILL 1 hr. + 30 min.
BAKE 10 min. per batch OVEN 350°F

1	cup unsalted butter (2 sticks)
1	cup granulated sugar
1	egg
1	egg yolk
1½	tsp. salt
1	tsp. vanilla
1	tsp. finely shredded lemon zest
½	tsp. ground white pepper
3	cups all-purpose flour
1	recipe Royal Icing

1. For clarified butter, in a small saucepan melt butter over low heat until milk solids rise to the top, about 10 minutes. Using a spoon, skim off milk solids until remaining butter is clear; discard solids. Pour clarified butter into a large glass bowl. Cover; chill 1 hour or until firm.

2. In the same large bowl add sugar. Beat chilled butter and sugar with electric mixer on medium-high speed until light and fluffy. Add egg and yolk; beat until fully incorporated. Add salt, vanilla, lemon zest, and pepper. Slowly beat in flour. Using hands, knead dough until smooth; divide in half. Wrap in plastic wrap; chill 30 minutes.

3. Preheat oven to 350°F. On a lightly floured surface roll each dough half to slightly less than ⅛-inch thickness. Using a 4-inch snowflake cookie cutter, cut out about 36 snowflakes. Arrange cutouts 1 inch apart on ungreased baking sheets.

4. Bake 10 to 12 minutes or until edges just start to brown. Remove from oven. Cool on baking sheets 5 minutes. Using a spatula, carefully remove cookies. Transfer to a wire rack; cool completely. Decorate cooled cookies with Royal Icing, as shown, or decorate with flooding icing.

Royal Icing In a small bowl stir together 2 cups powdered sugar,

1½ Tbsp. meringue powder, and 3 Tbsp. water until smooth. Spoon into a pastry bag fitted with a small round tip; set aside. For flooding icing, in a small bowl stir together 3 cups powdered sugar, 3 Tbsp. meringue powder, and 6 Tbsp. water. Spoon into a resealable plastic bag; set aside. Using piping icing, trace around edge of each cookie. Let dry 15 to 20 minutes. Snip a corner from the flooding icing

bags. Pipe inside lines of dried icing. Let stand 30 to 60 minutes to dry completely. Makes 36 servings.

Note To make cookie ornaments, use a straw to cut out a hole near one edge of the snowflake cutouts before baking. Use the straw to re-cut holes after baking, if necessary.

EACH SERVING *284 cal, 9 g fat, 39 mg chol, 165 mg sodium, 50 g carb, 0 g fiber, 2 g pro.*

One homemade pillowy marshmallow slowly melting into a pool of luxurious white hot chocolate is enough to make any moment special.

White Hot Chocolate

START TO FINISH 25 minutes

- 8 oz. white baking chocolate, coarsely chopped
- 4 cups milk
- ⅔ cup strong brewed coffee
- 1 Tbsp. rum
- 1 tsp. vanilla
  Homemade or purchased marshmallows

1. In a large heavy saucepan combine the white chocolate and ⅔ cup of the milk. Stir over medium-low heat until chocolate is melted. Add the remaining milk. Stir over medium heat until heated through. Stir in coffee, rum, and vanilla. Serve in mugs topped with marshmallows. Makes 8 servings.

EACH SERVING *220 cal, 11 g fat, 15 mg chol, 79 mg sodium, 23 g carb, 0 g fiber, 6 g pro.*

Salted Caramel Marshmallows

Because the marshmallows are flavored with purchased syrups, you can make a batch of salted caramel one day and peppermint the next. Don't eat them all at once—these delicate confections also make sweet gifts.

PREP 30 min. CHILL 4 hr.

- Nonstick cooking spray
- 4 envelopes unflavored gelatin
- ¾ cup water
- 3 cups granulated sugar
- 1 cup light-color corn syrup
- ½ cup peppermint syrup, salted caramel-flavored syrup, or other flavor
- ¼ tsp. salt
  Red or orange gel food coloring
  Powdered sugar

1. Line a 2-quart baking dish with parchment paper, 2 inches of paper extending over each side. Coat with nonstick cooking spray; set aside.
2. Pour gelatin in the bowl of a stand mixer fitted with the whisk attachment. Pour water over the gelatin. Gently whisk to combine. Let stand 10 minutes.
3. Meanwhile, in a large saucepan combine the granulated sugar, corn syrup, peppermint syrup, and salt over medium heat, stirring until sugar is completely melted. Bring sugar mixture to boiling over medium-high heat; attach a candy thermometer to the saucepan. Boil 2 minutes or until the thermometer registers 240°F. Remove from heat.
4. With mixer set to medium speed, carefully pour sugar syrup down the side of the mixing bowl. Increase speed to high; whisk until marshmallow mixture has quadrupled in size, is white and fluffy, and the bowl is cool enough to touch, about 122°F.
5. Using a rubber spatula coated with nonstick cooking spray, transfer marshmallow mixture to prepared pan; spread evenly.
6. Dip a wooden skewer into food coloring gel; swirl into marshmallow mixture. Chill marshmallow, uncovered, about 4 hours or overnight.
7. Remove marshmallow from refrigerator. Generously sprinkle powdered sugar. Remove marshmallow from pan; transfer to parchment paper. Remove any attached parchment paper. Generously sprinkle powdered sugar over the under side. Using a very sharp knife, cut marshmallow into 1½- to 2-inch squares. Place additional powdered sugar in a small bowl; dredge squares in powdered sugar to coat. Refrigerate in an airtight container up to 2 weeks. Makes 16 servings.

EACH SERVING *35 cal, 0 g fat, 0 mg chol, 10 mg sodium, 9 g carb, 0 g fiber, 0 g pro.*

Home Cooking

COMFORT FEAST Create a hearty, soul-soothing supper to savor at home. Chef Scott Peacock shows you how to make a meal that satisfies all season—as a special holiday dinner or a cozy night in.

Rich Beef Stew with Bacon and Plums

A few thoughtful additions elevate this dish beyond the average beef stew. "Even though it's a longer recipe, every ingredient and step serves an important purpose," Scott says. "The reward—deep luscious flavor—is worth the extra effort."

PREP 1 hr. 30 min. CHILL overnight
BAKE 3 hrs. 25 min.
OVEN 450°F/275°F/350°F

1   3½- to 4-lb. well-marbled beef chuck roast, cut 3 inches thick
6   oz. thick-sliced, center-cut applewood-smoked bacon
3   Tbsp. olive oil
1   medium butternut squash, peeled, seeded, and cut into 1-inch pieces (about 4 cups)
2   Tbsp. unsalted butter
2   cups diced yellow onion
1   leek, white part only, split lengthwise (reserving one long inner piece) and cut crosswise into slices
3   large cloves garlic, roughly chopped
2¾ cups dry red wine (such as Pinot Noir)
1   to 1½ cups chicken stock
1   stick cinnamon, broken
7   black peppercorns
2   whole cloves
3   fresh bay leaves (or 1 dried bay leaf)
1   Tbsp. tomato paste
¼   tsp. dried thyme
5   stems fresh parsley, leaves picked and chopped, stems reserved
1   cup pitted prunes, halved

1. Trim and cut roast into 2-inch pieces. Sprinkle evenly with 1 Tbsp. kosher salt. Cover; chill overnight.
2. Preheat oven to 450°F. Line a 15×10×1-inch baking pan with a silicone baking mat; set aside. Cook bacon in 1 Tbsp. hot oil over medium-low heat until browned. Remove and drain on paper towel, reserving 3 Tbsp. drippings. Crumble bacon; set aside. Place squash on prepared pan. Add 1 Tbsp. butter and 1 Tbsp. of the bacon drippings. Sprinkle lightly with salt; toss to coat. Bake 20 to 30 minutes or until tender and browned, stirring once. Remove from oven. Cover with waxed paper; set aside. Reduce oven to 275°F.
3. Add 2 Tbsp. olive oil to remaining 2 Tbsp. drippings in skillet; heat over medium-high heat. Blot beef well with paper towel; add to skillet in batches. Brown well on all sides. Remove; set aside.
4. Drain all but 1 tsp. fat from skillet. Add remaining 1 Tbsp. butter and onion. Sprinkle with salt. Stir over medium heat, scraping up browned bits from bottom of pan. Cook 3 to 4 minutes, stirring often, until onion just begins to soften. Stir in leek slices and garlic. Sprinkle with salt. Cook 4 minutes more. Transfer to a 3-quart baking dish; set aside. Pour wine into skillet. Bring to boiling; reduce heat. Boil gently, uncovered, until reduced to 2 cups.
5. Place beef and bacon over onions. Pour over reduced wine. Add stock to almost cover. Using kitchen string, tie cinnamon, peppercorns, and cloves in a piece of cheesecloth; tuck into beef mixture. Add bay leaves. Dollop tomato paste around beef. Sprinkle with thyme. Tie together parsley stems and inner leek piece; add to beef mixture. Place parchment paper over dish. Top with a triple layer of heavy foil. Seal tightly. Place on a rimmed baking sheet. Bake 2 hours. Uncover; add prunes. Cover; bake 45 minutes to 1 hour more or until meat is easily pierced with a knife. Uncover; skim off fat. Remove cheesecloth bag, bay leaves, and parsley stems; discard. Increase oven to 350°F. Add butternut squash to meat in dish. Bake, uncovered, 20 minutes, basting once or twice. To serve, sprinkle with parsley leaves. Makes 8 servings.
EACH SERVING 541 cal, 24 g fat, 115 mg chol, 1,348 mg sodium, 30 g carb, 4 g fiber, 38 g pro.

SCOTT SAYS
"Blot the meat well with paper towels before placing in the pan, and be sure to work in batches—you don't want to overcrowd the pan. This step builds incredible flavor."

Bend this simple, affordable meal to fit your schedule. You can easily do it all in one day or bits of prep over a few days.

SCOTT'S MAKE-AHEAD TIPS

• Up to 2 days before: "Cut up and salt the meat. It can rest in the fridge up to 2 days, and the flavor actually improves as the seasoning has time to permeate the meat," Scott says. "You can also make the entire stew the day before—and I think it's even better that way. It thickens and the flavors mature and ripen. Just skim off any fat from the top and warm through before serving."

• The day before: "Make the puddings and have the syrup for the compote prepped and ready to toss with the fruit just before serving."

• An hour before serving: "I actually prefer the broccoli at room temperature—it gets even more flavorful after it's been out of the oven for an hour or so, while you make the spoon bread."

Roasted Broccoli and Olives

"I like to use two or more varieties of green olives as well as some tiny black niçoise olives," Scott says. To finish, he sprinkles Maldon flaked sea salt; you can also season to taste with kosher salt.

PREP **20 min.** STAND **5 min.**
ROAST **20 min.** OVEN **425°F**

6 cloves garlic, peeled and gently crushed
1 tsp. kosher salt
¼ cup extra-virgin olive oil
2¼ to 2½ lbs. broccoli, washed, drained, and patted dry
½ cup mixed unpitted olives
  Freshly ground black pepper
  Flaked sea salt
½ lemon

1. Preheat oven to 425°F. Line a 15×10×1 baking pan with a silicone baking mat or parchment; set aside. In a small bowl combine garlic and ½ tsp. of the kosher salt. Using the back of a spoon, muddle garlic and salt until garlic begins to release its oil. Let stand 5 to 10 minutes. Stir in olive oil; set aside.
2. Trim broccoli stems; cut stalks lengthwise into halves and/or quarters. Place in prepared baking pan. Pour garlic oil and olives over; toss well. Sprinkle with remaining ½ tsp. kosher salt and the black pepper. Roast 20 to 25 minutes, tossing occasionally, until tender yet al dente. Transfer to a serving dish.
3. To serve, sprinkle with flaked sea salt; drizzle with additional extra-virgin olive oil. Squeeze over lemon juice. Makes 8 servings.

EACH SERVING *134 cal, 10 g fat, 0 mg chol, 427 mg sodium, 10 g carb, 4 g fiber, 4 g pro.*

SCOTT SAYS

"I'm very keen on a silicone baking mat for roasting—especially for vegetables, which have a tendency to stick—because you don't lose all those lovely browned bits of flavor at the bottom of the pan. It also allows you to use a little less oil and ensures more even cooking."

Cornmeal Spoon Bread

"Resist the urge to serve this dish straight out of the oven," Scott says. "It really needs 10 minutes or so to cool slightly and settle for the best taste. It will fall a bit, but that's OK!"

PREP 35 min. **COOL** 20 min.
BAKE 30 min. **OVEN** 400°F

- 5 Tbsp. unsalted butter, softened
- 4 cups milk
- 1 cup fine ground white cornmeal or regular cornmeal
- 1¼ tsp. kosher salt
- 1 tsp. sugar
- 4 eggs, separated
- ⅛ tsp. cream of tartar

1. Preheat oven to 400°F. Butter a 1½-quart soufflé dish with 2 Tbsp. of the butter; set aside.

2. In a large saucepan heat milk until just below boiling. Slowly whisk in cornmeal; bring to boiling. Cook, whisking constantly, over medium heat about 5 minutes or until mixture thickens and begins to pull away from the sides of the saucepan. Remove from heat; transfer to a large mixing bowl. Cool 10 minutes. Whisk in the remaining 3 Tbsp. butter, the salt, and sugar. Beat in egg yolks until well blended.

3. In a large clean mixing bowl beat egg whites and cream of tartar with a large clean whisk to soft glossy mounds. Stir one-third of the beaten egg whites into cornmeal mixture to lighten. Gently fold in remaining egg whites. Gently turn into prepared soufflé dish (batter will nearly fill the dish). Bake 30 minutes or until puffed and golden brown. Cool 10 minutes before serving. Makes 8 servings.

EACH SERVING *226 cal, 12 g fat, 122 mg chol, 403 mg sodium, 20 g carb, 1 g fiber, 8 g pro.*

SCOTT SAYS

"Folding the egg whites into the cornmeal mixture is all about cutting down and lifting the batter into itself. You are just trying to minimize smooshing the air, which gives the dish its lovely textures."

Buttermilk Pudding with Pomegranate Compote

"The tang of buttermilk is so refreshing after rich beef stew. It's light and bright with the spark of acidic pomegranate."

PREP 25 min. COOK 10 min. CHILL 2 hrs.

- ¼ cup cold milk or water
- 2 envelopes unflavored gelatin
- 2 cups heavy cream
- 1 cup sugar
- ½ cup crème fraîche
- 2 cups buttermilk
- ¼ cup freshly squeezed lemon juice
- ¾ tsp. vanilla
- ½ tsp. kosher salt
- 4 tsp. finely shredded lemon peel
- 1 recipe Pomegranate Compote

1. In a small bowl combine milk and gelatin.
2. In a saucepan bring heavy cream and sugar to a simmer over medium heat, stirring until sugar is completely dissolved. Immediately remove from heat; add gelatin, stirring until completely dissolved. Cool 5 minutes. Transfer to a mixing bowl. Whisk in crème fraîche until blended. Whisk in buttermilk, lemon juice, vanilla, and salt. Strain. Whisk in lemon peel.
3. Divide pudding among eight 8-oz. ramekins. Cover with plastic wrap; chill for 2 to 3 hours or until set. Serve with Pomegranate Compote. Makes 8 servings.

Pomegranate Compote In a medium saucepan combine ⅓ cup red wine (such as Pinot Noir) and ⅓ cup sugar. Bring to a simmer, stirring until sugar is completely dissolved. Simmer 5 to 7 minutes until slightly reduced and syrupy. Remove from heat; cool completely. In a medium bowl combine ½ cup pomegranate seeds and ¼ cup chopped navel orange sections. Sprinkle with ⅛ tsp. salt. Pour red wine syrup over. Stir in 1 tsp. lemon juice. Serve immediately.

EACH SERVING *493 cal, 28 g fat, 105 mg chol, 251 mg sodium, 53 g carb, 0 g fiber, 6 g pro.*

SCOTT SAYS
"When the gelatin is softened in the milk, it will look unpromising— kind of like a wad of gum—but you haven't done anything wrong. This step is key because it helps the gelatin dissolve into the hot cream."

Dinner on a Dollar

This vibrantly spiced dish featuring tomatoes and chickpeas makes a delicious midweek meal.

Tomato, Greens and Chickpea Skillet

Curry is a spice blend that often includes a combination of turmeric, mustard seed, coriander, and cumin. It needs to be cooked for a few minutes along with other aromatics, like onions and garlic, to remove its bitter taste.
START TO FINISH **25 min.**

- 3 Tbsp. olive oil
- 1 medium onion, chopped
- 1 clove garlic, minced
- 1 Tbsp. curry powder
- 1 14½-oz. can diced tomatoes, undrained
- ¼ tsp. salt
- 1 15- to 16-oz. can chickpeas, rinsed and drained
- 2 cups torn Swiss chard or spinach
- 4 eggs

1. In a large skillet heat 2 Tbsp. of the olive oil over medium heat. Add onion and garlic; cook and stir 5 minutes. Add curry powder; cook 1 minute more. Add tomatoes and salt; cook and stir 3 minutes more. Add chickpeas; cook and stir until heated through, about 3 minutes. Add chard; cook and stir until slightly wilted, about 3 minutes. **2.** Meanwhile, in another skillet heat remaining 1 Tbsp. olive oil over medium heat. Break eggs and gently slip them into the pan, one at a time. Season to taste with salt and pepper. Cook, covered, to desired doneness. Serve eggs with tomato-chickpea mixture. Makes 4 servings.
EACH SERVING *279 cal, 17 g fat, 186 mg chol, 675 mg sodium, 21 g carb, 2 g fiber, 12 g pro.*

Easy Bake

One versatile dough from baking guru Dorie Greenspan is all you need to mix and shape your way to a sparkling cookie plate collection.

KID FRIENDLY

Vanilla Holiday Cookies

PREP 25 min. FREEZE 1 hr.
BAKE 8 min. per batch OVEN 375°

- ¾ cup (1½ sticks) unsalted butter, softened
- ½ cup sugar
- ½ tsp. fine sea salt
- 2½ tsp. vanilla
- 2 cups all-purpose flour
  Royal Icing (see recipe, page 311) and/or desired decorations

1. In a large mixing bowl beat butter, sugar, and salt with an electric mixer on medium-low speed until smooth, about 1 minute. Reduce speed to low; beat in vanilla. Add flour all at once. Beat on low speed just until flour disappears into dough (dough may appear crumbly). Using your hands, work dough into a ball; divide in half.
2. Working with one dough half at a time, roll between sheets of waxed paper to ¼-inch thickness. Freeze between paper for 1 hour or until easy to handle.
3. Preheat oven to 375°F. Remove one dough piece at a time from freezer; let stand at room temperature 5 minutes. Using a 2-inch cutter, cut into shapes. Place 1 inch apart on prepared cookie sheets. Gather scraps; repeat rolling and freezing, if necessary, between waxed paper.
4. Bake one cookie sheet at a time for 8 to 10 minutes or until almost firm to the touch and golden on bottom and around sides. Remove; cool on wire rack. Decorate as desired. Makes about 24 cookies.
EACH COOKIE *106 cal, 6 g fat, 15 mg chol, 47 mg sodium, 12 g carb, 0 g fiber, 1 g pro.*

KID FRIENDLY

Cocoa Sandwich Cookies

1. Prepare dough for Vanilla Holiday Cookies, except whisk ⅓ cup unsweetened cocoa powder into flour before adding to butter mixture. (Dough may be stiff.) Roll dough to ⅛-inch thickness between waxed paper; freeze 30 minutes. Cut into shapes using a 1½-inch scalloped cookie cutter. Arrange 1 inch apart on ungreased cookie sheets. Bake at 375°F for 7 to 8 minutes or until edges are firm. Cool on wire racks. Just before serving, spread bottoms of half the cookies with ½ tsp. chocolate-hazelnut spread. Top with remaining cookies. Makes about 50 sandwich cookies.
EACH COOKIE *89 cal, 5 g fat, 7 mg chol, 27 mg sodium, 10 g carb, 0 g fiber, 1 g pro.*

KID FRIENDLY

Spiced Thumbprints

1. Prepare dough for Vanilla Holiday Cookies, except whisk 1 tsp. ground cinnamon, ½ tsp. ground ginger, and a pinch ground cloves into flour before adding to butter mixture. Shape dough into 1-inch balls. Roll each in granulated sugar to coat. Arrange 1 inch apart on ungreased cookie sheets. Using your thumb, press an indent into each ball. Bake at 350°F oven for 8 to 10 minutes or until bottom edges just start to brown. Transfer to wire rack. Repress indents, if necessary, with the rounded side of a measuring spoon. Fill indents with ½ tsp. apricot preserves. Cool on wire rack. Makes about 42 cookies.
EACH COOKIE *73 cal, 3 g fat, 9 mg chol, 28 mg sodium, 10 g carb, 0 g fiber, 1 g pro.*

KID FRIENDLY

Toasted Pecan Biscotti

1. Prepare dough for Vanilla Holiday Cookies, except stir 1 cup finely chopped toasted pecans (see tip, page 35) into dough when flour is almost incorporated. Divide dough in half. Shape each into a 10×1½-inch log. Arrange 3 inches apart on an ungreased cookie sheet. Lightly press each to a 2-inch-wide log. Bake at 350°F for 20 minutes or until lightly browned. Cool on cookie sheet on a wire rack 1 hour. Using a serrated knife, bias cut each log crosswise into ½-inch-thick slices. Place cut sides down on cookie sheet. Bake at 300°F for 8 to 10 minutes each side or until lightly toasted. Cool on wire rack. If desired, dip bottom of each slice in melted chocolate. Makes about 30 cookies.
EACH COOKIE *114 cal, 7 g fat, 12 mg chol, 38 mg sodium, 11 g carb, 1 g fiber, 2 g pro.*

KID FRIENDLY

Lemon Crescents

1. Prepare dough for Vanilla Holiday Cookies, except place the sugar and 1 Tbsp. finely shredded lemon zest in the mixing bowl first. Using fingers, rub ingredients together until sugar is moist and aromatic. Add salt and butter; mix as directed, Step 1. Pinch off 1-inch pieces of dough. Shape into 3-inch logs; curve into crescents. Place 1 inch apart on ungreased cookie sheets. Bake at 350°F for 8 to 10 minutes or until bottoms are lightly browned. Cool 2 minutes on wire rack. Sprinkle heavily with powdered sugar. Makes about 42 cookies.
EACH COOKIE *72 cal, 3 g fat, 9 mg chol, 27 mg sodium, 10 g carb, 0 g fiber, 1 g pro.*

Recipe Index

Nutrition information.

With each recipe, we give important nutrition information you can easily apply to your own needs. You'll find the calorie count of each serving and the amount, in grams, of fat, saturated fat, cholesterol, sodium, carbohydrates, fiber, and protein to help you keep tabs on what you eat. To stay in line with the nutrition breakdown of each recipe, follow the suggested number of servings.

How we analyze.

The Better Homes and Gardens® Test Kitchen computer analyzes each recipe for the nutritional value of a single serving.

- The analysis does not include optional ingredients.

- We use the first serving size listed when a range is given. For example: If we say a recipe "Makes 4 to 6 servings," the nutrition information is based on 4 servings.

- When ingredient choices (such as butter or margarine) appear in a recipe, we use the first one mentioned for analysis. The ingredient order does not mean we prefer one ingredient over another.

- When milk and eggs are recipe ingredients, the analysis is calculated using 2 percent (reduced-fat) milk and large eggs.

What you need.

The dietary guidelines below suggest nutrient levels that moderately active adults should strive to eat each day. There is no real harm in going over or under these guidelines in any single day, but it is a good idea to aim for a balanced diet over time.

Calories: About 2,000

Total fat: Less than 65 grams

Saturated fat: Less than 20 grams

Cholesterol: Less than 300 milligrams

Carbohydrates: About 300 grams

Sodium: Less than 2,400 milligrams

Dietary fiber: 20 to 30 grams

Low Fat icon.

Certain recipes throughout the book have an icon above the recipe title that indicates the recipe is low fat. For a recipe to earn this icon, it must meet certain nutritional requirements. For a main dish one serving should have 12 grams of fat per serving or less, one serving of a side dish should have 5 grams of fat or less, an appetizer serving should have 2 grams of fat or less, and cookies and desserts should have 2 grams of fat or less per serving. Occasionally the fat level will slightly exceed one of the recommended numbers, but typically they remain below the listed amounts.

Metric Information

The charts on this page provide a guide for converting measurements from the U.S. customary system, which is used throughout this book, to the metric system.

Product Differences

Most of the ingredients called for in the recipes in this book are available in most countries. However, some are known by different names. Here are some common American ingredients and their possible counterparts:

- Sugar (white) is granulated, fine granulated, or castor sugar.
- Powdered sugar is icing sugar.
- All-purpose flour is enriched, bleached or unbleached white household flour. When self-rising flour is used in place of all-purpose flour in a recipe that calls for leavening, omit the leavening agent (baking soda or baking powder) and salt.
- Light-color corn syrup is golden syrup.
- Cornstarch is cornflour.
- Baking soda is bicarbonate of soda.
- Vanilla or vanilla extract is vanilla essence.
- Green, red, or yellow sweet peppers are capsicums or bell peppers.
- Golden raisins are sultanas.

Volume and Weight

The United States traditionally uses cup measures for liquid and solid ingredients. The chart below shows the approximate imperial and metric equivalents. If you are accustomed to weighing solid ingredients, the following approximate equivalents will be helpful.

- 1 cup butter, castor sugar, or rice = 8 ounces = ½ pound = 250 grams
- 1 cup flour = 4 ounces = ¼ pound = 125 grams
- 1 cup icing sugar = 5 ounces = 150 grams

Canadian and U.S. volume for a cup measure is 8 fluid ounces (237 ml), but the standard metric equivalent is 250 ml.

1 British imperial cup is 10 fluid ounces.

In Australia, 1 tablespoon equals 20 ml, and there are 4 teaspoons in the Australian tablespoon.

Spoon measures are used for smaller amounts of ingredients. Although the size of the tablespoon varies slightly in different countries, for practical purposes and for recipes in this book, a straight substitution is all that's necessary. Measurements made using cups or spoons always should be level unless stated otherwise.

Common Weight Range Replacements

Imperial / U.S.	Metric
½ ounce	15 g
1 ounce	25 g or 30 g
4 ounces (¼ pound)	115 g or 125 g
8 ounces (½ pound)	225 g or 250 g
16 ounces (1 pound)	450 g or 500 g
1¼ pounds	625 g
1½ pounds	750 g
2 pounds or 2¼ pounds	1,000 g or 1 Kg

Oven Temperature Equivalents

Fahrenheit Setting	Celsius Setting*	Gas Setting
300°F	150°C	Gas Mark 2 (very low)
325°F	160°C	Gas Mark 3 (low)
350°F	180°C	Gas Mark 4 (moderate)
375°F	190°C	Gas Mark 5 (moderate)
400°F	200°C	Gas Mark 6 (hot)
425°F	220°C	Gas Mark 7 (hot)
450°F	230°C	Gas Mark 8 (very hot)
475°F	240°C	Gas Mark 9 (very hot)
500°F	260°C	Gas Mark 10 (extremely hot)
Broil	Broil	Grill

*Electric and gas ovens may be calibrated using celsius. However, for an electric oven, increase celsius setting 10 to 20 degrees when cooking above 160°C. For convection or forced air ovens (gas or electric), lower the temperature setting 25°F/10°C when cooking at all heat levels.

Baking Pan Sizes

Imperial / U.S.	Metric
9×1½-inch round cake pan	22- or 23×4-cm (1.5 L)
9×1½-inch pie plate	22- or 23×4-cm (1 L)
8×8×2-inch square cake pan	20×5-cm (2 L)
9×9×2-inch square cake pan	22- or 23×4.5-cm (2.5 L)
11×7×1½-inch baking pan	28×17×4-cm (2 L)
2-quart rectangular baking pan	30×19×4.5-cm (3 L)
13×9×2-inch baking pan	34×22×4.5-cm (3.5 L)
15×10×1-inch jelly roll pan	40×25×2-cm
9×5×3-inch loaf pan	23×13×8-cm (2 L)
2-quart casserole	2 L

U.S. / Standard Metric Equivalents

⅛ teaspoon = 0.5 ml	
¼ teaspoon = 1 ml	
½ teaspoon = 2 ml	
1 teaspoon = 5 ml	
1 tablespoon = 15 ml	
2 tablespoons = 25 ml	
¼ cup = 2 fluid ounces = 50 ml	
⅓ cup = 3 fluid ounces = 75 ml	
½ cup = 4 fluid ounces = 125 ml	
⅔ cup = 5 fluid ounces = 150 ml	
¾ cup = 6 fluid ounces = 175 ml	
1 cup = 8 fluid ounces = 250 ml	
2 cups = 1 pint = 500 ml	
1 quart = 1 litre	